TOWARDS A JUST IMMIGRATION POLICY

Towards a Just Immigration Policy

edited by

ANN DUMMETT

Cobden Trust

The Cobden Trust
21 Tabard Street
London SE1 4LA

© Action Group on Immigration
and Nationality and the individual
contributors, 1986

British Library Cataloguing in Publication Data

Towards a just immigration policy.
  1 Great Britain—Emigration and immigration
  I. Dummett, Ann   II. Cobden Trust
  325.41   JV7625

ISBN 0–900137–26–6

Typeset by Wilmaset, Birkenhead, Wirral
Printed by RAP Ltd., 201 Spotland Road, Rochdale OL12 7AF
Tel: 0706 44981

Contents

Preface

The material in this book was first prepared in 1983 for an AGIN Conference in that year. Since then, there have been numerous changes to the immigration rules in Britain, and of course all sorts of other changes, some administrative, some arising from Court decisions, in this country and elsewhere. Immigration law and its administration are in general subject to change, and no book on the subject can remain up to date in every detail for very long. A number of minor changes have been made where it has been possible to update items affected by recent developments, but the only chapter in the present work which has been substantially altered before publication is Sarah Leigh's account of family settlement problems. Otherwise, we ask readers to bear in mind that, inevitably, some details of the following accounts have been overtaken by events. However, the important thing is that the book as a whole is *not* a legal manual but a collection of ideas and information relevant to law reform. In this respect, it is anything but outdated: indeed there is little else available at all to guide and stimulate those who want to think about changing the law in a practical way.

The Editor wishes to thank *New Society* for permission to reproduce Richard Plender's "Rights of Passage", which first appeared in its pages. We regret that a very useful chapter by David Coleman on the shortcomings of migration statistics has been withdrawn; Mr Coleman has been appointed an adviser at the Home Office and felt that it was inappropriate that it should be included. Finally, the Editor, and the Action Group on Immigration and Nationality, under whose auspices the book was planned, wish to thank most warmly all contributors for their work on, and interest in, this book, which we hope all readers will enjoy.

EDITOR

Introduction

The Meaning of Reform

This book arises out of a concern to reform UK immigration law. On many other political questions, the idea of law reform would immediately raise a host of ideas in the reader's mind, arising from newspaper articles and broadcast discussions over the years, but on the subject of immigration it is necessary to say something about what 'reform' means, because, in this as in many other respects, immigration differs from other questions of current political importance. Broadly speaking, ever since immigration control over Commonwealth citizens (including some British people from dependent territories) was introduced in 1962, the argument has not been between two alternative policies but between proposals for racial restriction on the one hand and opponents of new restrictions on the other. The proposers have had a programme ('policy' would be too dignified a word for the series of laws and rules that have been brought into force) but opponents have had none: all that opposers have tried to do has been to stop the latest batch of controls and maintain the status quo. In short, there has been no attempt to think out what a rational, non-racial immigration policy would be. This book tries to begin to find an answer.

In 1981, the question of positive reform of immigration law was raised by the introduction of the British Nationality Bill in Parliament. That Bill modelled a new nationality structure very closely on the existing immigration-law structure established in the Immigration Act 1971, and therefore those who opposed the government proposals on nationality were forced to examine what was wrong with immigration law. They were not forced very far, but they did have to look at the 1971 Act in a new way, not as proposals on the table to be rejected but as a system, already in operation, establishing different rights and disabilities for different groups. They also had to look at it as a system so closely intertwined with British nationality law that any change to the one would require a change to the other. There is now an impetus to reform the law of nationality, an impetus impelled by the concern shown in 1981, and since, by the churches, by many lawyers, some journalists and, of course, the minority groups worst affected, but also at last by many members of the general public who had acquiesced unthinkingly for many years to immigration controls but who found the new nationality law too much to stomach. In practical terms, however, it will be impossible to revise nationality without paying some attention to immigration policy as well.

Where can we start? We need first to examine the basic assumption of existing debate: that there is no alternative between present controls on the one hand and an 'open door' policy on the other. This is an assumption that the Thatcher Government has emphasised, but it is not new; indeed there are people in all the main political parties who take it for granted. (It is worth emphasising, at this point, that the contributors to the present book include supporters of all the main parties, as well as some without party affiliation and some foreign experts and observers.) A moment's pause for reflection is enough to show that there is something wrong with this assumption, for in fact there have been many different systems of control since 1962, and one could argue that a return to this or that earlier set of rules would be a possible alternative to the present system. But at each stage these controls have aimed at excluding black people rather than white. It is taken for granted in the present book that a just immigration law cannot be based on racial discrimination. From our point of view, then, there is no point in reviving old rules: what is needed is a completely new approach.

What then of the supposed alternative: no control at all? This is thought by some people to be the only just policy, by others to be so absurd that it can be rejected out of hand. It is not examined in any of the chapters that follow. The purpose of this book is to demonstrate that there is a very wide range of possible alternatives to present policy, even if one assumes that some form of control over entry is necessary or desirable. Before dismissing a policy of no control, however, it is worth asking what the likely results would in fact be. First, an enormous saving of money and bureaucracy: there would be no more immigration officers, entry clearance officers or appeal system, no police time spent on tracing overstayers or illegal entrants. Secondly, the opportunity for families to be reunited here, and for refugees to enter freely and without anxiety. Thirdly, the opportunity for people engaged in organised crime and political violence to use the country as an easy refuge and base. Fourthly, the likelihood that people wishing, for any reason, to leave their own countries, would try to come here simply because every other country has an entry-control system: thus the total number of entrants would certainly increase. A vast increase in entry might possibly bring economic and cultural benefits here and there, but in the present economic situation it would be more likely, on the whole, to increase the number of residents suffering poverty, unemployment and bad housing. In other words, though it is impossible to guess what all the results would be, the lifting of controls would probably have some good and some bad results. To our knowledge, there has been no serious attempt to calculate these, since people who espouse the cause of the 'open door' believe in principle, and not on consequentialist grounds, that immigration control is wrong. The principle is not an absurd one: it can be justified on various grounds (including concern for the rights of the poor, belief in individual freedom of movement, and even the theory of *laissez-faire* economics, which involves the free movement of labour, though modern supporters of the free market are strangely hostile to the idea of no controls). Moreover, it was actually in operation in much of the world up to the end of the nineteenth century, with international law assuming that restriction of entry into a state by aliens was justified only as an exceptional measure, when national security was at stake. There is still an echo of this view in Sweden's Aliens Act of 1954, which stated: 'An alien is entitled, to the extent and under the conditions set out in this Act, to enter and leave Sweden, and also to stay in the country and to take employment here'. The assumption on which the discussion in this book is based is this: that once you have accepted that control is possible at all, even if it is minimal, an apparatus for maintaining control has to exist, and the way that this apparatus works will represent some kind of policy. Questions then arise about what the policy should be, and how it can be justly administered.

Since 1962, such questions have not been discussed in any fundamental way. Nor indeed were they discussed before then. It is too often forgotten that the UK had a system of control over alien entry since 1905 which was originally based on discrimination against Jews, and which was operated very largely at the discretion of officials in the Home Office. The aim has always been to restrict this group or that, never to give a positive welcome – unless, by implication, the exclusion from control of Commonwealth patrials after 1971 is taken to be a gesture of welcome to the white Commonwealth. The style of restrictiveness has spilled over into the way the UK receives visitors of all sorts; those separate queues at the immigration desks at our ports are unknown in other countries. It has also, of course, with far more important effect, spilled over into the way that people inside the UK see each other. The use of the word 'immigrant' here contrasts very much with the use of 'immigrant' in Canada, for example, as a direct result of the different policy aims and administrative structures of the two countries' immigration laws.

If we want some alternative to the existing system of control, on the one hand, and absolutely no entry controls, on the other, we have to do a lot of hard thinking about what immigration control system we really want. We therefore have to look at all sorts of relevant matters that have been sadly neglected: the requirements of international agreements, the relationship between migration and population, between migration and the economy, and the effects of our policies on other countries. Above all we have to look at migration *as a whole*: not only 'Commonwealth', or non-white, migration into the UK but at all other migration into it, from Ireland, from other European Community countries and from foreign countries in general. And we shall get a completely false and highly misleading picture if we do not look also at emigration as a whole: British people leaving, and former immigrants re-migrating overseas. How are we to find out the past facts and present trends? It is an important function of this book not only to raise new ideas about migration, but to indicate what information we already have and what sort of information needs to be collected if we are to have a useful basis for discussion.

The chapters which follow deal, to some extent, with the existing situation and with the past, for we are not starting from scratch, and we cannot devise a new policy that ignores the practical effects and *idées reçues* created by former laws and practices. But the main purpose is to look ahead, to search out new facts, to re-examine assumptions, and to be open to new ideas. The book tries to lay the foundation for an immigration policy for the future. There is a widespread tendency at the moment to shy away from thinking about the future at all, because it looks so gloomy in so many different ways, but one important message which emerges from what follows is that we should remember the importance of *political will* in changing the situation. It is too often assumed, on all sorts of questions, that some courses are possible and others impossible, without the assumptions being properly examined. Many political reforms have been carried out in the teeth of apparent impossibility. Soon afterwards, they look as if they had always been inevitable. If the determination exists, British immigration policy and its administration can be changed, and the present become a story from the benighted past.

I. Migration in the Modern World

There has always been international movement. Throughout recorded history and before written records, we have evidence of constant movement from one territory to another. People go either to settle, as workers or refugees, in a new land, or to make journeys for temporary purposes, as students or seasonal workers or visitors. In the present century, nation-states have imposed more detailed and stringent controls on such movement than ever before; at the same time, a body of international agreements between states has been created concerning rules of practice for such control.

The UK is a part of this world picture: as a country of immigration and of emigration, as a state bound by a number of international agreements, as a member of the Commonwealth and of the European Community, and as a metropolitan territory with overseas dependencies. It is also part of the world economy and part of the world political scene: its policies on movement therefore have international aspects quite as important as the domestic ones. Yet UK immigration policy and law are generally discussed in an entirely insular way. Part I looks at the international context, beginning with information on international law concerning nationality, immigration and human rights. The first two chapters describe legal standards and agreements: they can be used for reference when later chapters refer to treaties, conventions and cases, but their main purpose is to establish a solid framework for all the description and discussion which follows. The next two chapters are concerned with migration in Europe from the political, economic and social points of view as well as the legal. Finally, the development of policy, and present practice, in two Commonwealth countries and in the US is described, and different systems of administering immigration law can be compared.

Immigration, Nationality and the Standards of International Law[1]

GUY S. GOODWIN-GILL

*Legal Adviser in the office of the United Nations High Commissioner for Refugees**

Introduction

It has long been argued that immigration law and decisions on the entry, exclusion and expulsion of foreigners fall, like questions of nationality, within the realm of sovereign or absolute power, of the reserved domain of domestic jurisdiction. Each state retains, inherent in its sovereignty, the power to exclude all and any aliens; alternatively, the community's right of self-definition justifies a degree of exclusiveness and lesser responsibility towards the non-belonger.[2] In fact, however, no state today maintains a policy of total exclusion and it is evident, if infrequently admitted, that the movement of persons between states not only raises international issues, but also touches the rights and duties of the subjects of international law. The practice of states nevertheless provides ready evidence of the breadth of discretion which is both claimed and conceded to others;[3] yet, increasingly, other standards, with their origins in treaty and in general international law, are impressing themselves upon the conduct of states. Certain rules, such as those relating to nationality – the attribution of persons to a particular territorial unit and the identification of the entity which is legally responsible for them – have a well-established history. Others, such as those relating to the procedural rights of non-nationals, are emerging only now within the body of human

*The views expressed are the writer's personal views and have no official standing.

3

rights law. The following pages survey these developments in the overall context of general international law, and propose certain minimum standards which can be considered essential if immigration law and administration are to avoid censure.

The Implementation of International Legal Obligations[4]

The general duty of a party to a treaty to ensure that its domestic law is in conformity with its international obligations has been frequently acknowledged, both in the jurisprudence of the International Court,[5] and in the views of jurists.[6] Nevertheless, the principles declared do not include an obligation, *per se*, to incorporate the provisions of treaties or of general international law into domestic legislation.[7] The fundamental distinction is that between an obligation of conduct or means, and an obligation of result.[8] Though easier to declare than to apply, this distinction remains crucial in assessing a state's performance under its treaties. In practice, obligations of conduct are less frequent than obligations of result, and are most common where action is required in direct inter-state relations. Obligations of result, on the other hand, incorporating acknowledgement of the principle of choice of means, are most usually found where states are required to promote or create a certain situation within their own legal system.

Article 22(1) of the 1961 Vienna Convention on Diplomatic Relations, for example, declares a clear obligation of conduct: 'The premises of the mission shall be inviolable. The agents of the receiving state may not enter them, except with the consent of the head of the mission.'[9] Here the internationally required conduct is that of omission by the organs of the receiving state; in other cases, positive action may be called for. Thus, states parties to the 1965 Convention on the Elimination of All Forms of Racial Discrimination agree, *inter alia* 'to amend, rescind or nullify any laws or regulations which have the effect of creating or perpetuating racial discrimination wherever it exists.'[10] Similarly, the specific *enactment* of legislation may be demanded, as by Article 20 of the 1966 Covenant on Civil and Political Rights ('Any propaganda for war shall be prohibited by law').[11] In all these examples, the international obligation requires a specifically determined course of conduct; ascertaining that the obligation has been fulfilled turns on the simple question, whether the state's act or omission is or is not in fact in conformity with the internationally required conduct, the sufficient injury being the breach of legal duty.[12]

International obligations requiring the achievement of a specific result often expressly acknowledge the state's full freedom in its choice of means for implementation. Article 22(2) of the 1961 Vienna Convention on Diplomatic Relations declares the receiving state's 'special duty to take all appropriate steps to protect the premises of the mission,' but defines those steps no further. Article 10 of the International Labour Organisation Migrant Workers (Supplementary Provisions) Convention 1975, (No. 143) obliges 'Each Member for which the Convention is in force . . . to declare and pursue a national policy designed to promote and to guarantee, *by methods appropriate to national conditions and practice*, equality of opportunity and treatment . . .'[13] The obligation of result is especially common in standard-setting treaties (for example, treaties of establishment guaranteeing most-favoured-nation treatment), and in human rights instruments. Full freedom of choice may be implied from the terms of the treaty itself, or a preference for legislative measures may be indicated.[14] Nevertheless, although legislation might be thought appropriate, even essential, it is evidently only one way in which the internationally required result can be obtained. It is not so much the letter of the law which counts, as actual compliance with the requisite conduct. Indeed, the International Law Commission has noted:[15]

> . . . so long as the State has not failed to achieve *in concreto* the result required by an international obligation, the fact that it has not taken a certain measure which would have seemed especially suitable for that purpose – in particular, that it has not enacted a law – cannot be held against it as a breach of that obligation.

Two recent treaties require states to enact 'such legislative or other measures as may be necessary'[16] to give effect to rights; and to 'prohibit and bring to an end' certain conduct, 'by all appropriate means, including legislation as required by circumstances.'[17] In both cases the objective is clear, but the conduct/result distinction has become blurred. The context, however, is the protection of human rights and the elimination of racial discrimination, and this permits the inference that obligations of result are intended, which will have their effect within the domestic jurisdiction of states. At the same time, given the declared preference for legislative measures (or at least the adoption of rules), a state which elects to employ less formal methods of implementation may find it difficult to show, either generally, that it has fulfilled its international obligations; or specifically, that individuals intended to benefit from such provisions in fact possess effective remedies against their violation.

Words such as 'necessary' and 'appropriate' show that the state enjoys discretion in its choice of implementing measures, but the standard of compliance remains an international one. The question is one of effective or efficient implementation of the treaty provisions, *in fact* and in the light of the principle of effectiveness of obligations.[18] Just as taking the theoretically best appropriate measures of implementation is not conclusive as to the fulfilment of an international obligation, so failing to take such measures is not conclusive as to breach.[19]

The same principle applies with regard to a state's adoption of a potentially obstructive measure, so long as the measure does not itself create a specific situation incompatible with the required result; what counts is what in fact results, not enactment and promulgation, but application and enforcement. This was clearly understood by the European Court of Human Rights in its judgment in 1978 in *Ireland* v. *UK*. The applicant government argued, *inter alia*, that the laws in force in the six counties of Northern Ireland did not specifically prohibit violation of Articles 3, 5, 6, and 14 of the European Convention. In so far as those laws authorised or permitted such violations the UK, apart from its obligations to individuals, was in breach of a separate inter-state obligation arising from Article 1.[20] The Court doubted whether a contracting state was entitled to challenge a law *in abstracto*. A breach, no doubt, might result 'from the mere existence of a law which *introduces*, *directs*, or *authorises* measures incompatible with the rights and freedoms safeguarded,' but a challenge under Article 24 of the Convention (which enables inter-state applications) would succeed only if the terms of the law were 'sufficiently clear and precise.' Said the Court:[21]

> . . . the decision of the Convention institutions must be arrived at by reference to the manner in which the respondent State interprets and applies *in concreto* the impugned text or texts.
>
> The absence of a law expressly prohibiting this or that violation does not suffice to establish a breach since such a prohibition does not represent the sole method of securing the enjoyment of the rights and freedoms guaranteed.

The Court held that an examination *in abstracto* of the relevant legislation disclosed that it never introduced, directed or authorised recourse to torture or to inhuman or degrading treatment. It did find, however, that certain *administrative practices* violated Article 3 of the European Convention.[22]

In theory, at least, the test of implementation of an international obligation of result might appear as straightforward as that for an obligation of conduct: compare the result in fact achieved with that which the state ought to have achieved. Major problems of interpretation and appreciation can arise in practice, however, in view of the relative imprecision of the terminology employed in standard-setting conventions; the variety of the legal systems and practices of different states; the role of discretion, first, in the states's initial choice of means, and secondly, in its privilege on occasion to require resort to such remedial measures as it may provide; and finally, the possibility that the state may be entitled to avoid responsibility by providing an 'equivalent alternative' to the required result, such as compensation for arbitrary detention. The question whether a state has fulfilled an obligation of result must be examined therefore in the light of the initial means chosen for implementation, the remedies available in the event that an initially incompatible situation ensues, and the option, if permitted by the obligation, of substituting an equivalent alternative result in the event that the principal required result is rendered unattainable. In the field of standard-setting, local remedies are especially important; the beneficiaries of the obligations in question are generally private individuals, 'and the situation which affords them protection must obtain at the level of the internal law of the state in which they are active'.[23] Thus, the availability and effectiveness of local remedies will often determine the question of fulfilment or breach of obligation.[24]

The practical problems inherent in assessing breach or fulfilment of treaty standards are well illustrated by the position adopted by the UK with regard, in particular, to its ratification of various conventions, including the 1948 Genocide Convention; the 1950 European Convention on Human Rights; and the 1966 Covenant on Civil and Political Rights. Only in respect of the Genocide Convention has the UK adopted implementing legislation (the Genocide Act 1969). Article V of that Convention provides:

The Contracting Parties undertake to enact, in accordance with their respective Constitutions, the necessary legislation to give effect to the . . . present Convention and . . . to provide effective penalties.

No such forthright obligation of conduct figures in the other instruments.[25] The European Convention, in Article 1, declares that the Parties 'shall secure to everyone within their jurisdiction' the various rights and freedoms defined,[26] while Article 2 (1) of the 1966 Covenant obliges each State Party, 'to respect and to ensure to all individuals within its territory and subject to its jurisdiction the rights recognised . . . without distinction of any kind . . .' This last mentioned article, as already briefly noted, goes on to trespass within the traditional reserve of choice of means:

2. Where not already provided for by existing legislative or other measures, each State Party to the present Covenant undertakes to take the necessary steps, in accordance with its constitutional processes and with the provisions of the present Covenant, to adopt such legislative or other measures as may be necessary to give effect to the rights recognised in the present Covenant.

3. Each State Party to the present Covenant undertakes:

(a) To ensure that any person whose rights and freedoms are herein recognised are violated shall have an effective remedy, notwithstanding that the violation has been committed by persons acting in an official capacity;

(b) To ensure that any person claiming such a remedy shall have his right thereto determined by competent judicial, administrative or legislative authorities, or by any other competent authority provided for by the legal system of the State, and to develop the possibilities of judicial remedy;

(c) To ensure that the competent authorities shall enforce such remedies when granted.

The reference to 'such legislative or other measures as may be necessary' has been interpreted by one commentator as imposing 'a conditional obligation' as to conduct, supplementing the parties' basic commitment to the obligation of result declared in Article 2(1).[27] This provision nevertheless lacks the precision generally required of obligations of conduct, and clearly allows discretion in the choice of means. That discretion is in turn more closely controlled and structured than is common in statements of obligations of result, so that the practical choices open to states wishing to meet the demands of Article 2(2) and (3) are restricted by the inclusion of preferred means and declared objectives. It does not follow, of course, that states parties are required specifically to incorporate the convention.

United Kingdom practice has generally been to avoid the specific incorporation of standard-setting treaties, in particular, those dealing with human rights. British courts, on occasion, have invoked the provisions of the European Convention on Human Rights, on the assumption that the Crown, 'in taking its part in legislation would do nothing which was in conflict with treaties.'[28] But, while such treaties may serve as an aid to interpretation – the court decisions are by no means consistent with regard to the degree of weight to be accorded them – the self-evident fact of non-incorporation will rule out their forming the basis of a cause of action.[29]

The official position appears to be, that specific implementing legislation is rarely necessary, and still more rarely required as a matter of obligation. If existing provisions of the law appear to cover new treaty obligations, then ratification will proceed without any formal change in the law.[30] Such a practice contains, however, certain inherent weaknesses. First, the question whether municipal law conforms to treaty provisions under review permits few straightforward answers. Treaty language is frequently different, and often imports concepts not known to or readily assimilable in particular legal systems, such as the common law. Thus, there is no common law 'rule' specifically prohibiting torture, inhuman or degrading treatment. The objective is achieved by roundabout means, via tort and offences against the person, but between the international precept and the domestic practice, state responsibility may arise. In like manner, the absence of incorporation may give the impression of an absence of effective remedies against real, or claimed, or imagined violations of rights. Secondly, UK practice ignores the temporal element, making few if any allowances for developments in both municipal and international jurisprudence; laws compatible in 1950 may no longer be so in the changed circumstances of the 1980s. Finally, the appreciation of compatibility is itself an exercise riddled with imponderables, not the least being the direction likely to be taken by the judiciary, the appropriate weight to be accorded, now and in the future, to administrative discretion, and changes in the policies of the executive.

Such apparently theoretical apprehensions find regrettable support in the frequency with which the UK appears before the European Commission or European Court of Human Rights, and in the criticism levelled by members of other supervisory bodies, such as the Human Rights Committee. In 1979, for example, the latter examined the UK with regard to its report on the implementation of the Covenant on Civil and Political Rights. One expert noted that the UK had no written constitution and that the Covenant was not part of its internal legal order; if there were no laws, he wondered how the Committee could determine the degree of compliance with the Covenant.[31] Another expert believed that Article 2(2) required the adoption of specific measures and that it was not sufficient to declare that existing laws were consonant with the Covenant.[32] The UK's representative disagreed with the view that states were obliged to adopt positive measures; what mattered was the treatment that people received and the way in which the law worked in practice.[33]

The conclusion, of course, is technically correct, at the very least, but as an argument, explanation or justification, it is less than satisfactory. In assuming obligations with regard to human rights, states necessarily undertake to implement them effectively and in good faith. The choice of means may well be left to individual states, which can opt between legislative incorporation, administrative regulation, informal and *ad hoc* procedures, or a combination thereof. Specific *legislative* action, however, may well be essential, not only for the purpose of sufficiently identifying human rights, a task important in itself; but also to ensure the availability of an effective remedy against violation. Such formal, legal provisions would be neither purely cosmetic, nor finally conclusive of a state's compliance with its international obligations. Whether in any given case such measures, either together or alone, are sufficient conditions for effective implementation remains to be judged in the light of the actual workings of the municipal system as a whole.[34]

The Question of Nationality

A clear conception of nationality in its domestic sense is an essential basis for the framing of just and effective immigration laws. While still true that nationality matters fall in principle within the reserved domain of domestic jurisdiction,[35] this proposition begs many questions. International law may become involved, for example, by claims to exercise diplomatic protection, or by the question of responsibility to admit nationals expelled from other states, or by the claims of individuals to enter, return to, or leave a particular state, which are founded upon the claim also to be nationals of that state.

The right to a nationality receives mention but surprisingly little emphasis in human rights instruments. It is declared in Article 15 of the 1948 Universal Declaration of Human Rights, which also calls for no 'arbitrary' deprivation of nationality; the right of a child to a nationality is proclaimed in Article 24(3) of the 1966 Covenant on Civil and Political Rights, and it figures also in various regional instruments,[36] although not in the European Convention. Somewhat more common, however, is recognition of the right of a national to enter and not to be expelled from his or her own state.[37] Similarly, the right to leave has been acknowledged in international instruments and has received some support in the decisions of municipal courts.[38] Whatever the status of the right to emigrate or travel, that of entry is an essential, normal incident of nationality.

Both as an obligation between states and as an obligation deriving from the body of fundamental human rights, states are bound to allow their nationals to enter. For the purposes of general international law, this obligation extends, first, to those linked to the state by 'a social fact of attachment, a genuine connection of existence, interests and sentiments.'[39] Secondly, it extends to other groups for whom responsibility has been specifically undertaken. This would include, for example, nationals born and resident abroad and, in particular, those who retained nationality on the independence of former colonial territories. International responsibility towards such nationals may derive from unilateral acts or undertakings, such as independence statutes; or from bilateral agreement. Its existence may be further confirmed by administrative practices, such as the issue of passports; and by reliance by other states upon the appearance of nationality.[40]

General international law cannot be silent when it comes to determining to whom a state owes human rights obligations. The class of persons within or subject to the jurisdiction of a state[41] is not determinable solely by that state. Consequently, where rights or their exercise are tied to the link of nationality, the criteria for membership are determined, in part at least, by rules of international law. This is not to deny that states retain a large margin of appreciation in the process of self-definition or in the application of the connecting factors; but in no case may the process be employed to avoid international responsibility. So, for example, there is nothing intrinsically objectionable in the concept of patriality: it signifies those fundamental connecting factors which international law recognises as forming the basis of the link between individual and state.[42] Problems arise, however, where the concept is employed not to extend benefits but to deny rights, such as that of entry, to particular classes of nationals for whom responsibility is attributable to the state. The unlawfulness of the exclusion may be compounded where the affected group share similar racial or ethnic characteristics, and their treatment, in fact or in law, contravenes the normative provisions of the principle of non-discrimination.[43]

Considered from a slightly different perspective, general international law may not yet recognise an *individual's* right to enter his or her own state.[44] Nevertheless, the very act of denial of entry, besides being a denial of that essential protection which is due to every national, can also infringe other human rights, including those from which no derogation is permitted. Thus, the excluded national may be subjected, in the process of exclusion, or in the country of eventual destination, to inhuman or degrading treatment;[45] or to demeaning measures or humiliation affronting human dignity;[46] or to denial of family rights.[47] Once again, state responsibility in such actions will be further compounded by elements establishing breach of the principle of non-discrimination.

In framing nationality and immigration laws, states are bound in good faith to take account of and effectively implement their international legal obligations. These influence not only the general issue of identification of those who ought to benefit from national protection, but also individualised human rights questions, such as the right of entry, the right not to be subject to inhuman or degrading treatment, the right to the protection of and respect for family life, and to freedom from discrimination on racial or other arbitrary grounds.

Immigration Issues and the Standards of International Law

Mass movements of people, for employment or otherwise on a more or less permanent basis, continue to be a major feature of the international scene, and it is surprising that there has not been greater consensus either on the modalities for the promotion of migration, or on the protection of the rights of migrants and other non-nationals. A single, multilateral convention is lacking and applicable standards must therefore be sought in general international law and in the treaty relationships of states, often in areas apparently remote from the field of immigration.[48]

A summary of all relevant agreements is beyond the scope of the present chapter, which has the following limited objectives: (a) to examine the present status in general international law of certain fundamental human rights, so as to determine the minimum 'no derogation' standard applicable to both nationals and non-nationals; (b) to survey briefly a number of formal agreements between states governing migration matters; and (c) to review, also briefly, some of the standard-setting work undertaken by the International Labour Organisation and other institutions. Finally, certain conclusions will be drawn regarding the content and administration of immigration law, in the light of the requirement to ensure the effective and efficient implementation of international legal obligations.

(a) Human rights standards[49]

Article 13 of the Universal Declaration of Human Rights, as noted above, proclaims the right of everyone to leave any country, including his or her own. However, it is doubtful whether this principle has established itself within the category of fundamental human rights; states in their practice have accorded it only limited recognition and 'lawful' travel remains dependent upon the passport regime, with its municipal law origins. The issue of travel documents is seen by states as an area in which they enjoy unlimited discretion, while the impact of international controls on other inhibiting measures such as exchange control, education or emigration taxes is even more remote.[50] Also, apart from special situations involving returning nationals, treaties and refugees, little consideration has been given to the necessary corollary to the right to leave a country, namely, the right to enter another state or that state's duty to admit. In the absence of any such obligation, proclamations of the right to leave, the right of exit, travel or migration, are somewhat premature, if not redundant.

Once entry into a foreign state has been obtained, and in the absence of special treaty rules, international law expressly permits an unequal status for foreign nationals, for example, in regard to ownership of property and the holding of certain jobs. The alien's position remains anomalous and controversial. Obedience to the local law is required and yet foreign nationals continue to enjoy the diplomatic protection of their own state. They are also entitled to the protection of the local law, and much debate in the early part of this century concentrated on the supposed minimum content of that law. Perhaps the most that could be said, from the point of view of general international law, was that states were obliged to accord 'a somewhat indefinite standard of treatment' to foreign nationals.

Whatever the situation in customary law, however, treaties were long used by states to guarantee to each other's nationals particular standards, for example, in regard to access to the courts, freedom and security in the enjoyment of property and trade. The standards of most-favoured-nation and national treatment developed from the seventeenth century onwards and contributed to a limitation of territorial jurisdiction over foreigners. More recently, the Charter of the UN has been invoked as the basis for a 'standard of humanity', in an attempt to defuse the controversy which had hitherto divided adherents of the international minimum standard school, and those who argued that foreign nationals could not expect treatment better than that accorded to local citizens.

Since 1945, the UN has progressively developed human rights principles by reliance on Articles 55 and 56 of the Charter in successive resolutions, by the adoption of the Universal Declaration of Human Rights in 1948, and by the promotion of multilateral treaties. Within the UN organisation the work of other bodies, such as the ILO, has also contributed to the setting of standards. The constitution of this office, for example, stresses the need for social justice and the annex to the constitution affirms that '*all human beings*, irrespective of race, creed or sex, have the right to pursue both their material well-being and their spiritual development in conditions of freedom and dignity, of economic security and of equal opportunity'.[51]

Adopted by the UN General Assembly in 1965, the International Convention on the Elimination of All Forms of Racial Discrimination enunciates in Article 1 a principle of non-discrimination in terms of any distinction, exclusion, restriction or preference based on the grounds of race, which has the purpose or effect of nullifying or impairing human rights and fundamental freedoms.[52] Article 1(2) of the Convention does expressly permit certain distinctions and exclusions between nationals and others, but given the objective of the treaty, a state is not entitled to implement a policy of racial discrimination on the basis of this exceptional right.

In 1966 the General Assembly adopted two instruments of importance in the migration field: the Covenant on Economic, Social and Cultural Rights and the Covenant on Civil and Political Rights. Article 2(2) of the first-mentioned Covenant declares that states undertake to guarantee the various rights without discrimination of any kind, including specifically discrimination as to 'birth or other status'. An exception allows 'developing countries' to determine to what extent they would guarantee economic rights to non-nationals. However, apart from this provision, no special limitation on the rights of foreign nationals appears in other articles of the Covenant. These recognise, for example, the right of *everyone* to the opportunity to gain their living by work which is freely chosen and accepted,[53] and the right of everyone to the enjoyment of just and favourable conditions of work.[54] Whilst states may not be obliged to allow foreign nationals to work, if that privilege is granted, then they must be treated according to the same standard as applies to nationals.

Article 2(1) of the Covenant on Civil and Political Rights obliges a state to respect and to ensure the rights declared to 'all individuals within its territory and subject to its jurisdiction'. The anti-discrimination provision is widely drawn and includes national or social origin, birth or other status. Article 4(1), which permits derogation in certain circumstances contains a narrower statement of the principle of non-discrimination; this would allow distinctions between nationals and aliens, but measures of derogation must be consistent with states' other obligations under international law. No derogation is permitted, however, from those provisions which guarantee the right to life, or which forbid torture or inhuman treatment, slavery, servitude, or conviction or punishment under retroactive laws. The right to recognition as a person before the law and the right to freedom of conscience, thought and religion are also declared in absolute terms.[55]

The Covenant at large elaborates many of the rights and freedoms first proclaimed in the Universal Declaration. Thus, the right to liberty and security of the person, and to freedom from arbitrary arrest and detention is declared; *all* persons deprived of their liberty are to be treated with humanity and respect; freedom of movement for *everyone* lawfully within the territory of a state is proclaimed, as is the right to leave any country; aliens are entitled not to be arbitrarily expelled and, in common with citizens, enjoy the right to equality before courts and tribunals, the right to privacy, honour and reputation and the right of the family to protection by the state.[56]

The European Convention on Human Rights and the jurisprudence of the European Commission and the European Court have likewise reinforced the fundamental aspect of certain principles. The rights and freedoms apply equally to all within the jurisdiction of contracting parties, apart from one exception which allows states to impose restrictions on the political activities of non-nationals.[57] As with the 1966 Covenant, even where derogation is permitted, certain rights remain sacrosanct: life, freedom from torture or inhuman or degrading treatment, freedom from slavery or servitude, and from penalisation under retroactive criminal legislation.[58]

Underpinning the whole structure lies the rule of non-discrimination. The basic rights, such as the right to life, liberty and security of the person and the right to equality before, and equal protection of the law, clearly allow for no distinction between aliens and nationals. The principle of non-discrimination, which began with the efforts of the international community to outlaw racial discrimination, is clearly now of wider import and, in international law, connotes distinctions which are unfair, unjustifiable or arbitrary. Different treatment, as such, may be lawful, but only (i) if the distinction is made in pursuit of a legitimate aim; (ii) if the distinction does not lack an objective justification; and (iii) provided that a reasonable degree of proportionality exists between the means employed and the aims to be realised.[59] It falls to international law to answer the question whether alienage is, in the circumstances, a 'relevant difference' which justifies differential treatment, and the onus is thus on the party seeking to invoke exceptions to show objective justification and proportionality. Non-discrimination is frequently the core issue in migration matters; it offers the basis for a principled approach to questions involving non-nationals and their methodological analysis, as well as a standard for the progressive development of institutions and practices.

(b) Treaty standards

The number of treaties which directly or indirectly affect the status of foreigners is legion and their role has a long history. Early treaties, called 'capitulations', established completely separate legal regimes for the benefit of foreign nationals, while during the seventeenth, eighteenth and nineteenth centuries, bilateral treaties of friendship, commerce and establishment promoted the interests of the individual merchant. Treaties concluded since the Second World War have concentrated on securing certain minimum rights for foreign nationals engaged in trade, including the right to a hearing in the case of refusal of a residence permit, the right to counsel, to an interpreter, to communicate with one's consul, and for restrictions on the expulsion of long-term residents. More often than not, the earlier bilateral treaties of establishment simply provided that the nationals of each party should enjoy 'full protection and security', or that they should be accorded national treatment. These standards lacked certainty and were hardly adequate to secure effective non-discrimination; for example, the most-favoured-nation clause never actually prohibited a state from discriminating against aliens as a class. Nevertheless, in their historical context, such bilateral arrangements contributed generally to the development of minimum standards of treatment and to increasing recognition of the basic rights of non-nationals.[60] Other bilateral agreements[61] have promoted the movement of groups of migrant workers, and have concentrated on specific issues, such as recruitment, supervision of contracts of employment, facilitation of departure and reception, equal pay with nationals, family reunion, social security, accidents at work, unemployment insurance etc.

Defence of the interests of workers employed abroad is expressly included, in the Preamble to its Constitution, among the objectives of the International Labour Organisation. The ILO's standard setting activities have in turn produced a variety of conventions and recommendations[62] of benefit to migrant workers, the most important of which are: Migration for Employment Convention (Revised) 1949, (No. 97); Migration for Employment Recommendation (Revised) 1949, (No. 86); Migrant Workers (Supplementary Provisions) Convention 1975, (No. 143); Migrant Workers Recommendation 1975, (No. 151). Both conventions are in force and their major provisions are examined elsewhere in this work.[63] The following general remarks are of relevance, however, to the overall international context.

In its work of promoting and developing standards for migrant workers,[64] the ILO has expressly acknowledged the specially weak position of this group. It remains exposed to hostility and exploitation, and will commonly face major problems in assimilation or integration, as well as in the preservation of its national, ethnic and linguistic base.[65] Increasingly, however, the international community is coming to recognise that alienage in itself is a suspect basis for discrimination, that not only do the rights of the individual migrant worker deserve protection, but that states themselves stand to benefit from formal co-operation between countries of emigration and immigration.

As a general rule, ILO conventions give particular importance to the principle of choice of methods by states for the implementation of standards, as well as to the principle of progressive implementation. Basic human rights, of course, permit no distinction between nationals and non-nationals, and the 1975 Convention (No. 143), for example, affirms in Article 1 that 'Each Member for which this Convention is in force undertakes to respect the basic human rights of *all* migrant workers.'[66]

Other specific rights and interests covered by ILO standards justify separate comment and include, first, the reunification of families, especially in view of the prominence given to respect for family life in recent human rights instruments.[67] Clearly, a relevant factor is the type of migration involved, whether it be permanent or temporary and, if the latter, for what duration. Paragraph 15 of the 1949 Recommendation (No. 86) looked forward to family reunion only in respect of migrant workers admitted on a permanent basis, and was limited to the migrant worker's 'wife and minor children', with 'favourable consideration' to be given to other 'dependent' family members. Article 13 of the 1975 Convention (No. 143) goes somewhat further, applies to migrant workers generally and defines the family to include 'spouse and dependent children, father and mother'. Surprisingly, there is no obligation to permit reunion,[68] but the ILO recommendations in respect of family visits may go some way to maintaining family life.[69]

Secondly, there is the question of the migrant worker incapacitated for work, or who otherwise suffers loss of employment. Article 8 of the 1949 Convention (No. 97) expressly provides that a migrant worker admitted on a permanent basis should not generally be required to return home in the event of incapacity arising from illness or injury subsequent to entry. Article 8 of the 1975 Convention (No. 143) goes further, to provide that lawfully resident migrant workers shall not be regarded as in an illegal or irregular situation merely by the fact of loss of employment.

17

Likewise, provision should be made for appeal against termination of employment and for equality of treatment in matters such as reinstatement and compensation.[70] Thirdly, in the event of threatened expulsion, the migrant worker should enjoy the right of appeal, and the appeal itself should stay execution of the order of expulsion 'subject to the duly substantiated requirements of national security or public order'.[71]

Finally, there are the problems of illegal migration. One objective of the 1975 Convention (No. 143) is indeed the suppression of migration in abusive conditions, including illegal migration and illegal employment of migrant workers.[72] It requires states to take various measures to detect and suppress such activities, as well as to provide minimum legal protection to migrant workers whose situation is irregular; basic human rights are not conditional upon the circumstances of residence.[73] Doubtless, the illegal migrant is tending less to be seen as fair game, but there remain wide divergences of opinion as regards the precise standard of treatment which is due. At a seminar organised by the Intergovernmental Committee for Migration in April 1983, for example, there was no agreement even on the fundamental human rights which undocumented or irregular migrants should enjoy. Moreover, it was stressed that acceptance of basic rights should not imply a *de facto* recognition of the legality of status.[74] On the other hand, as one commentator has cogently argued, there are certain cases of illegal migration in which regularisation is demanded by the equities of the situation,[75] and some regard for acquired rights is probably essential at all times. The issue remains controversial, and the divisions of opinion are still more apparent in current debate within the UN on two topics – the proposed declaration on the rights of non-citizens and a convention for the protection of the rights of all migrant workers and their families.[76]

Certain aspects of migration have also been the subject of regional arrangements. For example, the European Convention on Establishment 1955 expressly provides that contracting states shall facilitate the entry of nationals of other parties, first, for the purpose of temporary visits and secondly, for prolonged or permanent residence, although the latter may be limited in the light of social and economic conditions.[77] The Protocol to the Convention, at the same time, declares a wide power of derogation and concedes that states shall have the right to judge by national criteria the reasons of *ordre public* or national security, which may justify the exclusion of other states' nationals. This Convention espouses generalities rather than details, but it was the first multilateral treaty in an area traditionally governed by bilateral agreements. While the obligation assumed is mainly to facilitate entry and residence, the EEC Treaty of Rome concerns itself with details and anticipates a local plan to be fulfilled by the co-ordination of national regimes, the objective being the free movement of labour. The EEC has objectives exceeding the scope of the present chapter, while its freedom of movement provisions have already been the object of ample study.[78] That freedom is itself theoretically limited to the nationals[79] of member states, yet the European Community suffered for many years from a labour shortage which necessitated the recruitment of migrant workers from third countries. There has also been some tendency to extend certain community benefits beyond the class of community nationals.[80]

For present purposes, it is sufficient to note that a principal foundation of the community is the abolition of discrimination on the grounds of nationality. Articles 48–57 of the Treaty of Rome propose freedom of movement of workers, nationals of the member states, and the right of establishment in the territory of a member state, for the purposes of employment, involvement in production or distribution of goods, or the provision of services. Any restriction on the exercise of these rights must be justified by reference to community law concepts of *ordre public*, public security and public health. In view of the very close relationships anticipated by the overall objectives of the EEC, interpretation of the relevant provisions could hardly be left to the judgment of individual governments, and questions of community law are therefore entrusted to the European Court of Justice established by the Treaty.

Already the Court has acknowledged that the notion of 'community worker' is itself a concept of community law; it does not arise from and is not governed by national law. It includes not only manual workers, but all employees; not only a present worker, but also one who, having left a job, is capable of taking another.[81] The Court has confirmed that both Article 48 and Regulations made under it confer enforceable rights on the individual, who likewise is to benefit from fundamental human and constitutional rights recognised by member states and in accordance with general international law.[82] Secondary community legislation, the regulations and directives, have given much substance to the principles of the founding treaties. Regulation 1612/68, for example, is of particular importance; *inter alia*, it prescribes specific rights in regard to non-discrimination in access to employment; equality of treatment concerning conditions of employment; equality of treatment as regards membership of trade unions[83] and the exercise of trade union rights; non-discrimination in housing. The right to family reunion is proclaimed and the migrant worker's family is defined to include spouse, children under 21 or, if older, dependent children, and dependent relatives of worker and spouse in the ascending line. The exercise of the right of settlement is conditional upon provision by the migrant worker of adequate housing, but once admitted, spouse and children under 21 are entitled to take up employment and children are to be admitted to schools on the same terms as nationals.

Other measures make provision in regard to social security, so that under Community law migrant workers maintain rights to social security benefits for periods spent working in any of the member states; entitlements follow the worker.[84] Recognition has also been given to the right to remain in the territory of a member state after having been employed there; such 'acquired right of residence' is granted both to the worker and to the worker's family.[85]

Secondary Community legislation has also made a substantial impression on the basic rights of the individual. Directive 64/221, for example, requires co-ordination of matters affecting *ordre public*, which is itself a concept of Community law allowing to member states a certain margin of appreciation in matters considered to affect the national interest.[86] The privilege of derogation is exceptional and the validity of its exercise will be assessed in the light of the fundamental obligations accepted by states under the Treaty of Rome, and the express limitations on the area of discretion imposed by the above-mentioned Directive. This Directive applies also to questions of entry, to the issue or renewal of residence permits and to expulsion; it expressly declares that no restrictions may be imposed on community workers which serve economic ends. In addition to substantive guarantees, it provides further for certain procedural guarantees, for example, decisions without delay, conditional entry, and appeal or review of adverse decisions.

The EEC Treaty and subordinate legislation have created a special regime for the benefit of migrant workers who are nationals of the member states. The relevant provisions may also incidentally benefit migrant workers from third states, and there have already been moves to improve the situation of this latter class, the objectives again being non-discrimination and equality of treatment in the matter of basic rights. In 1976, the Council of Ministers of the European Communities resolved on an action programme for migrant workers and their families. The need to improve the lot of those from third states was emphasised and the goal of equality was proposed in regard to living and working conditions, wages and economic rights. It was intended that realisation of this aim should be accompanied by joint action to suppress illegal migration. The following year the Council of Europe promoted for adoption by member states the European Convention on the Legal Status of Migrant Workers, and this entered into force on 1 May 1983.[87]

(c) Refugees

The most important international legal instruments affecting the situation and rights of refugees are the 1951 Convention and the 1967 Protocol relating to the Status of Refugees, to which 97 states are now party.[88] Moreover, as I have argued elsewhere, there is now clear evidence that 'refugees' are a class known to and enjoying the protection of general international law;[89] in particular, states are bound by the principle of *non-refoulement* and, save in very limited circumstances, may not return a refugee to a country in which he or she may face persecution.

There remains no legal obligation to accord to refugees asylum in the sense of a lasting solution, although in many countries recognition as a refugee is in fact both the necessary and the sufficient condition for the grant of residence and treatment equal and often superior to that required under the Convention. That treaty also imposes no requirement to establish a refugee status procedure, and prescribes no minimum procedural standards. States retain choice of means, therefore, and will often opt for a system which is consonant with existing judicial or administrative structures, and with their own conceptions regarding the appropriate standards of due process or natural justice.

The international legal requirements of effective implementation, however, imply the necessity of some sort of procedure if refugees are to be singled out and receive appropriate protection.[90] Legislation may well be the most appropriate vehicle for this purpose, although finally it is the actual working of the municipal system as a whole which will determine whether a state is fulfilling its international obligations. Specific proposals with regard to the processing of asylum applications in the UK appear elsewhere in this volume.[91]

One other aspect of the refugee problem demands attention, namely, the contribution which states can make to meet refugee needs worldwide. Clearly, the capacity of individual states to accept refugees for resettlement is conditioned by various factors, including the economic situation, immigration objectives and obligations, numbers of refugees directly arriving and settled locally etc. Principles of international solidarity and burden-sharing, however, argue for some degree of positive contribution.

Simply to allow admission to refugees who qualify anyway under existing immigration policies is a somewhat incomplete contribution: what is required is a commitment to those who do not qualify, or who may even be ineligible. Only in that way can some prospect of a new life be offered to so many who find themselves detained in camps or jails throughout the world, to the physically and mentally handicapped, to the socially disadvantaged.

Conclusions: Rights in Immigration and Nationality

Already there is a sufficient body of principles and rules which can rightly be called the international law of human rights.[92] Universal and regional differences allow for varying degrees of supervision and enforcement, but, backed overall by principles of state responsibility, the individual now possesses a certain standing in general international law with regard to the protection of his or her basic rights.

Nationality, for example, is not simply the concept which links the individual to this or that state.[93] It also symbolises a variety of international obligations operative at the inter-state level, and cognisable by competent intergovernmental organisations. Nationality, in its international legal sense, thus describes the class of persons for whom a particular state is legally responsible and to whom certain duties are owed, for example, to accord entry and otherwise to provide protection. 'Protection' in this context has both internal and external aspects: it implies the provision of effective domestic guarantees in matters such as life, liberty and security of the person; and the exercise of diplomatic protection of nationals abroad, including documentation and recognition of the right to return.[94]

Whatever the individual dimension in this sphere, it remains clear that nothing justifies differentiating between national and non-national in the matter of fundamental human rights – the right to life, and to protection against slavery, torture, cruel or inhuman treatment; the right to liberty and security of the person (including protection against arbitrary arrest and detention); recognition as a person before the law; equality before and equal protection of the law; freedom of conscience, thought and religion. The principle of non-discrimination, moreover, calls into question any other differential treatment which may be practised on non-nationals.

Such statements on fundamental rights, however, tend to provoke few dissentients. Their generality accommodates many shades of opinion, and what really counts is how the scheme of protection is worked out at the local level, particularly with regard to subsidiary rights and procedural guarantees.

Apart from its special duty to nationals, it is by no means clear that a state, under *general* international law, is ever bound to admit an alien.[95] Any absolute discretion which the state might claim, however, is circumscribed amply by treaty and other obligations towards human beings at large, and to identifiable groups and individuals in particular.

Migrant workers, for example, benefit from standards promoted universally and regionally by the ILO, the Council of Europe, the EEC and the like institutions in other parts of the world. It is widely accepted that, where migration is to be promoted, it should take place in appropriate conditions, with due regard to recruitment, placing, travel, reception and accommodation, as well as to the suppression of migration in abusive conditions and the exploitation of labour.[96] In the case of permanent or medium-term migration, the principle of family reunion requires implementation, as do measures generally which will assist with integration (including language tuition and educational opportunities for children). Non-discrimination implies equality of opportunity in the work field, in remuneration, job opportunity (though doubtless subject to recognised public service exceptions), trade union rights and benefits, social security, taxation, medical treatment and accommodation. Basic legal guarantees are also called for in those matters of greatest concern to migrant workers, including termination of employment, non-renewal of work permits and expulsion.

While not every country is in search of migrant labour or in need of immigration, this does not render it immune to the claims of non-nationals. In appropriate circumstances, therefore, a state may be bound to allow entry to the family members of nationals or resident aliens, or to previously resident aliens who benefit from acquired rights.[97] Under general international law, refugees and asylum seekers may be entitled to entry, if not durable asylum, through operation of the principle of *non-refoulement.* Once admitted, particularly if on a permanent or indefinite basis, there will be little if any justification for discriminating against the non-national in regard to employment, education, housing, social security, or freedom of movement. Indeed, positive steps may be called for in the protection and promotion of the cultural rights of non-national minorities, particularly if present in substantial numbers.

For their effective protection, rights require a procedural framework, founded upon due process and the rule of law. This means that those who claim a right, whether of entry or treatment, should have access to a procedure for the determination of their case, or for a remedy in the face of violation.[98] Not only are the basic requirements of natural justice called for, but in a developed system also the provision of advice, speedy decision-making, detailed statements of reasons for refusal of claims and remedies, and the opportunity for renewal or appeal.

Notwithstanding the tenor of the preceding argument, it must be admitted that state practice still accepts substantive and procedural limitations on the rights of non-nationals. Typically, it is claimed that entry may be refused or expulsion ordered where the alien constitutes a threat to national security, to public safety or to the general welfare of the community. An alternative argument, with origins in notions of national exclusiveness, would deny to non-nationals the full extent of due process rights, simply because the individuals in question are not part of, or sufficiently part of, the community. Certainly, one can concede discretion in self-definition, but to qualify both substantive and procedural rights by reference to the national/non-national distinction alone is too wide, and leaves too many claims unmet. The exceptions of national security, public safety, etc., not only require restrictive interpretation; their principled application also demands that they be related to the circumstances of each case.

Various rules applied or interpreted in various jurisdictions, however, militate against the principled approach; national exclusiveness can thus be employed to frustrate the attainment of a certain level of judicial and judicious administration. For example, deportation has frequently been described by courts as 'not a punishment', so that full due process rights may not apply, and prohibitions or cruel or inhuman treatment are held inapplicable.[99] Even under the European Convention on Human Rights, the jurisprudence adopted with regard to Article 6(1) and the interpretation of 'civil rights' has sanctioned serious limitations upon non-nationals' entitlement to substantive and procedural due process. Deportation, termination of a residence permit, and the grant or refusal of entry, have all been found by the European Commission not to involve civil rights.[100] Insofar as such disadvantages tend on balance to reduce the quality of justice without contributing significantly to the protection or promotion of a valid community interest, they must be considered suspect. Likewise, provisions which limit appeal or review rights to aliens lawfully in state territory restrict the scope for objective and effective examination of claims to refugee status, or to respect for family life, or for acquired rights.

Recent decisions by US courts hightlight the problems still emerging from the national/non-national distinction. In *Plyler* v. *Doe* (1982), for example, the Supreme Court struck down a state statute denying tuition-free public education to undocumented alien children.[101] In early 1984, on the other hand, the Court of

Appeals ruled not only that excludable aliens have no rights under the US Constitution (and therefore no entitlement to the benefit of the due process and equal opportunity clauses); but also that there are no inherent or implied limitations on the length of time for which excludable aliens may be detained; and that such aliens have no right to be informed of the opportunity to apply for asylum. National security and foreign policy considerations were adduced and confirmed as a sufficient justification for the broadest discretions.[102]

The view from the perspective of general international law is somewhat different. The import of human rights and related developments is that claims to offer a lesser degree of justice to particular groups or individuals should be called into question. The principle of effectiveness of obligations and the norm of non-discrimination cast doubt on each and every denial of substantive or procedural rights. The generality of human rights is due not because the individual is or is not a member of a particular group, and claims to such rights are not determinable according to membership, but according to the character of the right in question.[103] To many rights, legitimate exceptions attach, but the lawfulness of the latter in a given case depends upon their bearing a reasonable relationship to some greater community interest. Certainly communities retain discretion in the process of self-definition, but other, perhaps weightier principles also abound. The individualised aspect of fundamental human rights requires, at the least, a case-by-case consideration of claims, and the recognition that certain special duties are now owed to all persons.

Notes

1 I have already canvassed some of the ideas in this essay in *International Law and the Movement of Persons between States* (1978), *The Refugee in International Law* (1983), and in a paper presented in 1981 in Nicosia, Cyprus, at a conference on International Migration in the Arab World, 'International Covenants and Agreements governing International Migration' (UN doc. E/ECWA/POP/CONF. 4/WP. 7) I nevertheless hope that I have avoided tedious repetition.

2 Cf., Martin, 'Due process and the treatment of aliens,' 44 *University of Pittsburgh Law Review* (1983) p. 165; Aleinikoff, 'Aliens, due process and "community ties": A response to Martin,' *ibid.*, p. 237.

3 Cf., Nafziger, 'The general admission of aliens under international law,' 77 AJIL (1983), p. 804 who argues strongly in favour of a 'qualified duty of states to admit at least some aliens'.

4 The arguments which follow are further developed with regard to refugees in Goodwin-Gill, *Refugee, op. cit.*, pp. 140–148.

5 See, for example, 'Treatment of Polish Nationals in Danzig', PCIJ, Ser. A/B, No. 44, p. 24; 'Greco-Bulgarian Communities Case', PCIJ, Ser. B, No. 17, p. 32; 'Free Zones Case', PCIJ, Ser. A, No. 24, p. 12; Ser. A/B, No. 46, p. 167; Article 27 of the 1969 Vienna Convention on the Law of Treaties.

6 McNair, *The Law of Treaties* (1961), pp. 78–9; Brownlie, *Principles of Public International Law* (3rd. ed., 1979), pp. 36–8; and *System of the Law of Nations: State Responsibility, Part I* (1983), pp. 241–276.

7 The International Court has stressed that failure to enact legislation necessary to ensure fulfilment of international obligations will not relieve a state of responsibility; see 'Exchange of Greek and Turkish Populations Case', PCIJ, Ser. B, No. 10, p. 20.

8 See generally, International Law Commission, *Yearbook*, (1977), Vol. II, pp. 11–50; Brownlie, *State Responsibility*, passim.

9 Text in UN doc. A/CONF.20/13; Brownlie, *Basic Documents op. cit.*, p. 212.

10 Article 2(1)(c); text annexed to UN General Assembly resolution 2106(XX) of 21 December 1965; Brownlie, *Basic Documents*, p. 302.

11 Text annexed to UN General Assembly resolution 2200(XXI) of 16 December 1966; Brownlie, *Basic Documents, op. cit.*, p. 270. Some states have entered reservations to this article on the basis of its inconsistency with the freedom of expression recognised in Article 19. See reservations by Denmark, Finland, Iceland, Netherlands, New Zealand, Norway, Sweden, and the UK: UN doc. ST/LEG/SER.D/13, (Multilateral Treaties in respect of which the Secretary-General performs depositary functions; List of Signatures, Ratifications, Accessions, etc., as at 31 December 1979), pp. 111–120.

12 *Diplomatic and Consular Staff in Tehran*, (*USA* v. *Iran*), (1980), ICJ Rep., 3, 30–31. Cf., International Law Commission, Draft Articles on State Responsibility, Articles. 16, 20: *Yearbook*, (1977), Vol. II, pp. 10–11. In commenting on the irrelevance of harmful consequences actually resulting, the International Law Commission suggests as one example that Article 10(3) of the 1966 Covenant on Economic, Social and Cultural Rights ('. . . States Parties . . . recognise that . . . (child employment in certain circumstances) . . . should be punishable by law.') is breached by simple failure to enact legislation. This conclusion seems erroneous; Article 2(1) of that Covenant refers expressly to 'achieving progressively the full realisation of the rights recognised', while Article 10 alone in that instrument employs the ambivalent 'should'. The provision is thus rather an obligation of result, than of conduct.

13 See also Article 24 of the ILO Constitution, whereby every member state 'binds itself effectively to observe within its jurisdiction any Convention to which it is a party'.

14 See, for example, Article 2(1) of the 1966 Covenant on Economic, Social and Cultural Rights, and Article 2(2) of the 1966 Covenant on Civil and Political Rights.

15 International Law Commission *Yearbook*, (1977), Vol. II, p. 23.

16 Article 2(1) of the 1966 Covenant on Civil and Political Rights.

17 Article 2(1)(d) of the 1965 Convention on the Elimination of All Forms of Racial Discrimination.

18 See generally Brownlie, *State Responsibility, op. cit.*; also Lauterpacht, *The Development of International Law by the International Court* (Stevens 1958), pp. 257, 282ff. Article 31(1) of the 1969 Vienna Convention on the Law of Treaties; McNair, *The Law of Treaties, op. cit.*, p. 540f.

19 *Tolls on the Panama Canal* (1911–12): Hackworth, *Digest of International Law*, Vol. VI, p. 59 (views of the US); 'Certain German Interests in Polish Upper Silesia (Merits)', PCIJ, (1926), Ser. A, No. 7, p. 19.

20 Judgment of the Court, *Ireland* v. *UK*, (Application 5301/71), paras. 236ff. Article 1 of the European Convention provides: 'The High Contracting Parties

shall secure to everyone within their jurisdiction the rights and freedoms defined . . .'.

21 *Ibid.*, para. 240, (emphasis supplied).

22 *Ibid.*, paras. 241, 246.

23 The local remedies rule was originally framed with regard to the standard of treatment of aliens, but is now increasingly applied, in human rights instruments, to all persons regardless of status; see, for example, Article 26 of the European Convention on Human Rights; Articles 11(3), 14(7)(a) of the 1965 Convention on the Elimination of All Forms of Racial Discrimination; Article 41(1)(c) of the 1966 Covenant on Civil and Political Rights; Article 5(2)(b), Optional Protocol thereto.

24 International Law Commission *Yearbook*, (1977), Vol. II, p. 36.

25 The apparently clear statement of an undertaking to enact has not in fact prevented states from asserting that, in their case, legislation was not required because the offences to be suppressed were covered by existing laws, even though the latter might not mention genocide specifically. See UN doc. E/CN.4/Sub.2/416, (1978), paras. 498–504 (Ruhashyankiko, *Study of the Question of the Prevention and Punishment of the Crime of Genocide*).

26 In its judgment in *Ireland* v. *UK* (*supra*, note 20), the European Court of Human Rights noted: 'By substituting the words "shall secure" for the words "undertake to secure" in the text of Article 1, the drafters of the Convention also intended to make it clear that the rights and freedoms set out . . . would be directly secured to anyone within the jurisdiction of the Contracting States . . . That intention finds a particularly faithful reflection in those instances where the Convention has been incorporated into domestic law . . .' (para. 239).

27 Schachter, 'The obligations of the parties to give effect to the Covenant on Civil and Political Rights,' 73 AJIL (1979), p. 462 notes: 'It is not enough for a party to say that it respects and ensures rights (the obligation of result); it must also carry out the obligation to use the specified means required by Article 2 through its domestic legal system.'

28 See, for example, *Waddington* v. *Miah* [1974] 1 WLR 692, HL; *R* v. *Secretary of State, ex parte Bhajan Singh* [1975] 3 WLR 225, DC and CA; *R* v. *Secretary of State, ex parte Phansopkar* [1975] 3 WLR 322, DC and CA; *R* v. *Chief Immigration Officer, Heathrow Airport, ex parte Salamat Bibi* [1976] 1 WLR 979, CA; *R* v. *Secretary of State, ex parte Hosenball* [1977] 1 WLR 766 (per Lord Denning MR, at 779); *R* v. *Board of Visitors of Hull Prison, ex parte St Germain* [1978] 2 WLR 598 (per Lord Widgery CJ, at 606).

29 Some possible exceptions are considered by Mann, 'The enforcement of treaties by English courts,' in *Studies in International Law*, (1973), pp. 327–359; and 'Britain's Bill of Rights,' 94 LQR (1978) p. 512; *Laker Airways Ltd* v. *Department of Trade* [1977] 1 QB 643.

30 See *Hansard*, 25 May 1979, col. 1376 (Mr Raison), commenting on the UK's ratification but non-incorporation of the 1951 Convention relating to the Status of Refugees.

31 Mr Movchan, expert from the Soviet Union: UN doc. CCPR/C/SR.147, paras. 8, 9; (a more lively account appears in United Nations, Press Releases, HR/1792–4, 25, 26 April 1979). It may be noted in passing that the Soviet Union figures among those states which, despite the apparently express requirement of Article V of the Genocide Convention, have not found it necessary to enact specific legislation: UN doc. E/CN.4/Sub.2/416, para. 501 (*supra*, note 25).

32 Mr Sadi, expert from Jordan: UN doc. CCPR/C/SR.147, para. 13; Mr Movchan agreed: *ibid.*, para. 31. Schachter, 73 AJIL 462, 464f (1979) has doubted whether proposed US reservations designed, in the view of the State Department, to harmonise the treaties with existing provisions of domestic law, but in fact aiming to avoid any need to modify the said law, can be

regarded as compatible with the object and purpose of the Covenant, especially in the light of the obligations of conduct which he finds expressed in Article 2. He considers that the object of Article 2 is to require all parties to adopt measures wherever necessary to give effect to the Covenant; reservations intended to deprive Article 2 of all effect themselves challenge the general principle reflected in Article 27 of the Vienna Convention on the Law of Treaties.

33 Mr Richard (UK): UN doc. CCPR/C/SR.147, para. 18 and SR.149, para. 18; also Mr Cairncross (UK): *ibid.*, SR.147, para. 32.

34 Increasing importance attaches to international supervisory machinery such as that established by the ILO, or under the Covenant on Civil and Political Rights or the European Convention on Human Rights. The decisions of the European Commission and the European Court, in particular, have led to numerous changes in the law and practice of states. See generally, Sieghart, *The International Law of Human Rights*, (Clarendon Press, 1983), ss. 4, 5.

35 *Nationality Decrees Case*, PCIJ, Ser. B, No. 4, p. 23. Goodwin-Gill, *Movement of Persons, op. cit.*, pp. 4–21.

36 Article XIX of the 1948 American Declaration of the Rights and Duties of Man; Article 20 of the 1969, American Convention on Human Rights.

37 Articles 9, 13 of the 1948 Universal Declaration of Human Rights; Article 12(3), of the 1966 Covenant on Civil and Political Rights; Articles 2(2), 3 of the 1963 Fourth Protocol, European Convention on Human Rights; Article 22 of the 1969 American Convention on Human Rights; Article 12 of the 1981 African Charter on Human and Peoples' Rights.

38 Goodwin-Gill, *Movement of Persons, op. cit.*, pp. 29–38; see also Ingles, 'Study of Discrimination in Respect of the Right of Everyone to Leave any Country, including his Own, and to Return to his Country': (1964) UN doc. E/CN.4/Sub.2/229/Rev. 1. For nearly 20 years, this report was consistently ignored by the UN Commission on Human Rights. At its 1984 session, however, the Commission endorsed the proposal to appoint a rapporteur to analyse current trends and developments with respect to the right. The study was extended to cover the possibility of entering other countries, employment, the brain drain, labour compensation, and permissible limitations. Cf., *Haig* v. *Agee* (1981) 101 S Ct 2766; noted 75 AJIL (1981), p. 962 in which the US Supreme Court, reversing lowers courts, upheld (as a matter of statutory interpretation rather than of executive foreign affairs powers) the revocation of an individual's passport on the ground of likely serious damage to national security or US foreign policy.

39 *Nottebohm Case*, 1955 ICJ Rep., 4 at 23.

40 Goodwin-Gill, *Movement of Persons, op. cit.*, pp. 13f, 49, 101–103.

41 Sieghart, *op. cit.*, s. 6.3.

42 Cf., the nationality provisions of France and the Federal Republic of Germany: Goodwin-Gill, *Movement of Persons, op. cit.*, pp. 14–21.

43 *Ibid.*, pp. 92f, 102f, 164–167, 173–176.

44 The UK, for example, has not ratified the Fourth Protocol of the European Convention on Human Rights and has also made the following reservation to the 1966 Covenant on Civil and Political Rights: 'The Government of the United Kingdom reserve the right to continue to apply such immigration legislation governing entry into, stay in and departure from the United Kingdom as they may deem necessary from time to time and, accordingly, their acceptance of Article 12(4) and of the other provisions of the Covenant is subject to the provisions of any such legislation as regards persons not at the time having the right under the law of the United Kingdom to enter and remain in the United Kingdom. The United Kingdom also reserves a similar right in regard to each of its dependent territories.'

45 See Duffy, 'Article 3 of the European Convention on Human Rights,' 32 ICLQ (1983), pp. 316, 340–344.
46 The concept of human dignity, which percolates the whole realm of human rights law, clearly deserves elaboration; see Schachter, 'Human dignity as a normative concept,' 77 AJIL (1983), p. 848.
47 Goodwin-Gill, *Movement of Persons*, *op. cit.*, pp. 162–164; Mehl and Rapoport, 'Soviet policy of separating families and the right to emigrate,' 27 ICLQ (1978), p. 876.
48 See *infra*, note 76.
49 See *International Provisions protecting the Human Rights of Non-Citizens*: UN doc. E/CN.4/Sub.2/392/Rev.1 (1980), Study prepared by the Baroness Elles, Special Rapporteur of the Sub-Commission on Prevention of Discrimination and Protection of Minorities.
50 See *supra*, note 47.
51 Constitution of the ILO, Annex, Declaration concerning the aims and purposes of the ILO, Pt. II (a); text in Brownlie, *Basic Documents*, op. cit., p. 49.
52 As of 31 December 1983, 121 States were party to the convention.
53 Article 6.
54 Article 7.
55 Article 4(2). See also Annex III, Elles, *Human Rights of Non-Citizens*, (*supra* note 49), p. 57.
56 Articles 9, 10, 12, 13, 14(1), 17(1), 23(1), 26.
57 Schachter, 77 AJIL (1983) p. 848.
58 Articles 2, 3, 4(1) and 7.
59 See generally McKean, *Equality and Discrimination under International Law*, (Clarendon Press, 1983); Bossuyt, *L'interdiction de la discrimination dans le droit international des droits de l'homme*, (Bruylant, 1976).
60 See the categories of 'treaty trader' and 'treaty investor' in US immigration law: Goodwin-Gill, *Movement of Persons*, *op. cit.*, pp. 192–195.
61 See, for example, the wide variety of agreements cited in *Report of the Committee of Experts, International Labour Conference*, 'Migrant Workers', (1980), 66th Session, p. 44f, note 49.
62 Also of relevance are: Social Security (Minimum Standards) Convention 1952, (No. 102); Discrimination (Employment and Occupation) Convention 1958, (No. 111); Social Policy (Basic Aims and Standards) Convention 1962, (No. 117); Equality of Treatment (Social Security) Convention 1962, (No. 118); Employment Policy Convention 1964, (No. 122). To a varying degree, each proposes, in the context of its subject matter, the objective of non-discrimination between nationals and migrant workers. Certain exceptions are retained, however, and the 1958 Convention, (No. 111), for example, does not include 'nationality' amongst the prohibited grounds of discrimination, though this may be added by states parties after consultation with employers' and workers' organisations and other appropriate bodies. The 1964 Convention, (No. 122), which had full employment as its objective, may be applied to non-nationals at the discretion of states parties. The flexibility of many of these instruments allows states to implement non-discriminatory policies in the light of their own development, although certain others (such as the Convention on Freedom of Association 1948, (No. 87)), apply 'without distinction'.
63 See Hilary Kellerson, 'International Labour Conventions and Recommendations on Migrant Workers,' pp. 33–42, *post*.
64 Formally interpreted to cover those who migrate from one country to another for the purpose of being employed there other than on their own account.
65 See generally Watson, ed., *Between Two Cultures: Migrants and Minorities in Britain*, (Blackwell, 1977).

66 The Report of the Committee of Experts, International Labour Conference, *op. cit.*, pp. 68–69 proposed for inclusion within this category of rights – the right to life, to protection against torture, cruel, inhuman or degrading treatment or punishment, liberty and security of the person, protection against arbitrary arrest and detention, and the right to a fair trial.

67 See, for example, Article 8 of the European Convention on Human Rights; Articles 17, 23 of the 1966 Covenant on Civil and Political Rights.

68 Compare the EEC provisions, described below.

69 Paragraphs 17, 18 of the 1975 Recommendation, (No. 151).

70 *Ibid.*, paragraphs 30–33.

71 *Ibid.*, paragraph 33. Cf., Article 13 of the 1966 Covenant on Civil and Political Rights.

72 Article 2(1) of the 1975 Convention, (No. 143) defines migration in abusive conditions to include 'any movements of migrants for employment in which the migrants are subjected during their journey, on arrival or during their period of residence and employment to conditions contravening relevant international multilateral or bilateral instruments or agreements, or national laws or regulations.'

73 Equality of opportunity and treatment under Article 10 of the 1975 Convention, (No. 143) is limited to those lawfully in state territory; however, Article 9(1) requires further that illegal migrant workers, whose position cannot be regularised, should receive 'equal treatment' for themselves and their families in respect of rights arising out of past employment in matters of pay, social security, etc. Unless Part II of this Convention is accepted, 'equal treatment' in this context means not treatment equal to that accorded to nationals, but that accorded to lawfully present migrant workers. See also article 6 of the 1949 Convention, (No. 97), limiting application of its provisions to immigrants lawfully within state territory.

74 See Intergovernmental Committee for Migration, 'Sixth Seminar on Adaptation and Integration of Immigrants: Undocumented Migrants or Migrants in an Irregular Situation, Conclusions and Recommendations' (doc. MC/SAI/VI/GEN/VI).

75 Böhning, 'Regularising the irregular,' 21 *International Migration* (1983), p. 159.

76 The UN is currently at work on two issues which should promote the interests of migrant workers and non-citizens. In 1979, the General Assembly decided to create at its 35th session a working group open to all member states, to elaborate an international convention on the protection of the rights of all migrant workers (Res. 34/172). A similar working group was established in 1982 to conclude a draft declaration on the human rights of individuals who are not citizens of the country in which they live (Res. 37/169). See UN docs. A/C.3/38/5 (migrant workers) and A/C.3/38/11 (non-citizens) for latest reports of the working groups (1983).

77 Article 2; European Treaty Series, (ETS), No. 19. Goodwin-Gill, *Movement of Persons*, *op. cit.*, pp. 168–186.

78 In addition to general works on Community law, the following deal with specific aspects of free movement: Böhning and Stephen, *The EEC and the Migration of Workers*, (1971; Supp., 1972); Sundberg-Weitman, *Discrimination on Grounds of Nationality: Free Movement of Workers and Freedom of Establishment under the EEC Treaty*, (1977); Evans, 'United Kingdom Courts and European Community Law governing the exclusion or expulsion of migrants,' *Public Law*, (1981), p. 497.

79 'Nationals' is a term hardly free from doubt or ambiguity; see White and Hampson, 30 ICLQ (1981), pp. 247, 253f, 258; 31 ICLQ (1982), pp. 849, 850.

80 Cf., Regulation 1612/68, Articles 1, 2, 4, 5, 6; Regulation 1408/71, Articles 1, 2.

81 See *Vaasen-Goebbels* v. *Beamtenfonds vor het Mijnbedriff* [1966] CMLR 508; *Unger* v. *Bestuur der Bedrijfsvereniging voor Detailhandel en Anbachten*: [1964] CMLR 319; *City of Wiesbaden* v. *Barulli* [1968] CMLR 239; *R* v. *Secchi* [1975] 1 CMLR 383. There are certain reservations with regard to employment in the civil service or in the policy and decision-making levels of nationalised industries; cf., *Reyners* v. *Belgian State* [1974] 1 CMLR 305.

82 See *Nold* v. *EC Commission* [1974] 2 CMLR 338.

83 See Evans, 'The political status of aliens in international law, municipal law and European Community law,' 30 ICLQ (1981), p. 20; idem., 'European Community law and the trade union and related rights of migrant workers,' 28 ICLQ (1979), p. 354; Swart, 'The legal status of aliens: clauses in Council of Europe instruments relating to the rights of aliens,' 11 Neth. YB. I.L. (1980), p. 1.

84 Article 51 of the Treaty of Rome; Regulations 1408/71 and 574/72.

85 Regulation 1251/70.

86 O.J., Vol. 19, No. C34, p. 2; No. C45, p. 6 (14, 27 February 1976).

87 ETS No. 93. See also other relevant European agreements, such as the 1955 European Convention on Establishment: ETS No. 19; 1957 European Agreement on the Movement of Persons: ETS No. 25; 1961 European Social Charter: ETS No. 35; 1969 European Agreement on Au Pair Placement: ETS No. 68; 1959 European Agreement on the Abolition of Visas for Refugees: ETS No. 31; 1972 European Agreement on Social Security: ETS No. 78; 1980 European Agreement on the Transfer of Responsibility for Refugees: ETS No. 107; 1967 European Convention on Consular Functions: ETS No. 61.

88 Texts in Goodwin-Gill, *Refugee, op. cit.*, Annexes IV and V.

89 Goodwin-Gill, *Refugee, op. cit.*, pp. 17–19, 215–231.

90 *Ibid.*, pp. 147–148.

91 See Maureen Connelly, 'Refugees and Asylum-seekers: Proposals for Policy Changes,' pp. 159–168 *post*.

92 An important and practical survey is provided by Sieghart, *op. cit.*, (1983), ss. 1, 2, 4, 6, 7, 14, 22 and passim. See also Meron, ed., *Human Rights in International Law*, (Clarendon-Press, 1983), Vols. I and II.

93 In this essay, analysis of the nationality concept has been limited generally to questions of entitlement to entry and to participate in the community or body politic. The criteria for acquisition and loss, and their operation in practice, require separate study.

94 Cf., Goodwin-Gill, *op. cit.*, pp. 10–11.

95 Nafziger, however, has argued that 'a duty of states to admit at least some aliens manifests several specific values of global order: the encouragement of peace by easing demographic pressures, the enrichment of national cultures, the redistribution of economic resources, and the pursuit of such humanitarian objectives as satisfaction of family reunification and the basic human needs of migrants'. 77 AJIL (1983), pp. 804, 844f.

96 The phenomenon of 'contract migration', though not especially relevant to the UK, calls for careful study; the sale of labour between states offers ample opportunity for exploitation, in a situation in which nationals may well fail to obtain the protection due from their government.

97 Goodwin-Gill, *Movement of Person, op. cit.*, pp. 178–179, 255–261.

98 Cf., *Golder* v. *UK* (4451/70): 1 EHRR 524; *Campbell* v. *UK* (7598/77): 14 *Decisions and Reports* 186; Sieghart, *The International Law of Human Rights*, (1983), s.22.4.1.

99 See cases cited and comment in Goodwin-Gill, *Movement of Persons, op. cit.*, pp. 238–239, 257, note 3.

100 *Agee* v. *UK* (7729/76): 7 *Decisions and Reports* 164; *X* v. *UK* (7902/77): 9 *Decisions and Reports* 224; *Uppal et al* v. *UK* (8244/78): 17 *Decisions and*

Reports 149; *X, Y, Z, V and W* v. *UK* (3325/67): 10 *Yearbook* 528; Sieghart, *Human Rights*, s.22.4.5.

101 *Plyler* v. *Doe* 102 S.Ct. 2382 (1982). The Supreme Court concluded that denial of education would promote the creation of a sub-class of illiterates and add to the problems and costs of unemployment, welfare and crime.

102 *Jean* v. *Nelson*, 727 F. 2d 957 (11th Cir., 1984). The case arose out of a class action, one of many, by Haitian asylum-seekers.

103 Rosberg, 'Aliens and equal protection: Why not the right to vote?' 75 Mich L Rev 1092 (1977); Schachter, 77 AJIL (1983), pp. 848, 853.

International Labour Conventions and Recommendations on Migrant Workers

HILARY KELLERSON

Office of the Legal Adviser, International Labour Office

Introduction

It is important to be clear from the outset that the International Labour Organisation is competent to deal only with migration for employment, and hence with the protection of migrant workers and their families, not with immigration policies and problems in general. Secondly, the ILO has never taken a position on the question of whether or when candidates for immigration should have a right to be admitted for purposes of employment. Its programmes and standards deal with the position of those who have been lawfully admitted, not with the circumstances in which persons should be permitted to enter a country to take up employment.

That being the case, it is nonetheless the fact that the ILO has from its origins given an important place in its activities to the protection of workers employed in a country other than their own. At the present time, there are four international instruments adopted by the ILO on migrant workers, two dating from 1949 and two from 1975: the Migration for Employment Convention (Revised) 1949, (No. 97), the Migration for Employment Recommendation (Revised) 1949, (No. 86), the Migrant Workers (Supplementary Provisions) Convention 1975, (No. 143) and the Migrant Workers Recommendation 1975, (No. 151).

The distinction between the Conventions and Recommendations is that the former are designed to become binding international treaties on ratification by member states of the ILO whereas the Recommendations, as their name implies, contain non-binding standards and guidelines for national policy. These include both more detailed provisions concerning the implementation of measures provided for in the Convention which they accompany, and provisions on matters which were not felt suitable for inclusion in a Convention designed to create binding obligations.

Two general points are worth making about these ILO standards. First, they are not adopted by a purely governmental body, but by the International Labour Conference which is composed of two government delegates, one employer delegate and one worker delegate per member state, so that their text is the outcome of tripartite discussion, negotiation and compromise. Secondly, unlike other international instruments dealing with migrant workers – for example, the EEC rules and the European Social Charter as well as bilateral agreements – they are not based on reciprocity. This means that a state which ratifies Convention No. 97 or No. 143 undertakes to apply its provisions to all migrant workers lawfully in its territory whatever their country of origin, and not just to workers from the other states which have also ratified the Convention.

The 1949 instruments were, of course, adopted in a very different world from that in which we live today, and the needs they sought to regulate, and the context in which they did so, no longer correspond to the major problems facing a country like the UK today. Nonetheless, while certain of their provisions may have lost a good deal of their relevance, others remain fully relevant even in a greatly changed world.

Migration for Employment Convention (Revised) 1949, (No. 97)

Convention No. 97 contains, in the first place, provisions designed to ensure that adequate and accurate information on conditions and possibilities for employment is made available to potential migrants, and that a free service to assist them is maintained. It provides for measures to facilitate the departure, journey and reception of migrants for employment and contains in two Annexes detailed measures concerning the recruitment, placing and conditions of labour of migrants for employment recruited under government-sponsored arrangements for group transfer (Annex II) or recruited otherwise than under such arrangements (Annex I). The Convention also provides for medical services to ascertain the health of migrants on departure and arrival and to ensure adequate medical attention during the journey; for co-operation between the competent services, in particular the employment services, of the countries of emigration and immigration; and for the conclusion of agreements to regulate matters of common concern between countries where the number of migrants from one to the other is sufficiently large. The Convention thus deals, in the first place, with arrangements for the selection, recruitment, journey and reception on arrival of migrant workers.

Its other main provisions deal with the conditions to be accorded to migrant workers in the country in which they are employed. The following articles are worth quoting:

Article 6

1. Each Member for which this Convention is in force undertakes to apply, without discrimination in respect of nationality, race, religion or sex, to immigrants lawfully within its territory, treatment no less favourable than that which it applies to its own nationals in respect of the following matters:
(a) in so far as such matters are regulated by law or regulations, or are subject to the control of administrative authorities –
   (i) remuneration, including family allowances where these form part of remuneration, hours of work, overtime arrangements, holidays with pay, restrictions on home work, minimum age for employment, apprenticeship and training, women's work and the work of young persons;
   (ii) membership of trade unions and enjoyment of the benefits of collective bargaining;
   (iii) accommodation;
(b) social security (that is to say, legal provision in respect of employment injury, maternity, sickness, invalidity, old age, death, unemployment and family responsibilities, and any other contingency which, according to national laws or regulations, is covered by a social security scheme), subject to the following limitations:
   (i) there may be appropriate arrangements for the maintenance of acquired rights and rights in course of acquisition;
   (ii) national laws or regulations of immigration countries may prescribe special arrangements concerning benefits or portions of benefits which are payable wholly out of public funds, and concerning allowances paid to persons who do not fulfil the contribution conditions prescribed for the award of a normal pension;
(c) employment taxes, dues or contributions payable in respect of the person employed; and

(d) legal proceedings relating to the matters referred to in this Convention.

Article 8

1. A migrant for employment who has been admitted on a permanent basis and the members of his family who have been authorised to accompany or join him shall not be returned to their territory of origin or the territory from which they emigrated because the migrant is unable to follow his occupation by reason of illness contracted or injury sustained subsequent to entry, unless the person concerned so desires or an international agreement to which the Member is a party so provides.
2. When migrants for employment are admitted on a permanent basis upon arrival in the country of immigration the competent authority of that country may determine that the provisions of paragraph 1 of this Article shall take effect only after a reasonable period which shall in no case exceed five years from the date of admission of such migrants.

Article 9

Each Member for which this Convention is in force undertakes to permit, taking into account the limits allowed by national laws and regulations concerning export and import of currency, the transfer of such part of the earnings and savings of the migrant for employment as the migrant may desire.

This Convention has been ratified by the UK and the ILO Committee of Experts on the Application of Conventions and Recommendations, an independent body which is responsible for examining the reports which the UK is required to send in every two years on the application of the Convention, considers that its terms are respected by the UK.

Migrant Workers (Supplementary Provisions) Convention 1975, No. 143

The 1975 Convention No. 143, has two objectives: one is to develop the provisions of the Convention of 1949 on equality of opportunity and treatment, the other is to prevent and eliminate migrations in abusive conditions, i.e. 'any movements of migrants for employment in which the migrants are subjected during their journey, on arrival or during their period of residence and employment to conditions contravening relevant multilateral or bilateral instruments or agreements, or national laws or regulations.'

Under Part I of the Convention, which deals with migrations in abusive conditions, states undertake to take measures, in collaboration with one another, to detect and suppress illicit or clandestine movements of migrants and to ensure that the authors of manpower trafficking are prosecuted; and to make provision for the effective detection of the illegal employment of migrant workers and for the application of sanctions, which include imprisonment in their range, in respect of the illegal employment of migrant workers, the organisation of migrations in abusive conditions, and knowing assistance to such movements.

This part of the Convention contains two provisions designed to protect migrant workers against unfair treatment as a result of the application of its terms. First, Article 8 provides that a migrant worker who has resided legally in the territory for the purpose of employment shall not be regarded as in an illegal or irregular situation by the mere fact of the loss of his employment, which shall not in itself imply the withdrawal of his authorisation of residence or, as the case may be, work permit. This provision is designed to ensure that a worker who loses his job does not become an illegal immigrant overnight; the questions of how long he can remain in the country and whether he can seek other employment remain subject to the worker's existing residence or work permit and national legislation.

The second protective provision, Article 9, deals with the position of an illegal migrant worker who has been detected: it provides first that he should enjoy equality of treatment for himself and his family in respect of rights arising out of past employment as regards remuneration, social security and other benefits, and that in case of dispute over these rights he must have the possibility of presenting his case to a competent body. This provision is designed to ensure that he receives the wages and other benefits arising out of the work that he has in fact done, and that the employer cannot shelter behind the illegality of the employment to avoid paying him or making the appropriate social security contributions resulting from the employment. Secondly, Article 9 provides that in case of expulsion of the worker or his family the cost shall not be borne by them: this provision does not relate to travel expenses but simply the administrative costs of expulsion.

Part II of Convention No. 143 deals with equality of opportunity and treatment for regularly admitted migrant workers. Article 10 reads as follows:

Article 10

Each Member for which the Convention is in force undertakes to declare and pursue a national policy designed to promote and to guarantee, by methods appropriate to national conditions and practice, equality of opportunity and treatment in respect of employment and occupation, of social security, of trade union and cultural rights and of individual and collective freedoms for persons who as migrant workers or as members of their families are lawfully within its territory.

Article 12 sets out a range of measures to be taken to promote and encourage equality. Article 14 permits restrictions on free choice of employment for the first two years of residence, after which they must be lifted. However, the Convention does not deal with the question of residence rights: its effect is simply that, in so far as a worker is permitted to remain and work beyond a period of two years, he must thereafter be assured of free choice of employment. This is probably the most problematical provision of the Convention. The initial draft would have permitted restrictions on free choice of employment for the first five years, a period which would have permitted the UK and numerous other immigration countries to accept this provision of the Convention. As it is, none of the major countries of immigration has ratified or seems likely to ratify it.

Each of these Conventions is supplemented by a Recommendation dealing in greater detail with the matters covered by the Convention. It is only possible, in this chapter, to highlight some of the principal provisions of the Recommendations, whose full text can be referred to by those interested in their detailed terms.

Migrant Workers Recommendation 1975, (No. 151)

Recommendation No. 151, of 1975, spells out in some detail the various aspects of the concept 'equality of opportunity and treatment' as defined in Article 10 of the Convention (*supra*) and the measures which might be taken to promote it. One provision worth quoting is paragraph 5:

Each Member should ensure that national laws and regulations concerning residence in its territory are so applied that the lawful exercise of rights enjoyed in pursuance of these principles (i.e., effective equality of opportunity and treatment with nationals) cannot be the reason for the non-renewal of a residence permit or for expulsion and is not inhibited by the threat of such measures.

The question of reunification of families, dealt with in both Recommendations, is also the subject of a provision in Convention No. 143, which is not however in binding terms. Article 13 provides:

Article 13

1.   A Member may take all necessary measures which fall within its competence and collaborate with other Members to facilitate the reunification of the families of all migrant workers legally residing in its territory.
2.   The members of the family of the migrant worker to which this Article applies are the spouse and dependent children, father and mother.

This provision, like those of Recommendation No. 151, is wider in scope than Recommendation No. 86 which referred only to the admission of the families of migrant workers admitted on a permanent basis. However, the use of the term 'may' means that the Convention leaves the whole issue to the discretion of the government of each state.

Recommendation No. 151 is somewhat more positive although, of course, as a Recommendation, it is equally non-binding. It provides that all possible measures should be taken both by countries of employment and by countries of origin to facilitate the reunification of families as rapidly as possible. It also recognises the link between family reunification and housing, by providing, first, that a prerequisite for the reunification of families should be that the worker has for his family appropriate accommodation which meets the standards normally applicable to the country of employment, and secondly that states should take full account of the needs of migrant workers in their housing policies.

The final subject covered by Recommendation No. 151 which calls for particular mention is that of removal or expulsion of migrant workers from the country. Like Convention No. 143, it does not deal with the question of expulsion or deportation of illegal immigrant workers, which is left to national laws or regulations, except in one provision which is as follows:

8.   (1) Without prejudice to measures designed to ensure that migrant workers and their families enter national territory and are admitted to employment in conformity with the relevant laws and regulations, a decision should be taken as soon as

possible in cases in which these laws and regulations have not been respected so that the migrant worker should know whether his position can be regularised or not.

For the rest, it seeks to provide for the case of a migrant worker whose right to remain in the country has or may come to an end for one reason or another. Recommendation No. 86 had already laid down that a state should as far as possible refrain from removing a regularly admitted migrant worker from its territory on account of lack of means or the state of the employment market. Recommendation No. 151 goes on to provide that loss of employment should not in itself imply the withdrawal of the authorisation of residence, and that a migrant who has lost his employment should be allowed sufficient time to find alternative work, at least for the period during which he is entitled to unemployment benefit. It also provides that if he has appealed against the termination of his employment he should be allowed sufficient time to obtain a final decision on his appeal and that, if it is established that the termination was not justified but he is not reinstated, he should be allowed sufficient time to find alternative employment.

The provision of the Recommendation concerning expulsions is as follows:

> 33. A migrant worker who is the object of an expulsion order should have a right of appeal before an administrative or judicial instance, according to conditions laid down in national laws or regulations. This appeal should stay the execution of the expulsion order, subject to the duly substantiated requirements of national security or public order. The migrant worker should have the same right to legal assistance as national workers and have the possibility of being assisted by an interpreter.

It would seem from the context – although it is not spelled out – that this provision does not cover migrants who entered the country illegally and were thus never lawfully employed there (who are dealt with in paragraph 8, quoted above), but that it should apply to migrant workers whose situation has become irregular because they have failed to respect the conditions of their residence or work permit or overstayed, as well as to those whom it is proposed to expel (i.e. deport) for reasons extraneous to their employment or residence status.

Employment Policy Recommendation

Since one of the subjects we are considering is the relationship between immigration policy and economic policy it seems appropriate to add some brief indications of general principles contained on this aspect in ILO standards.

The whole focus of the 1949 migration for employment instruments was on the organisation and regulation of the movements of migrant workers who were needed in the industrialised countries. Indeed, paragraph 4 of Recommendation No. 86 provided that:

> It should be the general policy of Members to develop and utilise all possibilities of employment and for this purpose to facilitate the international distribution of manpower and in particular the movement of manpower from countries which have a surplus of manpower to those countries that have a deficiency.

By 1964, when the International Labour Conference adopted a Convention and a Recommendation on Employment Policy, the interests of the developing countries were beginning to be taken into account, as is reflected in paragraph 33 of the Employment Policy Recommendation:

> International migration of workers for employment which is consistent with the economic needs of the countries of emigration and immigration, including migration from developing countries to industrialised countries, should be facilitated, taking account of the provisions of the Migration for Employment Convention and Recommendation (Revised), 1949, and the Equality of Treatment (Social Security) Convention, 1962.

More recently, within the framework of the New International Economic Order, the emphasis is being placed rather on measures to promote employment in the home countries of potential migrants, and the return of skilled migrant workers to their home countries. The International Labour Conference examined in first discussion in June 1983 proposals for a new Recommendation on employment policy to supplement that of 1964. The proposed conclusions, prepared for examination by the Conference after consulting governments, contain the following section on international migration and employment:

XI. International Migration and Employment

33. The Recommendation should provide that a country which habitually or repeatedly admits significant numbers of foreign workers with a view to employment should, when such workers come from developing countries, consider the encouragement of appropriate intensified capital movements, the expansion of

trade and the transfer of technical knowledge as possible alternatives to migration for employment.

34.   The Recommendation should provide that a country which habitually or repeatedly experiences significant outflows of its nationals for the purpose of employment abroad might take regulatory measures by means of legislation, agreements with employers' and workers' organisations or in any other manner consistent with national conditions and practice in order to prevent malpractices at the stage of recruitment or departure liable to result in illegal entry to, or stay or employment in, another country, provided that such measures are not inconsistent with the right of everyone to leave any country including his own.

35.   The Recommendation should provide that, where unregulated departures from developing emigration countries attain a volume damaging to the country or region of origin, or where the outflows of manual and intellectual skills cause problems, the country of emigration and the main countries to which its nationals tend to go should conclude migration agreements with a view to enabling the country of origin of the migrants to discourage outflows which are not in its interest.

36.   The Recommendation should provide that developing emigration countries, in order to re-attract from abroad their nationals who possess scarce skills, should:

(a) provide the necessary incentives; and

(b) enlist the co-operation of the countries employing their citizens as well as of the International Labour Organisation and other international or regional bodies concerned with the matter.

Postscript – The Employment Policy (Supplementary Provisions) Convention, adopted in 1984, contains provisions along the lines of these proposals.

Migration in Europe

ÉRIC-JEAN THOMAS

UNESCO Study Director on Immigrant Workers in Europe

Introduction

At the beginning of the 1970s, most European countries did not consider immigration to be a major issue. Hardly any country, except perhaps Sweden, had even defined an immigration policy. Yet by the mid-1970s, all European countries had put a stop on immigration.

When I say 'Europe', I do not mean here to include Great Britain. Of course Great Britain is a part of Europe, but it has a special set of regulations of its own, and its system is very different from the so-called 'European style' of regulating immigration. Nor am I referring here to the migrant workers in Europe from within the free movement zones of the EEC and the Common Nordic Labour Market.[1] There are certain guiding principles and common factors between the mechanisms which are used by European countries to control immigration from outside the free movement zones, and I am going to discuss some of the consequences of those mechanisms upon the place and role of the migrant worker within the structure of the host country and upon his status in the host society.

In Europe, the immigrant can neither enter nor work in the territory of the host country without having a work permit and a residence permit. The issue of a work permit is a *sine qua non* for entering the host country's national territory, in almost every case. The aim of the host countries has always been to lay down conditions for the issue of work permits which would enable the country to obtain maximum benefit from the predicted labour. Of course, today, immigration is very low, but this means it has become increasingly important for countries to extract that maximum benefit, and it is with this aim in mind that the regulations on work permits have been elaborated and revised in the last few years.

43

Work Permits

There are two main control mechanisms in use. In one of these, the traditional model, several permits are issued one after another, and usually the immigrant worker's rights are increased with each successive permit. This system exists, for instance, in Sweden, France and the Federal Republic of Germany. Belgium and the Netherlands operate the second system, under which the employer, not the employee, is required to obtain the permit. In fact, the Belgian regulations now have some features of both systems, and lie halfway between them, but the new legislation in the Netherlands which came into force in 1979–80 has completely abolished the old work permit system and replaced it by a single employment permit to be obtained by the employer. This is interesting as it means that the burden of administrative procedure and satisfying the system of control is now placed on the shoulders of the employer and not the foreign worker.

Residence Permits

So far as residence permits are concerned, there is now a movement in Europe towards bringing work permits into line with residence permits. Legislative provisions today are tending to align the conditions for issuing the one with conditions for the other. Before this alignment took place, it was possible to have, in France or Germany for example, a foreign worker with a valid work permit but whose residence permit had terminated and was not renewed, or vice versa, a valid residence permit but no permission to work. But despite the attempts now being made at alignment, it is important to bear in mind that the granting of a residence permit is *always* subject to the judgment, that is the discretionary power, of the competent authorities, which are usually a special section of the police, in charge of the country's foreign population, coming under the Ministry of the Interior or Ministry of Justice.

Family Immigration

Family immigration raises three questions, which are not answered in the same way in all European countries. First, what does the concept of the family cover? Secondly, at what point after the head of the family has immigrated do other family members acquire the right to come? Thirdly, while the members of the family who are allowed to immigrate will as a matter of course obtain a residence permit, how far are they allowed to take up paid employment themselves? It would take too long to describe here in detail how all the European countries have tackled these three questions, but it must be emphasised that *nowhere* do the members of a migrant worker's family automatically have the right to work. It always holds true, all over Europe, that they must obtain the authorisation of the administrative authorities before they can undertake any gainful activity whatever, and it is always possible for the authorities to refuse them authorisation.

Economic considerations

It is quite clear that all these regulations are based upon economic criteria: work permit issue, residence permit regulations and family immigration regulations. What, then, is the place of the migrant worker within the economic structure, and how much does legislation modify and shape the role of the migrant worker within the host country's economic structure? First, although the frontiers have been closed against foreign workers for many years now in Europe, the foreign populations have been steadily increasing, largely because of the influx of family members. Consequently, the relative proportion of foreign labour has declined between 1975 and 1980. It has declined in France by 16 per cent, in Germany by 19 per cent and in the Netherlands by as much as 29 per cent, so it is quite an important change in the structure of the population. Secondly, there is a growing tendency for new immigrants to be skilled workers. And, thirdly, there is a very marked lowering of the average age of foreign communities, and of course an increase in the number of persons among them who are not of an age to work. It is increasingly apparent that there is a deep contradiction between the official position taken by European countries – that they are not 'immigration' countries, a policy position expressed in the legislation – and the facts: there has developed in each country a resident foreign population that is displaying, more and more, the characteristics of an immigrant community aiming at permanent settlement.

The modification that has taken place in the structure of the foreign population is a very important phenomenon. It has given rise to new behaviour patterns within that population, which call strongly into question a number of generally accepted ideas concerning the place of the migrant in the economy. In order to understand what is in fact the relationship between the legislation and the place of foreign workers in European countries' economies, I have recently directed a survey for UNESCO.[2] The

45

necessary studies for the survey were finished two and a half years ago and a report was published which appeared in English.

The report compared how the structure of qualifications for workers has been modified in different countries. The lowest level of qualification is to be found in France and Germany, and these are the very countries in which there is the greatest concentration of foreign workers in what are traditionally 'immigrants' jobs', and where there are no signs at all of a trend towards an even distribution of foreign workers among various economic sectors. The situation regarding professional qualifications is quite stationary in those two countries. In other countries in Europe, there *is* a trend towards a more even distribution of foreign workers in different kinds of occupation, and the average level of qualification is tending to rise. Now this means that, in the other European countries, the distribution of foreigners between various types of job is coming more and more into line with that of workers who are nationals of the host country. In France and Germany there appears to be a concentration of foreign labour in certain sectors only: those where working conditions have deteriorated and into which it has become more and more difficult to recruit workers who are nationals. If nationals were to be employed in them, there would first have to be a modification of the capital-labour ratio in those jobs and an upgrading of the tasks to be performed by the workers. This seems particularly hard to achieve at present because it would jeopardise the price structure. This is especially the case in France in the car industry. Similarly, in Germany the textile industry has come to rely heavily on foreign workers. If the textile industry were, tomorrow, to employ only German workers it would collapse, because the employers would be unable to pay the same salary that has to be paid to German workers in other sectors of the economy. This trend shows, therefore, that a very strong link exists between, on the one hand, the sectoral distribution of foreign workers and their level of qualifications and, on the other, the immigration regulations. The strictest regulations in Europe regarding work permits are found in France and Germany. In neither country does there exist a permanent work permit, and before a worker is permitted any freedom of choice or movement he must wait for four years in France and five in Germany. In Belgium or Sweden he can apply for a permit to change his job at the end of the first year. It can therefore be assumed that liberal laws and regulations are to some extent conducive to the occupational mobility of immigrant workers within the labour market. Stringent laws, on the contrary, accentuate the basic inequalities between national workers and foreign workers. For example, they increase the degree to which the latter are concentrated in certain economic sectors and in certain levels of low-grade occupation. When you have a work permit system which allows some freedom of choice and movement to the worker, he will be able to move about within the economy of the country, and perhaps to take a better job, and take advantage of the same opportunities that the economy is offering to nationals. The consequences are not only economic, but social and political. The immigration regulations have a direct effect upon the migrants' integration into the society of the host country.

Some European countries have tried to establish special programmes to satisfy what they see as particular needs of the migrants, but only a tiny minority of the foreign populations have benefited from these services. This situation is partly limited by financial factors, but a more important limitation has been the host country's choice between political options. Germany, Belgium and the Netherlands, for example, have always refused to see themselves as countries of immigration, and therefore they have never set up any structure to promote the integration of immigrants,[3] although large communities were in fact settling in their territories. Whether or not a country thinks of itself as a country of immigration is, apparently, less a matter of observing the facts than of taking a political position. To say, 'We are not a country of immigration' is a political decision, a choice to adopt a certain stance, setting one's face against reality. With the important exception of Sweden (which gave the right to vote in local elections to foreigners in 1976) European countries have not offered immigrants a real opportunity to participate in political life, and hardly any to participate in social life. Some experiments have been made in Belgium and the Netherlands but they were not at all successful. But the reason for their lack of success was not that foreign workers were uninterested in participating in the social and political life of the country, but that they did not want to do so through new, specialised structures specifically intended for migrants.

It has been demonstrated by the Swedish experience that what needs doing is not to create such special, extra structures but, quite simply, to extend the rights of migrants so as to bring their status as close as possible to the status of a national of the host country. It is a mistake to construct programmes for satisfying unimportant needs or creating artificial needs: what is important is to treat people as much as possible like one's own nationals. This alignment of status with that of nationals should, moreover, to be effective, be carried out as a united policy. The Netherlands has, for example, not wanted to be thought of as a country of immigration, and yet it has tried to plan and to experiment. There

47

have been some experiments concerning voting rights for foreign workers, and to increase social participation within the life of small communities, such as villages, but these attempts have not been made as part of a consistent reconsideration of policy but as gadgets, as means of filling gaps here and there.

Refugees

Refugees are often more highly qualified than migrants who are admitted as foreign workers, and they do not as a rule compete for the same kinds of job as those foreign workers. France and Sweden, which both now have very restrictive policies indeed towards foreign workers – Sweden having been the first European country to impose a sudden 'stop', in 1966–67 – both admit quite high numbers of refugees. Sweden has the highest percentage of refugees in its population in the world, including a number of *de facto* refugees who stood little chance of getting into any other country.

Conclusion

Finally, I wish to make a point which I believe is very important. Foreigners are usually regarded in law as abstract and interchangeable beings, who cannot benefit from most civil and political rights unless they have undergone a very long process of integration. They must be slowly assimilated somehow, and this process may culminate in their naturalisation. But this sort of thinking is completely out of date, and out of touch with reality. It is not compatible with the role that foreign workers play in the economy of the host country nor with the level of social and economic development which has now been obtained by workers in almost all the European countries. Moreover, a great deal of work has been done in recent years by international organisations to promote the social, economic and political rights of all. International instruments have been worked out, containing principles which are now an integral part of international law, and have been ratified by the countries of Europe. Observance of these principles tends towards the elimination of discrimination against aliens. Yet the immigration control mechanisms of the countries concerned are often marked by a degree of discrimination against resident foreigners.

Immigration control and the regulation of the status of aliens are largely the concern of the political authorities. That is not to say that these authorities ought to persist in setting political considerations against the application of legal principles, which have been worked out by international organisations, accepted and integrated into international law. Political authorities are not justified in trying to prevent this law from being developed, and adapted to contemporary realities.

Notes

1 Since 1954 there has been a common labour market between Iceland, Norway, Sweden, Denmark and Finland. There is also a common labour market between all the EEC countries except Greece and the rest: France, Federal Republic of Germany, Italy, Denmark, Belgium, the Netherlands, Luxembourg, Ireland, the UK.
2 *Immigrant Workers in Europe: their legal status: A comparative study*, (UNESCO Press, 1982) (available from HMSO).
3 The highly organised resettlement of citizens from Indonesia after the Second World War was not seen in the Netherlands as a programme for immigrants. The people concerned were not immigrants, but Dutch citizens.

Rights of Passage

RICHARD PLENDER

Barrister and Director of the Centre of European Law, King's College, London

Early this year six aliens died in a fire that broke out in a detention centre in West Berlin. They included three Tamils, a Tunisian, a Lebanese and a Pakistani. All were being held pending their expulsion.

The episode aroused strong emotions in West Germany, not least because it occurred shortly after the suicide of Kemal Altun, a young Turkish man, who had claimed political asylum. He jumped from the sixth floor window of a courthouse in West Berlin during the hearing of his appeal against a deportation order. Last month the tribunal granted Altun's application for asylum – posthumously.

These events are symptoms of a more general and continuing disorder. The recession has increased the pressure on immigration to West Germany and has made the so-called 'guest workers' (*Gastarbeiter*) more reluctant to return to their countries of origin. At the same time, it has led the West German authorities to try to reduce the size of the alien population. It is in this context that the case of Kemal Altun has to be understood. In 1976 there were 11,123 applicants for asylum in West Germany. By 1980, the figure had risen to 107,818. In 1969, almost 88 per cent of these applications succeeded. By 1979, the figure was 20 per cent.

This combination is by no means found in West Germany alone. In Britain, there are no reliable statistics to show the number of applicants for settlement (whether generally, or in one particular category). But the proportion of unsuccessful applicants seems to be increasing. The refusal rate of applications made in the Indian subcontinent for entry clearances for admission to the UK as wives or dependants rose from 33 per cent in 1977 to about 45 per cent in 1983. The number of persons 'removed' from the UK by the summary procedure created under the Immigration Act, 1971, grew from 80 in 1973 to 910 in 1980, and has remained above 600 in each year since. In addition, deportations rose to 969 in 1980, and have remained above 850 since.

There is a similar pattern in other west European countries. On the day after *Le Monde* carried the story of the fatal fire in West Berlin, an editorial writer, Jean Aimard, urged ministers and the mayor to take the Paris metro just once, to see for themselves the effect of an influx of Pakistanis, Tamils, Bangladeshis and Indians. Aimard argued that the conditions in some of the countries from which the aliens come mean that their entire populations could claim to be refugees. He added that, to gain admission to France, the alien need not be a refugee: he had only to claim to be a student of the French language, even if illiterate. Another contributor to the same day's issue of *Le Monde*, signing himself simply 'BR,' took the opposite view with equal vehemence. He claimed that, in the very heart of Paris, aliens are treated '*plus mal que des ordures*' – worse than dirt.

There have been many reports of friction between the indigenous and alien propulation in several west European countries in recent months. Even Switzerland and Sweden have failed to escape. The Swiss and Swedish governments, like West Germany and France, have set out on policies to restrict immigration.

The industrial states of western Europe have encountered an economic recession more or less simultaneously. At the same time, migrant workers, refugees and their dependants are present on our subcontinent in large numbers. In the 21 Council of Europe states as a whole, there are now 15 million aliens. Even that figure excludes the first generation born in west Europe to parents born abroad, and immigrants who already had the nationalities of the countries they settled in.

During the last major recession, between the wars, new restrictions were imposed on immigration throughout the industrialised world. These took the form of changes in both law and administration. The present recession has been no different.

In West Germany the law on work permits, and on the rules for qualifying as the spouse of an alien employee, were tightened up in 1981. In France, the Loi Bonnet of 1980, among other stipulations, conferred on the administration the power to exclude aliens on grounds of public order. Later legislation has added to the curbs. In Holland, the Act on the Employment of Foreign Workers, which came into force on 1 November 1979, imposed a number of new restrictions on immigration. In particular, it created 'an imperative ground' for refusing to issue a work permit wherever this would bring a firm above its allotted maximum number of foreign workers.

Austria, Belgium, Italy and Switzerland have all adopted new legislation on the status of aliens, as has the UK. The new UK Immigration Rules, drawn up in 1982, restrict the admission of husbands or fiancés of women other than British citizens. They lay down that where the wife or fiancée is a British citizen, her partner will be admitted only if he satisfies the authorities that the marriage is genuine. The British Nationality Act 1981, was clearly drafted with immigration in mind.

Obviously, however, the laws and policies applied in each west European state affect the pattern of migration in neighbouring countries. This is particularly clear in the case of refugees. All 21 member states of the Council of Europe are parties to the Geneva Convention on the Status of Refugees. This says that contracting states shall not return refugees to their countries of origin. On the other hand, neither that convention nor any other one obliges European states to grant asylum to any refugee. So European states which decline to admit refugees to their own territories are apt to send them to other 'safe' states through which they have travelled, or to neighbouring states. The spectacle of refugees travelling from one European country to another in search of asylum will be increasingly common and troublesome – unless some means to share responsibility for them is set up.

Even in more mundane cases, new controls in one European state can have a significant effect on migration to other states. In his article in *Le Monde*, Jean Aimard pinpointed four groups of immigrants to France, all of them coming from former UK dependencies – India, Pakistan, Ceylon and Bangladesh. It is no coincidence that migration to the UK from there has been cut back.

In short, the national regulation of international migration produces international repercussions. Multilateral co-operation would be necessary to tackle this.

In western Europe, in fact, there is even now, no shortage of treaties governing the reception, admission and treatment of aliens. They have been adopted under the aegis of such bodies as the United Nations, the International Labour Organisation and the Council of Europe. An elaborate system of EEC rules governs the treatment of migrant workers. But these do not go far enough. When aliens and immigrants' organisations have tried to use them, the limits have become clear.

In the UK and some other west European countries, a private litigant before a national court cannot rely on international convention as a source of law. In these 'dualistic' states, a treaty is regarded as a compact between sovereign powers. It gives rise to rights and duties for the signatory states but not for individuals. It is considered as enforceable (if at all) only before international tribunals.

The problem in the UK is illustrated in a leading case called *Salamat Bibi*. The applicant was a woman who arrived at Heathrow airport in March 1976 with two small children. She had no entry certificate, but she said that she was the wife of one Barkat Ali, who was waiting at the airport to meet her, and that he was the father of the two children. Barkat Ali confirmed this. Salamat Bibi was refused admission on the ground, among others, that she had no entry clearance in advance.

In her appeal, she tried to rely on Article 8(1) of the European Convention on Human Rights, which seeks to protect the right to family life. The Court of Appeal held that it was not open to her to do so. The case led Lord Denning to disapprove of some of his own remarks in an early judgment. In his words:

> Treaties and declarations do not become part of our law until they are made law by parliament. I desire, however, to amend one of the statements I made in . . . *Bhajan Singh*. I said then that immigration officers ought to bear in mind the principles stated in the convention. I think that would be asking too much of the immigration officers. They cannot be expected to know or to apply the convention. They must go simply by the immigration rules laid down by the Secretary of State.

This does not mean that the European Convention is no use at all to litigants in immigration cases. It establishes machinery for the enforcement of its terms. Countries which adhere to it may permit individuals to send petitions direct to the European Commission on Human Rights. From there cases may go to the European Court. France, Spain and Portugal have now agreed to permit the right of individual petition. It remains only for Cyprus, Greece, Malta and Turkey to follow suit.

The convention contains provisions which are useful for the protection of aliens. As the European Commission on Human Rights observed in 1958:

> A state which signs and ratifies the European Convention on Human Rights and Fundamental Freedoms must be understood as agreeing to restrict the free exercise of its rights under general international law, including the right to control the entry and exit of foreigners.

It was by invoking the European Convention on Human Rights that some East African Asians challenged their exclusion from the UK under the Commonwealth Immigrants Act, 1968. By invoking this convention the widow of Colonel Amerikrane obtained compensation after the authorities in Gibraltar returned him to his death in Morocco.

On the basis of the same convention, lawyers acting for two small children are currently challenging the recent deportation of the children's Turkish father from the UK. The children, Zeynep and Fatih Hasbudak, are British citizens and cannot be removed. If the deportation stands, the children will either be separated from their father or obliged to leave their own country: it is argued that either would breach the Convention.

Even so, the limitations on using the Convention are formidable. Several of the provisions most directly relevant to migrants are contained not in the Convention itself but in Protocols which need separate ratification. The right to enter one's own country is guaranteed by the fourth Protocol. This has not been ratified by Cyprus, Greece, Liechtenstein, Malta, Spain, Switzerland, Turkey – or Britain.

A specific European Convention on the Legal Status of Migrant Workers came into force less than a year ago. It contains a fairly detailed code on the treatment of aliens. But again there are limits. Only member states of the Council of Europe can ratify it, and it only applies to their nationals. So the new Convention does not cover most of Europe's migrant workers, who come from Maghreb countries of North Africa, the Indian subcontinent, Africa and the Caribbean.

Likewise, EEC law is marginally relevant to migrant workers from outside Europe. A common immigration policy has proved elusive. The Treaty of Rome contains protection for 'workers of the member states.' But the Council of Ministers in Brussels has interpreted this in such a way that only EEC nationals benefit.

On a world level, there are the UN Geneva Convention and the New York Protocol on the Status of Refugees. Their limitations have again become particularly apparent in the recession. They do not impose a positive duty to admit a refugee (as distinct from a duty to refrain from returning the refugee to his country of origin). In western Europe, a small step has been taken in the right direction by a European Agreement on the Transfer of Responsibility for Refugees. But this has received few ratifications; and it only covers fugitives who have been granted asylum in one west European state and wish to move to another. It does not help people who have yet to be granted asylum and who find themselves, in the jargon of the UN High Commissioner for Refugees, 'in orbit.'

What could be done, with sensible co-operation among the countries of Europe?

European countries could, for example, conclude a convention whereby refugees who find themselves in any of these states would be granted asylum in the country with which they have specific connections by ancestry, education, or language. If this sounds like too much of a *carte blanche*, each country could be given an annual numerical limit on the refugees they need accept. This would all save costs in fares, policing and administration, to say nothing of the saving in distress to fugitives.

There should be European co-operation on other aspects of international migration: on an appeals system, for example, or on the admission of visitors bearing travel documents other than those listed in the existing rules. This would help to avoid the difficulties which occur when countries (such as France) decline to admit certain visitors from neighbouring countries (such as black Britons bearing the so-called 'Post Office passport').

Co-operation of this kind need not lead to a rise in immigration into any European country. Some multilateral arrangements, which were designed to improve the conditions under which aliens live and work, appear to have helped to cut the volume of migration by increasing the *cost* of foreign labour.

This may be true of EEC legislation on the free movement of workers. In 1959, when the EEC had not yet embarked on this programme, about three quarters of the EEC's migrant workers came from the territories of other member states. By 1973 when the programme had been completed and the EEC had grown, about threequarters of the migrant workers within the nine states came from countries outside the community. In the year Britain joined the community, the number of Britons taking employment in other member states fell. There was also a fall in the number of nationals of other EEC countries taking jobs in Britain. It is cheaper to employ non-EEC nationals: they have fewer rights.

The case for extending the international protection given to aliens in western Europe is overwhelming, in economic, administrative and humanitarian terms. What appears to be lacking is the political will.

Immigration Law and Management in the United States, Canada and Australia*

PROFESSOR FREDA HAWKINS

University of Toronto

Introduction

Immigration policy, law and management are indivisible and must be considered together. Policy is by no means always expressed in legislation. Laws are not always implemented as their authors intended and sometimes not implemented at all. Management is deeply involved in policy-making in larger and smaller ways. All three factors change and evolve over time responding to changes in the political environment and in the community at large. Naturalisation or citizenship laws are less susceptible than immigration laws to political, administrative or economic influences, but they are not immune from them.[1] In this paper, we will examine the immigration and naturalisation laws of three of the major receiving countries in international migration in recent times, the United States, Canada and Australia, putting these laws into their political and administrative context. All three countries have handled immigration and related matters in somewhat different ways, but all three have had to face similar problems in managing this difficult to control and sensitive policy area. Finally, we will consider some of the major principles and issues which emerge from this comparative

*This is a revised and updated version of a paper given to a conference on 'International Migration in the Arab World', organised by The United Nations Economic Commission for Western Asia, Nicosia, 11–16 May 1981.

review. We begin with Australia which is, thus far, the least legalistic of these three countries in its approach to immigration.

Australia

Major changes have taken place in the 1970s in Australian immigration policy and management and in the interpretation and implementation of immigration law. The famous 'White Australia' policy has gone, just as similar policies disappeared in the previous decade in the US and Canada. A National Population Inquiry has been conducted over a three-year period beginning in 1971, followed by the publication in 1977 of a Green Paper on 'Immigration Policies and Australia's Population', and the organisation of a major review and public discussion of immigration objectives and policies. New methods of selecting and admitting immigrants (known as 'migrants' in Australia), based partly on the Canadian Point System[2] have been introduced. The concept of Australia as a multicultural society has been deliberately fostered by governments, as a response to the increasing numbers of Australians who are not now of British origin and to the increasing activity and politicisation of ethnic groups. Substantial improvements are being made in immigrant services following an official review of post-arrival services and programmes carried out in 1978. Two amnesties have been held to attempt to meet the problems of illegal immigration. Large numbers of Indochinese refugees have been accepted for permanent settlement. These and other developments have made the 1970s a remarkable and creative decade in Australian immigration. It has also seen the emergence, for the first time in the post-war period, of significant differences between the two major political parties, the Liberal-National Party Coalition and the Australian Labour Party over the objectives of national immigration policy and over the ways in which it is being implemented.

Australia has admitted close to four million immigrants and refugees since the Second World War II.[3] Immigration in the post-war period has been a matter of high priority for governments and has been linked throughout to population growth. The Second World War was a very traumatic experience for Australians – the first major threat to security which the Australian nation had experienced. From the fall of Singapore in 1942 onwards and with the collapse of British protection in the Pacific and the real threat of invasion by Japan, Australia felt an urgent need to build up its population which was a little over seven million in 1945. In this it was very successful, doubling its population, very largely through immigration, in 25 years without serious stress or strain – a remarkable achievement which has never had adequate international recognition. On 2 August 1945, Australia's first Minister for Immigration, Arthur A. Calwell announced on behalf of the Labour Government, a large-scale post-war immigration programme whose principle objective was 'populate or perish' as it came to be known. It had the support of all political parties, a consensus which continued until the early 1970s. Two per cent was regarded then as a desirable annual level of population growth to which immigration might contribute one per cent.

At the same time, a small planning staff was established within a new Department of Immigration created in 1946, and a blueprint worked out for a substantial degree of community participation in this national effort, including the creation of an Immigration Advisory Council in 1947 to advise on the settlement and adjustment of immigrants and an Immigration Planning Council in 1949. Both these advisory councils survived for many years with a record of very valuable service to the development and management of Australia's post-war immigration movement. Today Australia has one advisory council in this field: The Australian Advisory Council on Population and Ethnic Affairs. As part of this initial planning effort after the Second World War, it was also decided to provide reception centres and hostels for the large number of immigrants who were expected to arrive, as well as free and assisted passages, provided first for British migrants and British and Allied ex-servicemen and later extended to selected European countries. Although the Labour Government led by Ben Chifley was defeated in December 1949, the new Liberal Government under Robert Menzies simply continued these policies and programmes, as did their successors up to the critical moment in 1972, when the Australian electorate returned a Labour Government to power once again after a gap of 23 years.

White Australia Policy

The three major receiving countries discussed in this paper, the US, Canada and Australia, have all had 'white' immigration policies in the twentieth century. Australia was the first of the three to establish a racially discriminatory immigration policy in the Immigration Restriction Act 1901 and the last to get rid of it which it did in 1973. The US and Canada began to exclude non-white (generally non-European) immigrants after the First World War.[4] Canada was the first country to abandon this policy which was done in the Immigration Regulations of 1962. The US followed in the Kennedy Immigration Amendments of 1965 which became effective in 1968.

After the Second World War, there was a series of minor relaxations in Australia's firm adherence to a policy of total exclusion of non-Europeans in immigration, particularly as it began to recruit and select migrants from a wider group of countries outside Europe. The first of these relaxations related to the temporary residence of non-Europeans admitted for business reasons; to the eligibility of non-Europeans for naturalisation; and to the admission of 'distinguished and highly-qualified non-Europeans' and persons of mixed descent. But in 1966, a definite step was taken to make the admission and permanent settlement of non-Europeans somewhat easier. This was announced by the then Minister for Immigration, Hubert Opperman in the House of Representatives on 9 March. He said that from now on:

> applications for entry by people wishing to settle in Australia with their wives and children will be considered on the basis of their suitability as settlers, their ability to integrate readily and the possession of qualifications which are in fact positively useful to Australia. Those approved will initially be admitted on five-year permits and will then be able to apply for resident status and citizenship.

This fairly cautious measure did not result in the admission of more than a few thousand non-Europeans and persons of mixed descent annually, increasing to approximately 10,000 by 1971–72, but it did open the door to a limited extent and also established the principle of skill as an important criterion for admission and means of entry.

Meanwhile, Australians were becoming more critical of their national immigration policy, uncertain about its population goals and their possible effect on the environment and more concerned about Australia's relations with its neighbours in the Pacific, and the damaging effect of the White Australia policy on these relationships. Public opinion was also becoming more used to the many new elements in Australian society. The 1961 census had shown that of a total population of 10.5 million, 8 per cent were now non-British and European-born. The largest groups were Italians, 228,000; Germans, 109,000; Greeks, 77,000; Polish, 60,000; Yugoslavs, 50,000; and Hungarians, 30,000; with smaller groups of Austrians, Latvians, Russians and Ukrainians.

The final and decisive step in bringing the White Australia policy to an end was taken in 1973 by Gough Whitlam, Prime Minister in the new Labour Government. In a foreign policy statement in the House of Representatives, the Prime Minister said:

> Just as we have embarked on a determined campaign to restore the Australian aborigines to their rightful place in Australian society, so we have an obligation to remove methodically from Australia's laws and practices all racially discriminatory provisions and from international activities any hint or suggestion that we favour policies, decrees or resolutions that seek to differentiate between peoples on the basis of the colour of their skin. As an island nation of predominantly European inhabitants situated on the edge of Asia, we cannot afford the stigma of racialism.

Policy Developments in the 1970s

The Labour government of 1972–75, which was eventually dismissed by the then Governor General, Sir John Kerr in a major constitutional crisis, made some significant changes in immigration policy and management, bringing to an end the bipartisan support of Australian immigration policy which had been such a notable feature of the post-war period up to that point. Leading elements in the Australian Labour Party in 1972, including the Prime Minister, Gough Whitlam, were in favour of non-discrimination in immigration but they were not in favour of a steadily increasing population, the basic premise of post-war immigration policy thus far. Gough Whitlam himself was far more concerned with building a really responsible, caring society, both domestically and internationally, with an effective economic system producing a high standard of living for all Australians, than he was with population growth and the large-scale development it might ultimately bring. In immigration, he was chiefly concerned with removing the racist image which Australia had acquired through the widely-known White Australia policy, eliminating 'racist management', i.e., the unstated pro-European bias which he thought was a major feature of the Department of Immigration, and removing all traces of British preference in immigration and citizenship policies and practice.

The Labour government held office for three years only. In that time, and with three different Ministers for Immigration, it progressively reduced the immigrant intake from 140,000 in 1972–73 to 50,000 in 1975, introduced new migrant selection procedures and cut back on overseas advertising and promotion. At the same time, it provided more resources for settlement services and immigrant welfare. The Department of Immigration was merged with the Department of Labour and some of its major functions, including welfare and community services, English language training, immigrant accommodation, publicity and information were transferred to other departments. When the Report of the National Population Inquiry was tabled in the House of Representatives in 1975, the Labour government announced the creation of an Australian Population and Immigration Council, replacing the Immigration Planning Council created in 1949 to monitor demographic trends in Australia and advise the government on the economic and social consequences of changing population patterns.

The Labour government also made some significant changes in citizenship law; produced a Racial Discrimination Act which, among other things, established a new office of 'Commissioner for Community Relations'; encouraged the idea of Australia as a multicultural society – mainly through the speeches of the Prime Minister and the first Minister for Immigration, Al Grassby, who became the first Commissioner for Community Relations; and made some tentative moves towards the creation of an ethnic broadcasting service.

The Liberal-National Country Party Coalition (now the Liberal-National Party – the word 'Country' has been dropped by the National Party) led by Malcolm Fraser,[5] won a decisive victory in the election of December 1975 which followed the constitutional crisis and the dismissal of Gough Whitlam and his Government. Almost immediately, they set about reversing some of the major moves made by the Labour Party. First, they reassembled the former Department of Immigration, as they had promised to do while in opposition, restored nearly all its former functions and gave it the new title of Department of Immigration and Ethnic Affairs. Secondly, they began to restore life and vigour to the immigration programme and to set it once more on the path of population growth and expansion. It should be mentioned here that the Fraser Government was a government of firmly conservative persuasion. The Liberal-National Party represents, in a broad sense, the interests of business, industry, development and the middle and upper income groups, as well as the agricultural and rural communities of Australia. It is the party which now strongly supports immigration as a major instrument for population growth and economic expansion and it is the principal architect of Australia's present immigration policies and procedures.

In addition to these early moves, the Fraser Government engaged in a major review of existing immigration and population policies. A new method of selecting migrants, (Numerical Multi-factor Assessment System) based, to a considerable extent on the

Canadian Point System, was introduced in January 1979; and there were major developments in the fields of multiculturalism, immigrant services, the control of illegal immigration and other areas. The Numerical Multifactor Assessment System aroused unexpected hostility, however, partly because of its very detailed system of numerical weighting and partly because it was seen as emphasising skills at the expense of family reunion. On 29 October 1981, the then Minister for Immigration and Ethnic Affairs, Ian Macphee, made a statement in Parliament outlining the details of a new migrant selection system for Australia which had been in use since April 1982 (with certain modifications introduced recently by the new Labour government). The new system is actually closer to the Canadian Point System than NUMAS was in that it gives major emphasis to family reunion and does not attempt to attach numerical weightings to settlement factors as NUMAS did. As in Canada, the principal reasons for introducing a more structured selection system were to improve consistency in migrant selection; to ensure that assessments were made relating to all the factors relevant to successful settlement; and to establish a fair and non-discriminatory selection system which can be used anywhere in the world. For details of Australia's present migrant selection system, see Appendix I.

The main elements of the Fraser Government's immigration policy and procedures were outlined by its first Minister for Immigration and Ethnic Affairs, Michael MacKellar in a major speech to Parliament on 7 June 1978 and these are described in the following section. The Liberal-National Party was returned to power again in the federal election of 18 October 1980, but with a reduced majority. In that election, the Australian Labour Party made an unexpectedly strong showing with a national swing of 6.2 per cent in its favour and in the federal election of 5 March 1983, it won a triumphant victory under a new, dynamic and popular leader, Bob Hawke. We will now examine the major features of Australia's immigration policy and procedures as developed by the Fraser Government and then consider the extent to which these may be changed by the new Labour administration.

Immigration Policy and Procedures

The major statutory provision in Australian immigration is the Migration Act 1958. This Act, which has been amended in minor ways, simply vests very substantial discretionary powers in the Minister and through him his officials. These powers are, however, much more circumscribed than they were, particularly by the new selection procedures introduced in the 1970s which attempt to provide an objective and well-defined method of selecting immigrants which is open to scrutiny. The possibility of appeal against administrative decisions has also been a matter of considerable debate and creative development in Australia in the last few years and there are now improved opportunities for review and appeal against adverse decisions in immigration.

Nevertheless, the Minister for Immigration still has substantial powers. Although this system causes considerable difficulties because of the large number of representations which have to be dealt with – if the Minister can make the final decision, it is very important to talk to him directly – Australian governments thus far have had a great deal of confidence in it.[6] The argument which is always made for Ministerial discretion is that it permits a great deal of flexibility and the exercise of more compassion than is possible in a very legalistic system. Opinion on this is changing in Australia, however, and the possibility of a new Migration Act which would be much more explicit and detailed in relation to immigration policy and procedures than the present legislation is certainly being discussed.

Australia's present immigration policy, as defined by the Fraser Government and endorsed so far by the Hawke Government, with only minor changes of wording, is based on nine principles which were outlined by Mr MacKellar in his speech to Parliament in June 1978. These principles are not yet enshrined in the law, as similar principles are in Canada, but nonetheless they carry considerable weight. They have a common basis, as the Minister put it, in the interests of Australia and its people, together with compassion and international responsibility. Described very briefly, these principles are as follows:

(1) The Australian Government alone determines who will be admitted to Australia. Only Australian citizens or constituent members of the Australian community have a basic right of entry.

(2) Apart from the categories of refugees and family reunion, migrant entry criteria should (*must* in the new wording) be developed on the basis of benefit to the Australian community and Australia's social, economic and other requirements.

(3) The size and composition of the immigration movement should not jeopardise social cohesiveness and harmony within the Australian community.

(4) Immigration policy should be non-discriminatory. Policy will be applied consistently to all applicants, regardless of race, colour, nationality, descent, national or ethnic origin or sex.

(5) Except in the case of refugees, applicants should be considered for migration as individuals, or individual family units not as community groups.

(6) Standards of eligibility and suitability for migrants should reflect Australian law and social mores. (e.g., polygamous unions or the entry of child fiancés are not acceptable).

(7) Migration to Australia should be for permanent settlement (without any barrier to prevent departure). No guest worker system will be developed.

(8) All migrants will be free to choose their place of residence, but 'enclave settlement' will not be encouraged.

(9) Policies governing entry and settlement should be based on the premise that immigrants should integrate into Australian society, while having the opportunity to preserve and disseminate their ethnic heritage.

It is interesting to compare these principles with the ten principles or objectives which form Part I of the Canadian Immigration Act of 1976 which is discussed in the next section of this chapter.

While in office, the Fraser Government also introduced an important change in immigration planning. The familiar annual immigration targets in Australia were replaced by 'triennial rolling programmes', beginning with the period 1978–79 to 1980–81. This was intended to add a measure of stability to immigration and to provide a more reliable base for public and private sector planning. Due to the recession, however, annual levels have recently been reduced and in 1982–83, the original estimate of between 115,000 and 120,000 migrants was revised downwards to between 90,000 and 95,000. The present Minister for Immigration and Ethnic Affairs, Stewart West, has announced that the migration programme for 1983–84 will be held to a ceiling of between 80,000 and 90,000 with no growth proposed for the triennium unless economic conditions improve sufficiently.

This announcement was made as part of an important statement on the Labour government's immigration policy made by the Minister in the House of Representatives on 18 May 1983. In this statement, the Minister said that his Government reaffirmed the nine principles underlying Australia's present migration policy. The Labour government's policy, he said, would be to steer a middle course, rejecting demands for a massive reduction in intake and, at the same time, preventing major increases until the Government's economic policies stimulated recovery. Within the proposed ceiling, the Government was strongly committed to family reunion and to refugees. It also intended to restructure the points system to eliminate what were felt to be its more discriminatory features. Changes would include the removal of points awarded for knowledge of English and for occupational demand. The purpose of these and other changes, he said, were 'to remove to some extent an in-built bias in favour of highly skilled, English-speaking and financially well-off migrants'.[7]

The most critical part of this speech, however, related to the recruitment of skilled workers overseas and reflected the Australian Labour Party's strong views on this subject. Less reliance would now be placed, Stewart West said, on the migration programme as a source of skilled workers. While skilled migration would be needed to fill gaps for some time, the Government would develop a manpower planning approach to ensure that economic recovery was not held back by skilled labour shortages and conversely that immigration did not become an alternative to Australian training and re-training programmes, particularly for adults.

Responding to this statement in the House, the Opposition spokesman John Hodgman said that while the Opposition would endeavour to maintain a bipartisan approach to the question of Australia's migration policy, there were matters with which they strongly disagreed. On the basis of the statement just given to the House, it was their view that Australia now had 'a more authoritarian, a more rigid, a more discriminatory and certainly an anti-English speaking migration policy'.[8] Notwithstanding the Government's assertion that it had sought a middle course, it was in fact putting migration into reverse gear – and he produced arguments to show that migrant intake should actually be increased in difficult times because it provided a major stimulus to the economy. In addition, John Hodgman said, the Government had already indicated that it proposed to take away one of the essential elements of a proper migration policy, namely the exercise of ministerial discretion in appropriate cases.

It can be seen, therefore, that whereas Australia's two major political parties did, in fact, share a similar approach to immigration through the post-war period, at least until the late 1960s, they have today a rather different view of the major purposes of immigration in national development.

Citizenship

The grant of citizenship in Australia is governed by the Australian Citizenship Act 1948 (as amended). Citizenship may be acquired by birth in Australia, by birth abroad to Australian parents, or by grant of citizenship to persons resident in Australia under conditions prescribed by the Act. All matters pertaining to citizenship are the responsibility of the Department of Immigration and Ethnic Affairs.

A major amendment to the Act, introduced by the Whitlam

Government in 1973 provided that all persons, of whatever origin, could apply for citizenship after two and a half years residence in Australia. The Minister could then grant a certificate of citizenship provided the applicant had lived in Australia for at least three years, was of good character, had an adequate knowledge of English and of the responsibilities and privileges of citizenship and intended to reside in Australia permanently.

The Fraser Government, after a major review of the Australian Citizenship Act 1948, as well as a joint review of citizenship procedures by the Department of Immigration and Ethnic Affairs and the Public Service Board, produced further amendments to the Act in 1982 designed (1) to remove all discriminatory aspects giving preferential treatment on the basis of national origin, sex or marital status; (2) to eliminate anomalies and reduce subjectivity in criteria for citizenship; (3) to clarify and simplify administrative requirements in the application of the Act and (4) to provide for independent review of decisions to deny persons citizenship. In addition, following agreement between Commonwealth and State Ministers responsible for immigration and ethnic affairs, the Commonwealth Electoral Act was amended to provide that Australian citizenship would replace British subject status as the nationality criterion to enrol, to vote and to nominate as a candidate for election to Parliament.

According to a press report received as this study goes to press, the Hawke Government has now introduced further changes in citizenship requirements. In legislation introduced in Parliament on 7 December 1983, the Australian Citizenship Act 1948 was amended to include a new oath of allegiance and the elimination of British subject status. Reference to the Queen was deleted, qualifying periods for citizenship cut, a right of appeal established and English language requirements eased. The Minister for Immigration and Ethnic Affairs described these changes as the most far-reaching since the introduction of the Citizenship Act in 1948. They came into force in 1984.

Canada

Canada and Australia have many things in common: similar historical origins, one shared official language, federal political systems combined with a British form of parliamentary democracy, and territories of continental size with only small populations of 25 and 15 millions respectively. Both countries have impressive resources, many of them as yet undeveloped. Both are highly urbanised and both have very large areas of difficult and intract-able country – Canada's frozen north and Australia's arid or semi-arid lands.

Canada and Australia have both been countries of immigration since the earliest days of settlement and both continue to rely on it for population growth and economic development. Because of Canada's proximity to the US, however, her close ties with the American economy and continued reliance on US defence of North America, population growth has been a matter of much less urgent concern in Canada than it has in Australia. Until the early 1970s, hardly any Canadian politicians, and no Canadian political party in the post-war period, showed more than nominal interest in issues of population growth and distribution. It was only as the international community itself became vitally interes-ted in population problems, and when the United Nations began planning in the early 1970s for a World Population Year in 1974, that Canada followed suit. Today, however, it still has no clearly-established population policies.

There are several other important differences between these two countries in the immigration field which should be men-tioned. One is the advantage which Canada has had in what might be described as a 'tri-partisan approach to immigration policy'. Throughout the post-war period, the Liberal Party, the Progressive Conservative Party and the New Democratic Party, the major parties on the federal political scene, have been in agreement on Canadian immigration policy and practice, differ-ing only in minor matters. There is another important difference relating to immigration and citizenship laws. Both Canada and Australia created departments of immigration in the immediate post-war period as well as a basic immigration statute – the Canadian Immigration Act 1952 and the Australian Migration Act 1958. Both were based on the central principal of ministerial discretion in all immigration matters from selection and admis-sion to deportation. While Australia has, as we have seen, continued to make use of its 1958 Act without altering it in major ways, Canada, and particularly the Canadian Parliament, has never been happy with such extensive use of ministerial discre-tion and has attempted to change or modify the Act first by regulation beginning in 1962, and finally by the passing of a new Immigration Act in 1976. Canada also established an indepen-dent Immigration Appeal Board in 1967. Canadian parliamenta-rians have also expressed a continuing concern that *reasons* be given for exclusion and removal in immigration (including security cases) as well as for denial of citizenship. In addition there has been a continuing effort to reduce the degree of discretion allowed to immigration officers at overseas posts and entry points.

Canada and Australia share a common political heritage, but with one vital difference. The majority of Australians are still of British origin and Australia has one major charter group. Canada's background, on the other hand, relates both to Britain and to France. There are two charter groups and two official languages and its political system reflects this important fact. Some 44 per cent of the Canadian population today is believed to be of British origin, 27 per cent is of French origin and 30 per cent or a little less of other national origins.

Post-War Developments in Immigration

There have been four major developments in Canadian immigration policy and practice since the end of the Second World War. The first occurred in 1962 when, as already mentioned, Canada brought her 'White Canada Policy' to an end, after a period of some 40 years covering the difficult, economically-troubled inter-war years, the war itself when immigration virtually ceased, and the immediate post-war period when Canada, like Australia, began to recruit and admit immigrants from a much wider range of countries. The decision to adopt a universal policy, free from any kind of racial or national origin discrimination, and based on skills, family reunion and compassionate considerations (mainly relating to refugees), was not taken as a result of any public outcry against the former policy, or of any particular urging by Parliament. It was a deliberate decision taken in the first place by senior officials, and particularly those concerned with foreign affairs, in the belief that Canada could not function effectively in the international community, or in the new multiracial Commonwealth, if it remained vulnerable to the accusation of racial discrimination in immigration. It was the same approach as that taken by Gough Whitlam in Australia eleven years later.

The second critical development occurred in 1965–66 when Canada embarked on a major programme of development in the manpower and employment field. Immigration became part of a new, high-priority Department of Manpower and Immigration with a very large budget, and labour market considerations became from then on a particularly important element in immigration policy and management. In 1966, the Canadian Point System for the selection and admission of immigrants, worked out by Canadian immigration officials, was adopted. It represented an attempt to find an objective and straightforward way of assessing and selecting potential immigrants which would be comprehensible both to immigration officers and to applicants, and could be used in all countries. It was an essential management tool in the light of the new universal policy and would later be adopted with modifications by Australia.

As in Australia, the past decade had been a period of intense review and development in the immigration field. A major review of Canada's immigration and population policies was undertaken by the Liberal Government in the autumn of 1972 which resulted in the publication of a Green Paper on Immigration Policy which was tabled in the House of Commons in February 1975. This led in turn to the appointment of a Special Joint Committee of the Senate and the House of Commons on Immigration Policy, which was asked to examine and invite the views of the public on the fundamental questions of immigration policy and population growth and distribution which were discussed in the Green Paper. This review process was the third of the significant developments mentioned above.

The Special Joint Committee which was an all-party Committee and proved to be a very able one, then embarked upon nearly 50 public hearings across Canada and produced an excellent Report to Parliament in November 1975. Sixty out of 65 of the Committee's recommendations were accepted by the Liberal Government and they form some of the major elements in the new Immigration Act which was passed by the Canadian Parliament in the following year.

Very briefly, the Committee believed that Canada should continue to be a country of immigration for demographic, economic, family and humanitarian reasons, and that immigration should be directly related from now on to population growth. A new Immigration Act should contain a clear statement of principles, and operational details and procedures should be specified in regulations. Canada's present non-discriminatory immigration policy should be continued and should be expressed explicitly in the new Immigration Act. The provinces should be involved in the decision-making process in immigration and should be consulted by the Minister prior to the annual announcement in Parliament of the number of immigrants to be admitted during the following year. The point system should be retained with certain modifications, but some substantial changes were required in the control and enforcement area, as well as a general liberalising and modernising of what are now called 'the inadmissible classes'. Immigration, the Committee believed, was a long term investment in human resources. Unless it were continued, Canada's future economic development might actually be held back by serious labour shortages in the near future.

Canada's new Immigration Act is an innovative and effective piece of legislation which provides the essential structure of Canada's present immigration policies. In the main, the Act does what the Special Joint Committee and many other Canadians who contributed to the short but useful national debate on immigration which took place in 1975, hoped it would do. As the Minister said when originally tabling the Bill in the House of Commons, the Act explicitly affirmed, for the first time, the fundamental objectives of Canadian immigration law: family reunion, non-discrimination, concern for refugees and the promotion of Canada's demographic, economic, social and cultural goals. It removed inequalities in the existing law; it provided a modern flexible framework for the future development of immigration policy; and it made future immigration levels a matter for open decision and public announcement in advance by government.

The major provisions of the Act fall into certain well-defined areas including (a) Canadian immigration policy, (b) immigration planning and management, (c) admissible classes, (d) inadmissible classes, (e) control and enforcement, (f) refugees, (g) other provisions. The following are some brief comments in each of these areas.

(a) Canadian Immigration Policy

As recommended by the Special Joint Committee, the basic principles and objectives of Canadian immigration policy are set out very clearly in Part 1 of the Act. This is a completely new provision in Canadian immigration law. There are 10 objectives in all and it may be useful to quote several of the most significant ones. Part 1 opens with a statement that immigration policy should be designed and administered in such a manner as to promote the domestic and international interests of Canada, recognising the need:

(1) to support the attainment of such demographic goals as may be established by the Government of Canada from time to time in respect of the size, rate of growth, structure and geographic distribution of the Canadian population;

(2) to encourage and facilitate the adaptation of persons who have been granted admission as permanent residents to Canadian society by promoting co-operation between the Government of Canada and other levels of government and non-governmental agencies in Canada with respect thereto;

(3) to ensure that any person who seeks admission to Canada on either a permanent or temporary basis is subject to standards

of admission that do not discriminate on grounds of race, national or ethnic origin, colour, religion or sex;

(4) to fulfil Canada's international legal obligations with respect to refugees and to uphold its humanitarian tradition with respect to the displaced and persecuted; and

(5) to foster the development of a strong and viable economy and the prosperity of all regions of Canada.

This part of the Act also makes it clear that the admission of immigrants and the admission and stay of visitors to Canada are a matter of privilege and not of right.

(b) Immigration Planning and Management

The Act contains several original and constructive provisions relating to the planning and management of Canadian immigration, reflecting a desire on the part of the Federal Government to involve the provinces more closely in planning and decision-making, as well as making this process more open to public consultation and scrutiny. Section 109 of the Act makes consultation with the Provinces by the Minister mandatory and enables him to enter into agreements with a province or group of provinces relating to immigration. Section 7 requires the Minister, after consulting with the Provinces and 'such other persons, organisations and institutions as he deems appropriate' to announce annually in Parliament the number of immigrants which the Government proposes to admit during any specified period of time. There have now been five annual announcements of immigration levels. Like Australia, Canada now has a three-year planning cycle (introduced in 1982) and like Australia also, annual levels have been reduced recently on account of the recession. On 1 November 1983, the present Minister of Employment and Immigration, John Roberts, announced that Canada plans to admit 90,000 to 95,000 immigrants in 1984, compared to the 1983 range of 105,000 to 110,000. The 1985 and 1986 levels have been set at 100,000 to 110,000 and 105,000 to 120,000 respectively, but are subject to annual review and adjustment.

(c) Admissible Classes

Former categories established for the purpose of admission to Canada in various ways no longer apply. Instead there are first, a 'family class' which refers to the immediate family and dependent children but also includes parents of any age sponsored by Canadian citizens; secondly, refugees; and thirdly, other applicants consisting of immigrants selected on the basis of the Point System, including independent applicants and nominated (i.e., more distant) relatives. The point system is elaborated in the

Immigration Regulations attached to the Act. In addition, the Act requires all visitors who wish to study or work temporarily in Canada to obtain prior authorisation abroad. Once admitted, visitors may not normally change their status. Under the Act also, temporary workers who change jobs and students who change their course of study without proper authorisation plus all visitors who remain beyond the period for which they were admitted will be subject to removal. The Act also provides for moderately stiff penalties against employers who knowingly employ persons who are living and working in Canada illegally.

(d) Inadmissible Classes

Part 3 of the Act which deals with 'Exclusion and Removal' begins with a wholly revised section on inadmissible classes. Substantive changes have been made in the new Act reflecting far more liberal and sensible attitudes to the question of exclusion. The Act simply identifies certain broad classes of persons whose entry to Canada might endanger public health, welfare, order, security or the integrity of the immigration programme. Grounds for exclusion now include a degree of health impairment, judged on an individual's total health profile, which would constitute a threat to public health or safety, or cause excessive demands to be made on health or social services; the lack of means of support or evident capacity to acquire them; criminal offences of a severe character without evidence of rehabilitation; involvement in criminal activity (such as organised crime); or in espionage, subversion or acts of violence (such as terrorism and hijacking).

(e) Control and Enforcement

The Immigration Act makes some major changes in the control and enforcement area including provisions which seek (1) to improve the conduct of inquiries relating to persons subject to removal from Canada;[9] (2) to provide new ways to protect the fundamental rights of persons subject to an inquiry; and (3) instead of simple deportation in all cases requiring removal, as laid down in the 1952 Act, to offer three different instruments for removal depending on the gravity of the case, namely a deportation order, an exclusion order and a simple departure notice.

(f) Refugees

As we have seen, Canada's commitment to fulfil its international legal obligations in relation to refugees and 'to uphold its humanitarian tradition with respect to the displaced and the persecuted' is established as a fundamental principle of immigration policy for the first time in Canadian immigration law. The Act also codifies and improves existing procedures relating to the determination of refugee status. It provides for the establishment by regulation of special selection standards for refugees, as well as special admissible classes, in order to meet the needs of groups of displaced persons who are *de facto* refugees, but do not qualify under the existing definition of a refugee. The Act also formally establishes a Refugee Status Advisory Committee to advise the Minister on the determination of refugee status in individual cases, replacing an unofficial committee which had been in existence for some years.

(g) Other Provisions

(i) *Immigration Appeal Board*. The new Immigration Act incorporates most of the provisions of the Immigration Appeal Board Act of 1967 which established, for the first time in Canada, a fully independent body for the hearing of immigration appeals which is totally independent of government. The Act preserves the authority and independence of the Board, but defines its jurisdiction more precisely. It also provides for the appointment when necessary of more members to assist the Board in meeting regional demands and dealing with increased workloads. The Board is primarily concerned with appeals against removal from Canada. The appeal provision in the Act stipulates that, where a removal order is made (except for persons ordered to be deported by the Governor in Council for reasons relating to the safety and security of Canada), all permanent residents, and people holding valid returning resident permits but nevertheless found by an adjudicator to have lost their permanent resident status, have a full right of appeal to the Board on either legal or any other grounds. In addition, persons defined as refugees according to the provisions of the Act, as well as visa holders seeking admission to Canada have a full right of appeal on either legal or compassionate grounds, except in cases involving subversion or terrorism in which case an appeal can only be made on legal grounds. The Act also makes it possible for all eligible persons to appeal directly on humanitarian or compassionate grounds without first contesting a valid removal order, although they may also appeal on legal grounds if they wish.

(ii) *Security*. The Immigration Act contains completely new provisions relating to the 'Safety and Security of Canada'. Essentially this establishes a procedure whereby the Minister of Employment and Immigration and the Solicitor General can certify, on the basis of confidential information available to Canada's security agencies, that a person is a security risk and should be deported. This certificate then serves as conclusive evidence which may be placed before an adjudicator. Where the person in question is a permanent resident, the case will be examined not by an adjudicator, but by an independent advisory panel to be known as the Special Advisory Board. The function of this Board is to review the information submitted by the Ministers and to give advice on other questions involving considerations of national security and public order.

(iii) *Immigration Regulations.* The 1952 Act placed considerable reliance on the power to make regulations, established under the Act, in certain important areas which were defined in very broad terms. One of the best known of these was 'the prohibiting or limiting of admission of persons by reason of (1) nationality, citizenship, ethnic group, occupation, class or geographical area of origin, (2) peculiar customs, habits, modes of life, or methods of holding property, (3) unsuitability having regard to the climatic, economic, social, industrial, education, labour, health or other conditions or requirements existing . . . (4) probable inability to become readily assimilated or to assume the duties and responsibilities of Canadian citizenship . . .'. There is nothing like this in the new Act. The Act does establish the power of the Governor in Council to make regulations, but it specifies each separate matter on which regulations are or may be required; and if a particular matter is not so identified, no regulations will be possible without an amendment to the regulation-making powers. The list of matters on which regulations may be made is a long one, but it is very useful to have it there in print.

For reasons of space, we cannot examine the contents of the Immigration Regulations themselves which followed the Act and are known as Immigration Regulations 1978, except to say that they contain precise descriptions of the admissible classes and Point System among many other matters.

Since the new Immigration Act was proclaimed on 10 April 1978, there have been no major changes in Canadian immigration policy and law and relatively few administrative changes, adjustments or special programmes. Following this successful national effort in the 1970s to produce a new, modern and acceptable Immigration Act – an effort which was long overdue – this area of public policy has tended to recede into the background. In the first year or two since the Act was passed, simply making it work was a major undertaking, involving extensive staff training, revision of existing forms and procedures preparation of new manuals, re-writing data systems and similar activities. New forms of consultation with the provinces and with the voluntary sector had to be put in place. Where public attention and concern has been aroused, it has tended to focus on refugees, on the problem of illegal immigrants (which was the subject of a special study commissioned by the government and some subsequent administrative action) and on the annual immigration levels.

It should be mentioned here that Canada has been more successful in developing good immigration policies and programmes than it has in finding an appropriate and effective location for immigration management. Three different departments or agencies have been responsible for immigration in Canada during the post-war period: The Department of Citizenship and Immigration (1950–1965), the Department of Manpower and Immigration (1966–1977) and the Canada Employment and Immigration Commission created in 1977 through an amalgamation of the former Department of Manpower and Immigration and the Unemployment Insurance Commission. Immigration is managed today by a relatively small group of senior managers within the Canada Employment and Immigration Commission which is a very large agency indeed, organised to a considerable extent on a regional basis. Responsibility for the welfare and settlement of immigrants and refugees in Canada today is shared between the Commission, the Department of the Secretary of State and the provinces. The Department of the Secretary of State is responsible for all matters relating to citizenship. These divisions of responsibility, as well as the lack of unified, overall management are proving to have serious disadvantages.

Citizenship

Canadian citizenship is determined by the Canadian Citizenship Act of 1974 as amended and the Canadian Citizenship Regulations. A Canadian citizen is a person who has Canadian citizenship by birth or through a process of naturalisation. Dual citizenship is permitted under Canadian law. A citizen of Canada has the following rights:

(1) the right to full political participation (only a Canadian citizen may vote and run for political office in federal and some provincial elections);
(2) foreign travel and freedom of return (the privilege of travelling outside Canada on a Canadian passport and the right to re-enter Canada);
(3) full economic rights (some public service, business and professional positions and some commercial enterprises may be held only by Canadians).

Permanent residents who have been lawfully admitted to Canada and have lived in Canada for three years may apply for citizenship. Applicants must be 18 years of age or older; must have lived in Canada for a total time of three years within the four years immediately before an application for citizenship is made; must speak either English or French well enough to make themselves understood in the community; must have some knowledge of the rights and responsibilities of Canadian citizenship and of Canada's political system, geography and history; and must take the Oath of Citizenship.

The United States

The population of the US is now estimated as over the 233 million mark, but immigration, always the subject of keen public interest and concern, continues at maximum levels while the problems of controlling it are, as ever, a matter of vigorous debate. Some would argue that immigration to the US is, in fact, out of control, after a decade in which the country has taken in more new residents (legal and illegal immigrants, plus large numbers of refugees) than at any other period in its history. As in Australia and Canada, however, important changes in immigration law have taken place in the past few years.

The Constitution of the US grants to the Congress authority to determine immigration policy under the power 'to regulate commerce with foreign nations and among the several states and with the Indian tribes' (Article I, Section 8, Clause 3), and this power is both fully used and jealously guarded. The concern and activities of the Congress in this field have been described by the author in the following way:[10]

As in no other country, Congress not only makes immigration policy, but keeps existing legislation and its relevance to current needs under constant scrutiny, so that immigration policy is in a state of continuous evolution. The Senate and House Committees on the Judiciary and their sub-committees play a vital role in this process, as do the individual members of Congress who make immigration a major and often a lifelong concern. As in no other country, the way in which these Congressional committees operate, and the contacts maintained by individual members, permit a significant input in the policy-making process, from the considerable number of national organisations, voluntary agencies and individuals who are concerned about immigration and the development of immigration policy.

As well as interacting continuously with the Congressional committees, the bureaucracy is also remarkably accessible, comparatively speaking, to the voluntary sector and to informed opinion outside its ranks, and both the policy-making process in immigration and management itself are characterised by an openness and degree of democratic discussion not found elsewhere. This special kind of political environment is an outcome in part of the profoundly legalistic character of US immigration policy and management in which the law, its operation and evolution are the central focus of the entire system.

Responsibility for immigration in the US lies with the Department of State together with the Department of Justice and, to a lesser extent, the Department of Labour, the US Public Health Service and other agencies. The Secretary of State is responsible for the administration and enforcement of the immigration laws, as they relate to the issue or refusal of immigrant and non-immigrant visas overseas by consular officers; and he is authorised to establish regulations, prescribe forms and procedures and perform such other acts necessary to carry out his responsibilities. Within his department, these responsibilities are delegated to the Head of the Bureau of Security and Consular Affairs, who is now an Assistant Secretary. Within the Bureau and under the direct jurisdiction of the Assistant Secretary is the Visa Office which is headed by a Deputy Assistant Secretary. The Visa Office is responsible for the co-ordination of consular visa work at numerous posts throughout the world.

The Attorney-General is responsible for the administration and enforcement of immigration and nationality laws as they affect aliens after they arrive in the US. These responsibilities are delegated to the Immigration and Naturalisation Service of the Department of Justice which is headed by a Commissioner who is also a presidential appointee. The duties of the Immigration and Naturalisation Service, which is one of the principal law enforcement agencies in the US, include the inspection of persons to determine their admissibility to the US; adjudicating requests for benefits under the law; preventing illegal entry into the US; investigations, apprehension and removal of aliens in the US in violation of the law; and the examination of applicants wishing to become citizens.[11]

With the exception of the citizenship and citizenship education programme of the Immigration and Naturalisation Service, neither the federal government nor the states provide their own unique services for immigrants. Direct funding for service agencies is generally only provided in special circumstances, such as those relating to refugee movements. Practical help for immigrants and refugees is offered by a network of voluntary organisations, including sectarian agencies, nationality organisations and groups, non-sectarian helping agencies such as the International Institutes and many other community organisations. There are also several important national organisations and coalitions in this field such as the American Council for Nationalities Service and the American Council of Voluntary Agencies.

Post-War Developments in Immigration

There have been four significant stages in the evolution of American immigration law since the end of the Second World War. The first was the Immigration and Nationality Act 1952, known as the McCarran-Walter Act, which was passed by Congress, over President Truman's veto. It was the result of five years of intensive Congressional study and is still, in fact, the basic immigration statute in the US, although it has been amended in significant ways.

The Act's most noteworthy provision – and the main reason for President Truman's veto – involved the preservation and development of the national origins quota system created in the early 1920s which was the basis of the US 'White America Policy'. The McCarran-Walter Act added to this system by establishing the concept of the 'Asia-Pacific Triangle', an area embracing some twenty countries with about half the world's population. These countries were given, for the first time, minimum annual quotas of 100 immigrants each with 185 for Japan and 105 for Chinese persons outside China.

Despite substantial support in Congress at the time, the Act aroused considerable opposition and a fierce battle was fought in the ensuing years between the traditional forces of restriction and liberality, in which liberality eventually triumphed. (During the next few years, in fact, Congress enacted more than 30 public laws which in effect nullified the national origins quota system, by widening the loopholes in it and providing for the admission of special groups of non-quota immigrants.) The McCarran-Walter Act did, however, have some positive features. Among other provisions, it codified and brought together for the first time all the existing laws on immigration and naturalisation and established a system of preferences (still within national quotas) which has become a major feature of US immigration policy.

The next very important stage in the evolution of immigration policy took place in 1965 when a further Immigration Act (generally known as the 1965 Amendments or Kennedy Amendments) became law under President Johnson. This Act, which had originally taken the form of recommendations to Congress by President Kennedy, a long-time advocate of immigration reform, abolished the national origins quota system and with it the racially discriminatory policies of the previous 44 years.[12] It established American immigration policy on its present basis: universality, family reunion, the needs of the US labour market, particularly for skills and talents which are outstanding or in short supply, and concern for refugees. It was the beginning of an attempt which is still in progress to build a unified immigration system which would apply to prospective immigrants from any part of the world. The major provisions of the Act are listed below:

(1) The national origins quota system was to be abolished as of 1 July 1968 and the Asia-Pacific Triangle provision was to be repealed immediately.

(2) For the Eastern Hemisphere, an overall ceiling of 170,000 immigrant visas, exclusive of parents, spouses and children of US citizens, was established on the first-come first-served basis with a ceiling of 20,000 visas annually for each foreign state.

(3) For the Eastern Hemisphere also, seven preference categories were established, four for the purpose of family reunion, two for professional and skilled or unskilled workers and one for refugees.

(4) For natives of the independent countries of the Western Hemisphere, an overall ceiling of 120,000 visas, exclusive of parents, spouses and children of US citizens, was established as of 1 July 1968 unless Congress provided otherwise.

(5) Aliens seeking permanent admission for purposes of employment must obtain a certification from the Department of Labour before a visa can be issued. The certification is based on a determination that sufficient workers are not available in the US and that admitting the alien will not adversely affect similarly employed workers in the labour force. (This is a very important new departure, whose purpose was to protect American workers and to forge a stronger link between immigration and national manpower policies.)

Note: The preference system as it stands today is described in Appendix I together with the Canadian Point System and Australia's new Migrant Selection System.

The 1965 Act, admirable though it was in many ways, left several things undone. It did not deal in an adequate or conclusive way with Western Hemisphere immigration, although the Act provided for a Select Commision to look into the matter. Nothing was done to improve the law relating to refugee policy and refugees. The Labour certification programme, introduced in the Act, has not proved very effective and the chronic question of illegal immigration, which occurs on a very large scale in the US, has become even more severe since the Act was passed. The Act has also resulted, along with other factors, in major changes in the national origins of US immigrants with a striking global shift from north to south, both within Europe and in the world generally. Asia, Latin America and the Caribbean have been the significant growth areas in American immigration since 1965.

Congress passed two further Bills in 1976 and 1978 (Public Laws 94–571 and 95–412) which worked towards a more unified system. The first extended the Eastern Hemisphere selection system to the Western Hemisphere (but retained the same overall ceilings). The second combined the two ceilings into an overall worldwide total of 290,000 with the same per country limitation of 20,000. Under the three most recent Immigration Acts, the parents, spouses and children of adult US citizens have been exempt from these ceilings. In 1978, Congress also created a Select Commission on Immigration and Refugee Policy which reported to President Reagan in February 1981. It recommended an increase in legal immigration, enforcement measures to deter and reduce illegal immigration – now the major political issue in immigration in the US – and a one-time amnesty for all illegal immigrants resident in the US before 1 January 1980.[13]

On receipt of the Select Commission on Immigration and Refugee Policy Report, President Reagan appointed his own task force to review the Commission's proposals and in October 1981 the recommendation of this task force were incorporated in legislation (the Reagan bill). While the provisions of this bill were being considered in committee, the Chairman of the Senate subcommittee on immigration, Senator Alan Simpson, together with the Chairman of the House immigration subcommittee, Congressman Romano Mazzoli offered a new compromise immigration reform Bill which, they believed, would draw broad support. This was described in the following way in the *Congressional Quarterly*:—

HR 1510 and its Senate counterpart are designed to curb the flow of illegal aliens into the country. The primary enforcement tool would be an escalating system of fines, plus possible criminal penalties against employers who knowingly hire illegal aliens. The legislation would also revise and expand the temporary foreign worker programme that exists under current law. It would give legal status to perhaps millions of undocumented workers already in the country. In addition, it would streamline existing procedures for handling asylum, deportation and exclusion cases.[14]

The Senate Bill, S.529 was passed on 18 May but the House Bill suffered an unexpected and very disappointing setback. At a routine press conference in mid-October, House Speaker Tip O'Neill – without apparently consulting other Democratic leaders – announced that he would prevent the immigration reform bill from even reaching a vote. His principal reason for doing this appeared to be the opposition of Hispanic leaders and the fear that passage of the bill would cost the Democrats Hispanic votes in 1984. It is reported that Congressional leaders in both houses and both parties, as well as Administration officials, have been trying to find ways of salvaging the Bill and bringing it up for a vote next year if at all possible.

One further piece of legislation should be mentioned and that is the new Refugee Act which was passed by Congress in 1980. Among its major provisions, this Act broadened the concept of 'refugee' to match the definition in the UN Convention and Protocol relating to the Status of Refugees. It raised refugee visas to 50,000 a year through to 1982; thereafter the annual limit will be determined by the President after consultation with Congress. It provided federal support for refugee resettlement. It created the statutory office of US Co-ordinator for Refugee Affairs with the rank of Ambassador at Large, as well as an Office of Refugee Resettlement within the Department of Health and Human Services.

In the opening paragraph of this section, reference was made to the vigorous debate now in progress on current immigration issues in the US. A leading authority on American immigration has described the major national concerns in this field today in the following way:

> In sum, seven issues define the major areas for current immigration policy debate: illegal migration; population growth; the needs and absorptive capacity of the US labour force; the new geographic focus on immigration from Latin America and the Caribbean; the development of pluralism in the US, especially in regard to the size and spreading influence of Spanish-origin groups and the substantive and symbolic importance of language maintenance; foreign relations on a bilateral and multilateral level: and negotiating an international refugee resettlement policy and US administrative mechanisms for admitting refugees . . . (These) immigration issues will probably be the main policy topics under discussion in the near future. . . .[15]

It should be noted that all these issues, sometimes in slightly different forms and sometimes with different degrees of priority are also major concerns for Canada and Australia.

Under the Constitution of the US, Congress has the power to establish a uniform rule of naturalisation and, since the passage of the first naturalisation law in 1790, has placed the authority to naturalise in the courts. Naturalisation is, therefore, a judicial process and takes place in over 450 federal and state courts throughout the US.

Under US law, a person born in the US, with few exceptions, has a claim to US citizenship. Persons born in countries other than the US may also have a claim to US citizenship if: (1) either parent was born or naturalised in the US; or (2) either parent was a US citizen at the time of the birth of the applicant.

To qualify for naturalisation, an applicant:

(i)   must be at least 18 years old;

(ii) must have been lawfully admitted to the US for permanent residence;

(iii) must have resided continuously within the US for at least five years immediately preceding the date on which the petition is filed, and during that period must have been physically present in the US for periods totalling at least half that time – two and a half years; must have lived at least six months of the five-year period in the state in which the petition is filed; must maintain residence within the US from the date the petition is filed until admitted to citizenship; and must intend to reside permanently in the US;

(iv) must be able to understand, read, write, and speak English, unless exempt under certain special provisions;

(v)   must have a knowledge and understanding of the fundamentals of the history and of the principles and form of government of the US; be attached to the principles of the Constitution of the US, and well-disposed to the good order and happiness of the US;

(vi) must be of good moral character.

Conclusions: A Useful Model

Some important lessons can be learned from a study of the immigration policies, laws and methods of management of the US, Canada and Australia, all countries with a very substantial intake of immigrants and refugees in the post-war period. It is very instructive also to look at the problems which they have all had to deal with in this policy area and to consider how similar their responses have been.

During the post-war period, and indeed earlier, the immigration policies and laws of these three countries have been evolving in very similar ways with only minor differences of pace and style of operation. Today these policies and laws have the following major features which form a very useful set of guidelines for immigration management:

(1) Immigration policy is designed to serve specific national interests such as population growth and/or labour force requirements, but also embraces humanitarian and compassionate concerns including family reunion and refugee resettlement.

(2) A major effort has been made to eliminate all forms of racial and other kinds of discrimination in immigration.

(3) A unified and consistent system of selection and admission has been developed which can be applied on a worldwide basis. It is recognised that this system needs periodic review and adaptation to current economic and other circumstances.

(4) National policy objectives, as well as immigration laws and regulations are clearly and explicitly defined. (This statement applies to the US and Canada today and to all three countries in relation to policy objectives. Australia has not yet revised her basic immigration statute, the Migration Act 1958, but is now using immigration regulations which are much more clearly defined and explicit than formerly).

(5) Official decisions relating to immigration and naturalisation are subject, with certain exceptions, to review and appeal. (The US, Canada and Australia all have their own review procedures and appeal systems).

(6) Public participation and consultation in some form is regarded as essential. (In the US, this is achieved through the normal working of the political system described earlier. In Canada, consultation with the provinces and voluntary sector is mandatory before annual immigration levels are announced in Parliament. Canada also has a Canada Employment and Immigration Advisory Council. Australia has the Australian Council on Population and Ethnic Affairs, as well as a network of councils and committees in the area of settlement services.

(7) Effective programmes for the regulation of temporary employment with due regard to the rights and welfare of temporary workers are an essential part of immigration management, particularly in the light of worldwide increases in illegal immigration.

Within the space of a short chapter dealing with three countries, we cannot look into a very important aspect of immigration, namely welfare assistance and settlement services for immigrants and refugees. Nor is there space to discuss in detail some of the very important questions relating to control and enforcement in immigration, including the major problems of illegal immigration. But in these areas too the common experience and individual approaches of the US, Canada and Australia are equally interesting and instructive.

Notes

1 Canada and Australia use the word 'citizenship' rather than 'naturalisation'. The US uses both terms.
2 See Appendix I.
3 See Appendix II for comparative admission figures.
4 US efforts to exclude the Chinese, however, date back to 1875. Discrimination against the Chinese is an early phenomenon in all three countries.
5 Malcolm Fraser has now retired from party politics. His place as Leader of the Liberal Party and of the Liberal-National Party Coalition has been taken by Andrew Peacock.
6 This may change, however, under a Labour Government.
7 Hansard, House of Representatives, 18 May 1983, p. 663.
8 *Ibid.*, p. 665.
9 Under the Immigration Act 1976, a new category of immigration officers, known as 'Adjudicators' was created, replacing a former category of 'Special Inquiry Officers'. Adjudicators are given special legal training and are responsible for immigration inquiries, which take place when there is some doubt as to the status of a person or persons applying for admission to Canada at border or other entry points. Conditions for the conduct of immigration inquiries, as well as the rights to counsel and other matters affecting those subject to an inquiry, are clearly defined in the Act.
10 Freda Hawkins, *Immigration Policy and Management in Selected Countries*, Supplementary Study to the Canadian Green Paper on Immigration Policy, (Ottawa, 1975), p. 12.
11 *Ibid.*, pp. 12–13.
12 The first of the Acts establishing a national origins quota system was passed by Congress in 1921. It provided for a ceiling on total immigration with national quotas strongly favouring Western and Northern European countries.
13 It is estimated that more than a million illegal immigrants enter the US every year and many more are turned back. In the year ending 30 September 1983, US border guards apprehended 2 million illegal aliens, a 40 per cent increase over the previous year.
14 *Congressional Quarterly*, (25 June 1983), p. 1312.
15 Charles B. Keely, *US Immigration: A Policy Analysis*, The Population Council (Public Issues Series), (New York, 1979).

Appendix I

United States Preference System

Persons who desire to immigrate to the US are divided into two general categories: (a) those who may enter the US as permanent residents without any restriction on numbers, and (b) those who are restricted by the mandatory world ceiling of 290,000 annually. Those who may enter without numerical restriction include the spouses and minor unmarried children of a US citizen and the parent of a US citizen who is over the age of 21; as well as immigrants who lived in the US as lawful, permanent residents and are returning to the US, after a temporary residence abroad, practising ministers of religion with their spouses and children; and certain present and former employees of the US Government with their spouses and children.

All other immigrants are limited to 20,000 a year from each independent country and 600 from a dependent territory. The total annual number of all such immigrants may not exceed 290,000. Persons in the above category who wish to immigrate to the US are subject to the follow preferences:

(1) *First preference:* Unmarried sons and daughters of US citizens. (Not more than 20%).

(2) *Second preference:* Spouse and unmarried sons and daughters of an alien lawfully admitted for permanent residence. (20% plus any not required for first preference).

(3) *Third preference:* Members of the professions and scientists and artists of exceptional ability. (Not more than 10%).

(4) *Fourth preference:* Married sons and daughters of US citizens. (10% plus any not required for first three preferences).

(5) *Fifth preference:* Brothers and sisters over 21 years of age of US citizens. (24% plus any not required for first four preferences).

(6) *Sixth preference:* Skilled and unskilled workers in occupations for which labour is in short supply in US. (Not more than 10%).

| (7) *Seventh preference:* | Refugees to whom conditional entry or adjustment of status may be granted. (Not more than 6%). |
| (8) *Non-preference:* | Any applicant not entitled to one of the above preferences. (Any numbers not required for preference applicants). |

Note: The third and sixth preferences, as well as non-preference, all now require a job offer. There are no blanket certifications.

Labour Certification

Unless an intending immigrant is an immediate relative of a US citizen, or is in one of the special categories listed above, or is entitled to first, second, fourth or fifth preference status, or is a refugee, he must obtain a certification from the Department of Labour that there are no able, willing and qualified workers available for his proposed employment in the US.

Canadian Point System

The Immigration Act 1976, s. 6 sets out three basic classes of admissible immigrants: (a) the family class, (b) convention refugees and (c) the independent and other immigrants who apply on their own initiative. The third class includes assisted relatives, retirees, entrepreneurs and the self-employed as well as independent applicants. With the exception of retirees, all immigrants in this class are assessed against selection criteria in the Point System with certain modifications in some cases. Not every independent applicant has to meet all the ten selection criteria. Applicants are assessed only according to those factors which actually relate to their ability to become successfully established in Canada. Entrepreneurs (who have recently been given higher processing priority) and the self-employed, for example, are not assessed on occupational demand or arranged employment factors. Assisted relatives (with relatives in Canada who have signed statements promising to support them for a period of five years) are not assessed on the arranged employment, location or language factors.

To be admitted to Canada as a permanent resident, every immigrant selected according to the Point System must receive a minimum number of assessment points. Entrepreneurs must be awarded at least 25 points. Assisted relatives must earn 20 to 35 points, depending on their relationship to the Canadian resident who has promised to help them. All other applicants must earn at least 50 out of a possible 100 points before they can be issued with immigrant visas. In addition to earning a minimum number of points, applicants must meet certain mandatory requirements regarding the job experience and occupational demand factors. For example, any applicant who does not receive at least one point for the job experience factor must either have a pre-arranged job in Canada and a signed testament of the prospective employer's willingness to hire an inexperienced person, or be qualified and prepared to work in a designated occupation (one in an area of Canada identified as having a shortage of workers in that occupation). Furthermore, except for entrepreneurs and the self-employed, immigrants selected under the Point System must be awarded at least one point for occupational demand – unless they have arranged employment in Canada or are willing to work in a designated occupation.

Some discretion is allowed to the interviewing immigration officer to recommend to his director that an applicant who has not achieved the required number of points should nevertheless he regarded as suitable for admission and *vice versa*. Applicants who have been refused admission may request both a statement of the reasons for refusal as well as a review of their case. The following chart summarises the Point System.

Immigration Selection Criteria*

A Summary of the Canadian Point System

Applicable to:

Factors	Criteria	Max. Points	self employed	entrepreneurs	assisted relatives	others
1. *Education*	One point for each year of primary and secondary education successfully completed.	12	●	●	●	●
2. *Specific Vocational Preparation*	To be measured by the amount of formal professional, vocational, apprenticeship, in-plant or on-the-job training necessary for average performance in the occupation under which the applicant is assessed in item 4.	15	●	●	●	●
3. *Experience*	Points awarded for experience in the occupation under which the applicant is assessed in item 4 or, in the case of an entrepreneur, for experience in the occupation that the entrepreneur is qualified for and is prepared to follow in Canada.	8	●	●	●	●
4. *Occupational Demand*	Points awarded on the basis of employment opportunities available in Canada in the occupation that the applicant is qualified for and is prepared to follow in Canada.	15	●		●	●
5. *Arranged Employment or Designated Occupation*	Ten points awarded if the person has arranged employment in Canada that offers reasonable prospects of continuity and meets local conditions of work and wages, *providing* that employment of that person would not interfere with the job opportunities of Canadian citizens or permanent residents, and the person will likely be able to meet all licensing and regulatory requirements; *or* the person is qualified for, and is prepared to work in, a designated occupation and meets all the conditions mentioned for arranged employment except that concerning Canadian citizens and permanent residents.	10				●

*Members of the family class and retirees are not selected according to these criteria; Convention refugees are assessed against the factors listed in the first column but do not receive a point rating.

A Summary of the Canadian Point System (*cont.*)

Applicable to:

Factors	Criteria	Max. Points	self employed entrepreneurs	assisted relatives	others
6. *Location*	Five points awarded to a person who intends to proceed to an area designated as one having a sustained and general need for people at various levels in the employment strata and the necessary services to accommodate population growth. Five points subtracted from a person who intends to proceed to an area designated as not having such a need or such services.	5	● ●		●
7. *Age*	Ten points awarded to a person 18 to 35 years old. For those over 35, one point shall be subtracted from the maximum of ten for every year over 35.	10	● ●	●	●
8. *Knowledge of English and French*	Ten points awarded to a person who reads, writes and speaks both English and French fluently. Five points awarded to a person who reads, writes and speaks English *or* French fluently. Fewer points awarded to persons with less language knowledge and ability in English or French.	10	● ●		●
9. *Personal Suitability*	Points awarded on the basis of an interview held to determine the suitability of the person and his/her dependants to become successfully established in Canada, based on the person's adaptability, motivation, initiative, resourcefulness and other similar qualities.	10	● ●	●	●
10. *Relative*	Where a person *would* be an assisted relative, *if* a relative in Canada had undertaken to assist him/her, and an immigration officer is satisfied that the relative in Canada is willing to help him/her become established but is not prepared, or is unable, to complete the necessary formal documentation to bring the person to Canada, the person shall be awarded five points.	5	● ●		●

Australia's Migrant Selection System

Australia's present migrant selection system comprises five eligibility categories: (1) Family Migration, (2) Labour Shortage and Business Migration, (3) Independent Migration, (4) Refugees and Special Humanitarian Programmes, (5) Special Eligibility.

Family Migration includes spouses; unmarried children if part of the family unit; children under 18 years for adoption from overseas; orphaned unmarried relatives under 18 years of age, special need relatives; fiancé(e)s; parents of retiring age; parents of working age; aged dependent relatives; last remaining brother, sister or adult child outside Australia; non-dependent children and non-dependent brothers and sisters.

Labour Shortage and Business Migration includes occupations in demand; employment nominees; business migrants and self-employed applicants.

Special Eligibility includes migrants entering Australia from New Zealand under the Trans-Tasman Travel Arrangement (whereby persons holding New Zealand passports are generally exempted from visa requirements and economic employment assessment); self-supporting retirees and creative and sporting talents.

Most applicants for migrant entry, (with certain exceptions) are assessed under a Point System relating to economic adjustment in which the pass mark is 60 points, and must also contain a satisfactory rating on settlement factors from an immigration officer. The exceptions i.e., those who are not subject to an economic/employment/ assessment, consist of all family migrants (with the exception of non-dependent children and non-dependent brothers and sisters) as well as refugees and migrants entering Australia in the Special Eligibility category. A satisfactory rating on settlement factors may be required in all cases. The following chart summarises the Point System.

Economic/Employment Assessment

A summary of the Australian Point System

	Points
1. *Skills*	
Professional, Technical and Skilled Workers	
when qualifications are fully recognised in Australia	10
if not fully recognised	6
Service Occupations	6
Clerical, Commercial and Administrative	6
Semi-skilled	6
Rural and Unskilled	2
2. *Employment*	
Employer Nominees and Business Migrants	16
Other Arranged Employment	10
Occupations in Demand	10
3. *Age*	
25–35	8
23–24	6
37–38	6
20–22	4
38–39	4
Under 20	2
40–45	2
46 and over	0
4. *Education*	
Completed Tertiary	8
Full Secondary	6
Part of Secondary	5
Other	3
5. *Employment Record*	
Outstanding	10
Good	8
Satisfactory	5
Poor	0
6. *Economic Prospects*	
Labour Shortage and Business Migrants	25
Full Sponsorship by Australian Citizen	28
Full Sponsorship by Resident (not citizen)	25
Good	15
Satisfactory	10
Minor Problems Likely	5
Major Problems Likely	0
7. *Growth Area*	
To settle in a Designated Growth Area	6

Note: In exceptional cases, immigration officers may allot a maximum of 8 extra points where a candidate fails to obtain the necessary 60 points.

Appendix II

Post-war Admissions

TABLE 1
Immigration to the US 1946–1981

Year	No of admissions	Year	No of admissions
1946	108,721	1965	296,697
1947	147,292	1966	323,040
1948	170,570	1967	361,972
1949	188,317	1968	454,448
1950	249,187	1969	358,579
1951	205,717	1970	373,326
1952	265,520	1971	370,478
1953	170,434	1972	384,685
1954	208,177	1973	400,063
1955	237,790	1974	394,861
1956	321,625	1975	386,194
1957	326,867	1976	398,613
1958	253,265	1976*	103,676
1959	260,686	1977	462,315
1960	265,398	1978	601,422
1961	271,344	1979	460,348
1962	283,763	1980	530,639
1963	306,260	1981	596,600
1964	292,248		

*Transition Quarter covering change in fiscal year now ending 1 October.

TABLE 2
Immigration to Canada 1946–1981

Year	No of admissions	Year	No of admissions
1946	71,719	1964	112,606
1947	64,127	1965	146,758
1948	125,414	1966	194,743
1949	95,217	1967	222,876
1950	73,912	1968	183,974
1951	194,391	1969	161,531
1952	164,498	1970	147,713
1953	168,868	1971	121,900
1954	154,227	1972	122,006
1955	109,946	1973	184,200
1956	164,857	1974	218,465
1957	282,164	1975	187,881
1958	124,851	1976	149,429
1959	106,928	1977	114,914
1960	104,111	1978	86,313
1961	71,689	1979	112,096
1962	74,586	1980	143,117
1963	93,151	1981	128,618

TABLE 3
Australia: Settler Arrivals 1959–60 to 1980–81

Year	No of admissions	Year	No of admissions
1959–60	105,887	1970–71	170,011
1960–61	108,291	1971–72	132,719
1961–62	85,808	1972–73	107,401
1962–63	101,888	1973–74	112,712
1963–64	122,318	1974–75	89,147
1964–65	140,152	1975–76	52,748
1965–66	144,055	1976–77	73,189
1966–67	138,676	1977–78	75,732
1967–68	137,525	1978–79	68,749
1968–69	175,657	1979–80	81,271
1969–70	185,099	1980–81	111,900

United States Immigrant and Non-immigrant Visas

EDWARD S. GUDEON

United States lawyer resident in London

Introduction

United States laws limit new immigrants (that is, permanent entrants), other than immediate relatives and certain special immigrants or persons admitted for asylum, to a total of 270,000 a year. There is no such numerical limit on non-immigrants (temporary entrants), but they must qualify for admission. The US Immigration and Nationality Act (hereinafter called 'the Act') lists numerous grounds for exclusions of aliens because of undesirable conduct or traits (e.g. membership of a subversive organisation, such as the Communist Party, certain criminal activity, illiteracy or insanity etc.,) but these grounds for exclusion can frequently be waived for non-immigrants and in limited circumstances for immigrants as well. The Act however states that 'every alien shall be presumed to be an immigrant until he establishes to the satisfaction of the consular officer, at the time of application for a visa, and the immigration officer, at the time of application for admission, that he is entitled to non-immigrant status'. And the Act defines an immigrant as 'every alien except an alien who is within one of the . . . (specified) classes of non-immigrant aliens . . .'.

Thus the principal barrier in the way of obtaining non-immigrant status is an applicant's inability to demonstrate that he or she is not an intending immigrant. Furthermore, the alien who wishes to enter with non-immigrant status must establish eligibility for the *specific* non-immigrant status claimed.

Procedure for Temporary Entrants

An application for a visa must be submitted on Optional Form 156, with passport, photograph and supporting documents. An American consular officer employed by the Department of State issues visas abroad, but there are some non-immigrant visas which require prior approval of a petition by the Immigration and Naturalisation Service in the US; for example, H and L visas. The visa is not a guarantee of entry: once it has been endorsed in a passport, it indicates status and validity, but there is a double-check system. The second check is made by the Immigration and Naturalisation Service (which comes under the Department of Justice) at the American port of entry. If the applicant is admitted, Form I-94 is issued, stating the date and place of admission and the alien's status and period of stay.

If the alien, once in the US, wishes either to extend his or her stay or to change status, an application can be filed in the US. But if the alien departs from the US after changing status, a new visa in that status will be required for re-entry. If the alien has taken unauthorised employment in the country, the result will usually be denial of an application to extend the visa or change status, and will trigger deportation proceedings.

Non-immigrant Statuses: General Requirements

B visas

A tourist visa, designated B-2, is issued to visitors coming for pleasure, and a visitor's visa for business purposes, designated B-1, to travellers on business. 'Pleasure' includes reasons of health, tourism, amateur musical, sports or similar events without remuneration, participating in conventions etc. B-1 status prohibits 'skilled or unskilled labour' purposes, but allows business activities in the US defined in the State Department's regulations as 'legitimate activities of a commercial or professional character' that do not include 'purely local employment or labour for hire'. If the principal site of the business, and place where profits accrue, is a foreign country, B-1 status will normally permit some incidental labour in the US. A combined B-1/B-2 visa may be issued if appropriate. B-1 and B-2 visas are the most common and frequently-issued types available to an alien who has 'a residence in a foreign country which he has no intention of abandoning and who is visiting the US temporarily for business or temporarily for pleasure'. B visa entrants may be granted permission to remain for up to 12 months and extensions may be obtainable in increments of six months.

E visas

There is a separate system of temporary admission for 'treaty aliens', who are issued with E visas. E-1 visas for treaty traders, and

E-2 visas for treaty investors, are issued to aliens of certain countries pursuant to treaty (including British citizens if the alien concerned is resident actually and permanently in the UK and has his or her domicile there):

(1) 'solely to carry on a substantial trade principally between the US and the foreign state of which he is a national', or

(2) 'solely to develop and direct the operations of an enterprise in which he has invested, or of an enterprise in which he is actively in the process of investing, a substantial amount of capital'.

'Substantial trade' means that the volume of trade between the US and the other country party to the treaty must aggregate at least 51 per cent of the total volume of trade conducted by the alien or his employing firm. 'Substantial capital' means that the amount personally invested by the alien in an enterprise productive of goods or services be deemed sufficient for the particular business so as to give it a viable chance of commercial success. In this context, 'substantial' is deemed to be a term relative to the nature of the business. State Department regulations provide that the treaty investor visa (E-2) is not available to an investor with a small amount of capital in what is deemed to be a marginal business solely for the purpose of earning a living.

An alien need not himself be the trader or investor if he is suitably employed. A treaty trader employee must be employed in a supervisory or executive position or have specific qualifications that make his or her services essential. A treaty investor employee must be employed in a responsible capacity as a major managerial or executive employee or as a highly trained and specially qualified technical employee.

The accompanying spouse and minor (under 21) unmarried children are given the same visa as the principal alien. Although work by them is not affirmatively authorised, the Immigration and Naturalisation Service does not treat them as violating their status if they are employed.

E visas are valid for five years and treaty entrants receive a one-year permit on each entry (endorsed on the I-94 form on entry). Visas may be extended indefinitely as long as the principal applicant maintains E status. No petition form is required. Application may be made to an American consular official abroad on Optional Form 156 with supporting documents. Eligibility requires evidence of intent to depart from the US at the end of one's stay, but does not require the applicant to demonstrate that he has a foreign residence he has no intention of abandoning.

L visas

The status of intracompany transferee (L-1) is available to an alien who immediately prior to application for admission to the US has been continuously employed outside the US by a firm, corporation or other legal entity for 12 months or more as a managerial or executive employee or in a capacity involving specialised knowledge, and who seeks to enter temporarily to continue to render services for the same employer or a subsidiary or affiliate thereof in a capacity that is managerial, executive or involves specialised knowledge. The issue of an L-1 visa requires prior approval by the Immigration and Naturalisation Service of a petition (Form I-129B) filed in the district office of the Immigration and Naturalisation Service where the alien will be employed, with supporting documents attached. It may be granted initially for up to three years; extensions may thereafter be obtained in one-year increments for the period of demonstrated need. No work permit (labour certification) is required, and the holder's spouse and minor unmarried minor children receive L-2 visas but are not allowed to work.

H visas

Temporary workers allowed to take paid work include professional aliens and aliens of distinguished merit and ability (H-1); skilled and unskilled workers in short supply (H-2), and trainees (H-3). H visas are sometimes referred to as temporary work permits, and require the applicant to demonstrate that he has 'a residence in a foreign country which he has no intention of abandoning'. They also require prior Immigration and Naturalisation Service approval of a petition (Form I-129B) filed, in most cases by a prospective employer. An H-1 visa may initially be granted for up to two years. Extensions may be granted in increments of 12 months for the period of demonstrated need.

H-1 status is available for professionally qualified aliens (e.g. doctors, lawyers, architects, teachers) and aliens of distinguished merit and ability substantially above that ordinarily encountered (e.g. a well-known athlete). A petitioner must demonstrate that the alien's particular skills are required temporarily in the US, and the alien must demonstrate that he or she possesses the required qualifications and seeks temporary entry to accept this employment. No work permit is required for the holder of an H-1 visa.

H-2 status is available for skilled or unskilled workers coming temporarily to perform temporary services or labour when domestic workers are unavailable. A work permit is normally required. The prospective employer must petition the Immigration and Naturalisation Service to classify the alien as an H-2 worker.

H-3 status is available to an alien coming temporarily as a trainee in an organised training programme, and the prospective employer must file a petition with the Immigration Naturalisation Service. No work permit is required. The accompanying spouse and minor unmarried children of H-visa holders are given H-4 visas and are not authorised to work.

Other non-immigrant visas

These are for students (F-1 and M-1); a fiancé or fiancée (K): officials of foreign governments (A); exchange visitors (J-1); representatives of foreign information media (I); international organisation aliens (G); transits (C); crewmen (D); and NATO representatives (NATO).

Immigrant Statuses

Aliens desiring to immigrate to the US are divided into two categories: (a) those not subject to the annual numerical limitation of 270,000 immigrant visas per year, and (b) those who are restricted by the annual numerical limitation.

(a) Immigrants not numerically restricted

Immediate Relatives
These include children of US citizens if the children are unmarried and under the age of 21, parents of US citizens if the US citizen is over the age of 21, and spouses of US citizens.

Special Immigrants
These include permanent resident aliens who are returning to a residence in the US from a temporary visit abroad, certain ministers of a religious denomination whose services are needed by such religious denomination in the US, certain recommended employees and former employees of the US Government abroad, and certain foreign medical graduates who entered the US before 10 January 1978.

(b) Immigrants with numerical limitations

First preference
This includes unmarried sons and daughters (over 21 years of age) of US citizens.

Second preference
This includes spouses and unmarried sons and daughters of aliens lawfully admitted as permanent residents.

Third preference
This includes members of the professions or persons of exceptional ability in the sciences or arts.

Fourth preference
This includes married sons and daughters of US citizens.

Fifth preference
This includes brothers and sisters of US citizens if the citizen is over 21 years of age.

Sixth preference
This includes persons performing skilled or unskilled labour, not of a temporary or seasonal nature, for which a shortage of employable and willing persons exists in the US.

Non-preference
This includes other immigrants, including retirees and investors.

It should be noted that non-preference immigrant visas have been unavailable since mid-1978 and will remain so for the foreseeable future unless there is a change in the laws by Congress.

The alien must establish eligibility for the immigrant status claimed.

Some grounds for exclusion may be waived for family members. Labour certification (work permit) is required for the third, sixth and non-preference categories, unless they are 'exempted' as follows. Exemption from the individual work permit requirements (advance or 'blanket' certification) is available to the following aliens with prearranged permanent employment and who are otherwise qualified for an immigrant visa: (1) physical therapists, (2) certain foreign medical graduates and professional nurses, (3) persons of exceptional ability in the sciences or arts, (4) persons coming to perform religious work, and (5) executive and managerial employees of international corporations or organisations who have been continuously employed for 12 months or more outside of the US and who are coming to work in an executive or managerial position for the same employer in the US or a US subsidiary or US affiliate thereof and the US employer has been 'doing business' in the US for at least one year.

Immigrant status also may be obtained under The Refugee Act 1980. The Act defines a refugee as 'any person who is outside any country of such person's nationality or, in the case of a person having no nationality, is outside any country in which such person last habitually resided and who is unable or unwilling to avail himself or herself of the protection of that country because of persecution or a well-founded fear of persecution on account of race, religion, nationality, membership in a social group, or political opinion'.

The Refugee Act provides that the number of refugees will not exceed a certain number, unless the President determined that additional admissions are 'justified by humanitarian concerns or is otherwise in the national interest', and the number is determined by the President in consultation with Congress. Admissions of refugees are limited to those determined by the President in consultation with Congress to be 'of special humanitarian concern to the United States'.

Applications for refugee status are submitted and processed outside the US and such status is unavailable to a refugee who has been 'firmly resettled' in a third country, or who has engaged in the persecution of others, or who is not otherwise admissible as an immigrant.

A refugee is admitted conditionally for one year. After one year, the refugee and his or her family can obtain immigrant status.

Major changes to US immigration laws could happen through the introduction of various Bills in Congress in the near future.

II. The United Kingdom past and present

This section does not set out to provide a full historical account of UK immigration law, but to contrast the familiar terms of debate on control, over the last 25 years, with two neglected factors. One of these is the view taken by immigrants themselves. Debates in the House of Commons are conducted exclusively by white people: a few of these are 'immigrants' in the proper sense of the word, being naturalised aliens or white Commonwealth citizens who were born overseas and have settled here, but none is an 'immigrant' in the sense that has been discussed and legislated upon since 1961. Newspaper and broadcast reports of immigration issues have therefore relied almost entirely on arguments in the form: what shall *we* do about *them*? The assumptions underlying such arguments have made it easy for politicians and the Press to slip into talking of 'public opinion' as the opinion of indigenous white people only, even when referring to an area with sizeable immigrant settlement. In other words, the immigrants themselves usually come into the matter only as objects with which policy must deal, or people who are a little less than other people, not having their own individual existences and views, as varied as those of the native majority, or even people who are not really there at all.

Even more neglected, however, have been the very matters which one would suppose the framers of any immigration policy would look at first: population and the economy. Until now, these matters have been considered only in a very narrow way, if at all, by the law makers. And the laws have been very little criticised by economists and demographers. If you ask an economist at random what he or she thinks about immigration and the economy, the instant reaction will be to answer in terms of either racial discrimination and the job market (an issue which in fact affects both immigrants and native citizens), or Commonwealth immigration in the 1960s. The notion of looking at immigration as a whole, including Irish and foreign settlement and excluding people born in the UK, is just not there. Demographers are more aware of immigration as a whole, and of the relationship between immigration and emigration as well, but the figures asked of them by politicians and the press do not usually deal with these matters but with essentially racial issues, like the number of children being born in particular areas to parents of New Commonwealth and Pakistan origin. The chapters in this section consider immigration, properly speaking, in a light that is quite unfamiliar to most people in the UK, and contain some surprises. They also demonstrate vividly another more general, neglected truth: that the motives for collecting particular statistics, and the means of collecting them, must be known if the figures themselves are to be understood and correctly evaluated.

The United Kingdom Immigration Policy: The Need for Reform

USHA PRASHAR

Director of the Runnymede Trust

Introduction

> Immigration Law in this country has developed mainly as a series of responses to, and attempts to regulate particular pressures, rather than as a positive means of achieving pre-conceived social or economic aims.

(Home Office's written memorandum submitted to the House of Commons Select Committee on Race Relations and Immigration, February 1977).

The British policy towards immigration has traditionally been *laissez-faire*. Changes in the direction of immigration control have largely come about under the pressure of events rather than as the outcome of the country's anticipation and purposeful planning.

Development of Immigration Policy in the UK

The largest group of immigrants to come to the UK during the nineteenth century was the Irish. This immigration could be regarded as internal migration, since Ireland was at the time part of the UK. In the decades preceding the First World War Jewish immigration took place and this wave of immigration provided much of the ammunition for the political campaign against 'alien immigration'. Initially, the campaign was slow to get off the ground but eventually the agitation against 'alien immigration' mounted, and a Royal Commission was appointed to enquire into the desirability of legislation. In 1903 it reported in favour of limiting immigration.

The Conservative Government passed the Aliens Act 1905. It gave powers to control 'undesirable and destitute aliens'. The significance of the 1905 Act lay in the breach with the principle of the previous years that the UK should be freely open to immigration from overseas, both for economic self interest and humanitarian concerns. The antecedents of the 1905 Act were significant in that much of the anti-alien agitation was profoundly racist in character.

In 1914 more draconian immigration legislation was enacted. The Aliens Restriction Act 1914, envisaged largely as a security measure, gave the Home Secretary powers to prohibit immigrants from landing and to deport immigrants. The Act also imposed a requirement that all aliens register with the police. The Act did not apply to British subjects and hence was not applicable to the overseas dominions and colonies of the British Empire. Although the 1914 Act was introduced for temporary security reasons, it was renewed by means of the Aliens Restriction Act 1919. The main provisions of this Act together with amendments contained in a number of subsequent parliamentary orders continued in force until the Immigration Act 1971.

The main features of the 1914 and 1919 Acts and subsequent Orders in Council were that aliens could be refused entry into the UK at the discretion of an immigration officer; that for aliens without a visible means of support, only a short stay in the UK was permissible unless the immigrant secured a work permit issued by the Ministry of Labour; and the aliens could be deported by the courts or by the Home Secretary if such an act was deemed 'conducive to the public good'.

The Second World War produced a substantial addition of immigrants to the population, mainly Polish immigrants. To assist this group, the Polish Resettlement Act 1947 was passed. The Act was one of the few constructive legislative initiatives in the field of immigration since it established a Polish Resettlement Corps with the express purpose of resettling the Polish immigrants. The distinctive features of the resettlement effort was the recognition that resettlement had dimensions other than economic, and that it embraced not only housing, but health, welfare and education. Resistence to Polish settlement was strongest amongst the trade unions.

During this time, due to shortage of manpower for certain kinds of work, notably hospital work, agriculture, coal mining, textiles and building considerable numbers of Europeans, that is, Lithuanians, Ukranians, Latvians and Yugoslavs, were recruited to work in Britain under a number of different schemes. Conditions for these were harder – work permits were issued for 12 months and transfers between jobs were not permitted, although extensions within specific jobs were allowed. They were not allowed to bring in their dependents.

The work permit scheme did not originally apply to the citizens of the British Commonwealth, who under the British Nationality Act 1948 were allowed to enter the UK freely, to find work, to settle and to bring their families. Partly encouraged by employers and the government, increasing numbers of Commonwealth citizens from former British colonies and dependencies did precisely that. Substantial numbers from the Caribbean, Guyana, India, Pakistan, Africa, Malaysia and Hong Kong flowed in during the 15 years from 1948 onwards.

The rising tide of 'coloured' immigration led to an increasing social unease about immigration and to political agitation for its control. Consequently the status of Commonwealth immigrants was steadily whittled away in a succession of legislative and administrative measures: the Commonwealth Immigrants Act 1962; the Commonwealth Immigrants Act 1968; and the Immigration Act of 1971, and Britain retreated from the principles of the British Nationality Act 1948.

Under the Commonwealth Immigrants Act 1962 a system of employment vouchers for Commonwealth immigrants was introduced, and employment vouchers for unskilled and semi-skilled workers were progressively phased out. Vouchers for those with specific skills or qualifications or with specific jobs were successively cut and eventually abolished. The Commonwealth Immigrants Act 1968 specified that holders of UK passports issued outside the UK would be subject to immigration controls unless the holders or one of their parents or grandparents, had been born, naturalised or adopted in the UK or in a Commonwealth country already self-governing in 1948. The result of this Act was to create a new class of citizens who were 'stateless in substance though not in name'.[1] In practice Britain has been steadily admitting this new class of non-patrial UK passport holders from East Africa under a quota scheme, with the intention of regulating the flow. The Immigration Act 1971 replaced the Commonwealth Immigrant Acts of 1962 and 1968 and provides the framework of the current law on controls of admission to the UK. The practice to be followed in the administration of the Act is set out in the Immigration Rules. Under the 1971 Act those who qualify as patrials do not need work permits to take up employment or to settle permanently in the UK. All other categories are subject to immigration control. The category of patrial is important not simply in relation to immigration in the UK, but also because patrials constitute the class of citizens entitled, under the Treaty of

Accession 1971 between the UK and the EEC to the benefits of European Communities membership as UK 'nationals'.

On three occasions – 1962, 1968 and 1971 – restrictive legislation was enacted to control and limit immigration from the New Commonwealth. The result has been confusion, myth making and the devaluation of the concept of nationality and citizenship. Moreover the proliferation of categories of UK citizens created a justifiable impression that immigration control is applied on racial grounds. The British Nationality Act 1981 follows the lines of existing immigration control and perpetuates the unsatisfactory situation created by the Immigration Act 1971.

Administration of Immigration Control and Race Relations

The consistent thread in British race relations policy has been the determination of successive administrations to restrict immigration from the new Commonwealth. The assumptions and myths on which this policy is based are:

(1) Strict immigration control is a prerequisite to good race relations.
(2) Britain is a small crowded island which cannot absorb unlimited numbers of immigrants.
(3) There is fear that the British way of life is under pressure due to 'coloured' immigration.

Against such thinking the numbers of immigrants coming in from the new Commonwealth and the control of such immigration have come to be seen as the central concern of Britain's immigration policy. A brief look at the administration of immigration control and changes, which have been made to the Immigration Rules since 1971 show that legal, social and moral considerations have been secondary. The debate which we have had since 1974 about male fiancés highlights the concerns which have underlined the immigration law policy and practice.[2] Injustices of the entry clearance system for people from the Indian sub-continent seeking entry to the UK as dependents of someone settled here are well documented.[3] The system for appealing against decisions made by immigration officials is inadequate and again has been widely criticised.[4] Specific aspects of immigration policy and practices, and the need for reform, are discussed in greater detail elsewhere in this work.

Increasing concern has also been expressed about the operation and enforcement of the immigration laws within the UK. For instance the police and immigration service have wide powers to search, question and detain people suspected of being 'illegal entrants'. There are numerous cases of workplaces and homes being raided by police and immigration officers, of innocent people being questioned and sometimes held in police stations, and of people being questioned in the street by police officers about their immigration status and asked to produce their passports. In recent years access to the National Health Service[5] and Social Security benefits[6] has become dependent upon immigration status. The link between the Social Security Regulations and the Immigration Rules has caused some hardship among black communities. The Social Security Act 1980 and the regulations made under it exclude the following from receiving supplementary benefits: illegal entrants, deportees, people who stay beyond their permitted time, and those who are allowed into the UK so long as they do not have recourse to public funds. This link means that local DHSS officers, in order to establish eligibility for benefits, check passports. Because passports have become such a crucial document in the lives of black people these checks only succeed in making them feel more insecure and enhancing their feelings that they must first prove their right to be here before enjoying equality of treatment. The rationale behind the present policy is that it is illogical to support people from public funds who have no right to be here. However, this argument ignores the fact that complexities of immigration law, its discriminatory effect, the ever expanding definition of who is and is not an illegal entrant and the unequal status of women both in regard to Social Security Regulations and Immigration Rules have caused considerable hardship among black communities.

The hardship caused to black families due to unjust immigration policies and practices is there for any one to see. It is clear that these laws have a profoundly negative effect on the lives of black communities. Their lives are determined by considerations arising out of immigration and nationality laws and influence their views and perceptions about life in the UK. Racial matters, therefore, cannot be divorced from debates about immigration and nationality because it is the total experience of black communities in this society which determines whether or not they feel a legitimate part of society, develop a sense of belonging and realise their full potential. It is therefore necessary to reform the immigration laws in order to break their close association with race. This link has had a profoundly detrimental effect on the development of race policy.

Conclusion

Given the above description, the case is now overwhelmingly strong for a complete reform of immigration law. To date immigration law, its administration and any debate about immigration has been based on racial considerations. Consequently the debate has been emotive and dogmatic. It has blocked any rational discussion of the real issues involved. What is needed is a rational examination of the assumptions and myths which have determined the character of immigration policy. We need to look at immigration and emigration in the context of the population, economic, social, moral, and legal policies. The alternatives for the UK are well argued by Ann Dummett.[7] Suffice it to say here that any considerations about the reform of immigration policy should be guided by the following:

(1) National policy objectives, as well as immigration laws and regulations should be clearly and explicitly stated: immigration policy though often designed to serve specific national interests such as population growth and/or labour force requirements should embrace humanitarian and compassionate concerns, for example greater freedom of movement, uphold the rights of the individual, family reunion, concern for rights of refugees and their resettlement. In other words national policy objectives should be guided by the principles laid down by the international law.

(2) It should be free from all forms of racial and other kinds of discrimination. The system of selection and admission should be fair and consistent.

(3) Control and enforcement of immigration law should also be guided by the national policy and objectives and principles laid down by international law.

(4) Official decisions relating to immigration and naturalisation should be subject to review and appeal.

Notes

1 Ann Dummett, *Citizenship and Nationality* (Runnymede Trust, 1976).
2 'Race and Immigration' (Runnymede Trust No. 154/April 1983).
3 See for example M. Akram *Where Do You Keep Your String Beds?* (Runnymede Trust, 1974); *Firm But Unfair* (Runnymede Trust, 1976); M. Akram and J. Elliot, *Appeal Dismissed* (Runnymede Trust, 1977).
4 P. Gordon, *The Pivot of the System* (Runnymede Trust, 1982).
5 *Health Charges, Race Relations and Immigration Status* (Joint Council for the Welfare of Immigrants, 1981).
6 See Hugo Storey 'United Kingdom Immigration Controls and the Welfare State', pp. 183–195 *post*.
7 Ann Dummett, *A New Immigration Policy* (Runnymede Trust, 1978).

Immigration in Perspective: Population Development in the United Kingdom

HEATHER BOOTH

SSRC Research Unit on Ethnic Relations, University of Aston, Birmingham

Introduction

It is well known that Britain's early history involved her invasion by many different groups of people including the Saxons, Danes, Celts, Romans, Vikings and finally, in 1066, the Normans. The entry of aliens in later times has been more peaceful, but they were not always welcome. Evidence of early black immigration is found in the hostility expressed towards them. As early as 1596, Elizabeth I ordered, albeit unsuccessfully, that all black people in Britain should be sent 'abroad', and five years later issued a proclamation expressing her discontent at the 'great number of Negroes and Blackamoors which, as she is informed, are crept into this realm' and commanding that the 'said kind of people shall be with all speed avoided and discharged out of this her majesty's dominions'.[1] Efforts of this sort to remove black people and to prevent black immigration (except slaves) continued for some time. In contrast, various European traders, craftsmen and refugees entered Britain at this time in much greater numbers but without the kind of hostility experienced by black people.[2]

Today, black immigration to the UK is still, if not more so, a subject of concern, and that concern is still wholly out of keeping with the actual significance of immigration of this kind for the development of the population. Indeed, migration has never been an important factor in the development of the population of the UK.

Population development before 1945

After the Norman Conquest the population of England was about 1.25–1.5 million, rising to 3.5–4 million by the mid-fourteenth century. It was reduced considerably by the Black Death and other plagues, and by the reign of Elizabeth I again stood at about 4 million. By 1700 there were about 6 million people in England, and about 7.5 million in Great Britain by 1760. It was in the second half of the eighteenth century that the population began to grow rapidly. This was entirely due to natural increase, rather than net migration, brought about chiefly by a falling death rate due to medical advances and an improved standard of living, but also by earlier marriage and an increased birth rate.[3] By 1820, the population of Great Britain stood at about 14.5 million, with similar increases in Ireland. It was during this period of rapid expansion that emigration to the New World began.[4]

Census taking in Britain began in 1801. In that year there were 8.9 million people living in England and Wales, with a further 1.6 million in Scotland. The population grew at a slightly higher rate in England and Wales than in Scotland, to reach 15.9 million and 2.6 million respectively in 1841. With the introduction of birth and death registration in 1837, it was possible to determine the extent to which natural increase contributed to population growth: it follows that it was also possible to gain some idea of the magnitude of net migration. Table 1 shows these calculations for England and Wales. Though the levels of net migration do not correspond directly with other estimates,[5] they do provide a consistent series of data for over 100 years and roughly indicate the relative and negative contribution of migration to population growth over time. It is clear from Figure 1 that until very recently natural increase, and not migration, has been by far the more important factor in the development of the population. Indeed, the role of net migration during this period has been merely to cushion Britain slightly from the full effects of natural increase. In this there are direct and indirect effects: not only do the migrants leave themselves, but as young adults they take with them future births.

If natural increase was the major influence on population growth, it was births rather than deaths that determined changes in the size of that increase. The number of deaths occurring in England and Wales since 1841 has not changed appreciably, especially over the 100 years from 1861 to 1960, as Figure 1 shows. In contrast, the number of births has fluctuated considerably, rising from 5.5 million in 1841–50[6] to more than 9 million in each of the two 10 year periods from 1891 to 1910, and then falling to only 6 million during the 1930s.

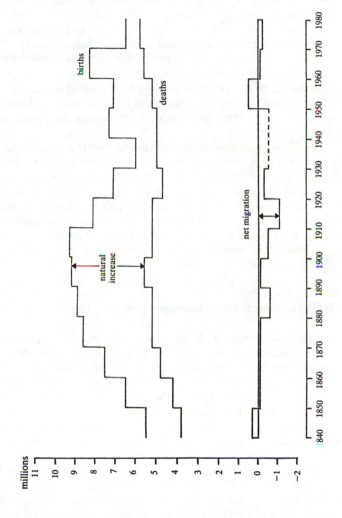

FIGURE 1
Components of population change, England and Wales, 1840–1980

These numbers of births and deaths provide us with the absolute sizes of natural increase, but they conceal the real trends that were taking place. The population to which they relate grew from 16 million in 1841 to 40 million in 1931; 5.5 million births in 1841 to 1850 was thus a very different proposition to 6 million in 1931 to 1940. The same is true of deaths. Falling mortality increased the expectation of life at birth from 42 years in 1851, to 49 in 1901, to 62 in 1931 for females, and from 40 to 46 to 58 respectively for males. Figure 2 shows the crude birth and death rates for England and Wales since 1841–50. Again, the birth rate has been more erratic than the death rate, but an overall downward trend has occurred for both. The fact that the birth rate has decreased faster than the death rate has meant that natural increase has declined over time. This in turn has contributed to the falling growth rate of the population.

The Second World War brought a change in these developments. Not only did it contribute to an increase in births by pulling Britain out of the depression, it also provided a harsh reminder of the need to maintain an adequate population for defence. Government propaganda linked this with the 'need' for women to return to their traditional role as wives and mothers, thereby giving up their jobs to their menfolk returning from war. During the 1940s, the number of births increased by 1.2 million, and natural increase rose similarly.

Overseas Population Movements before 1945

Insignificant though net migration has been in comparison to natural increase in determining population growth, the components of net migration merit attention. Net flows, as indicated in Figure 1, give no indication of the size of flows into and out of the country; they merely reflect the difference between these flows. The few data that permit estimates of migration flows are unreliable, but various estimates have nevertheless been made giving some guide not only to the size of flows but also to the origins and destinations of migrants.[7]

During the eighteenth century, about 1.5 million people left the British Isles for the New World. About a third of these were Ulster Presbyterians, and a further 50,000 were convicts. In the nineteenth and first third of the twentieth centuries, more than 20 million people left Britain for the New World. Many of these were victims of industrialisation, such as farm labourers and domestic staff. To encourage emigration at this time a special system of state aid was introduced, but economic crisis and the gold rush of the

FIGURE 2
Crude birth and death rates and rate of growth, England and Wales, 1840–1980

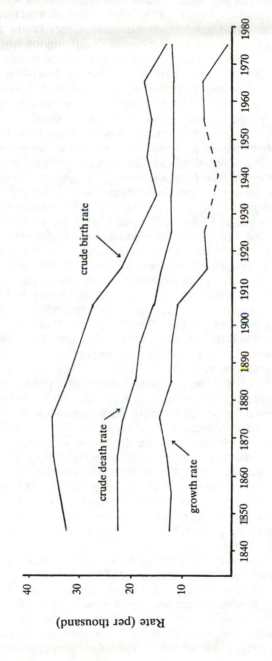

Source: Office of Population Censuses and Survey, *Birth* Statistics Series FM1; growth rate from data in Table 1.

113

mid-nineteenth century increased emigration regardless of financial incentives. From 1841 to 1845 a total of 400,000 people left the UK, rising to more than 1 million from 1846 to 1850. Assisted passages, paid out of colonial funds, to Australia and New Zealand alone were granted to 340,000 emigrants between 1847 and 1869. Indeed, Britons accounted for 80 per cent of all Europeans emigrating from the Old World in 1845 to 1850, and 50 per cent in 1850 to 1875. Emigration was seen as a means both of relieving population pressure at home, Britain being regarded as overpopulated at that time, and of populating the Commonwealth with British people. From 1857, industrial boom at home and the American Civil War reduced emigration but never to less than 600,000 for any five-year period. After 1875, emigration recovered, soon reaching even greater levels: 1.2 million people left Britain in each of the three five-year periods from 1881 to 1905, 1.7 million left in 1906 to 1910 and 1.8 million in 1911 to 1915. Most were destined for the US, but later emigrants were more likely to head for the Colonies. In fact, a great many of the emigrants from the UK were Irish. Between 1815 and 1850 almost 80 per cent of the 2.4 million emigrants were Irish. Slightly more than half of these left in 1845–50 with almost as many again leaving in 1851 to 1855.

Of course, the Irish also constituted the major part of immigration to the UK. Arrivals began in the eighteenth century and reached their height in the 1840s and 1850s after the famines of 1846 to 1850. By 1871, 2.5 per cent of the population of England and Wales were born in Ireland, as were 6.2 per cent of the population of Scotland. A further 101,000 people, or less than 0.5 per cent of the population of England and Wales, were alien, and of these a third were German. In Scotland less than 0.2 per cent or 4,700 were alien, again a third of them German.[8] The late nineteenth century saw the decline of Irish migration to Britain and the rise of a new migratory flow, that of the Russian Jews. By 1901, Russians and Poles (from Russian-Poland) had displaced Germans as the largest alien group, with 83,000 in England and Wales compared to 49,000 Germans. Even so, the Irish-born population continued to dominate with 427,000 in England and Wales comprising 1.3 per cent of the population, and 205,000 in Scotland or 4.6 per cent.

Despite these immigrant flows, the balance of migration was generally negative. Between 1871 and 1931 net migration from England and Wales was over 2 million,[9] and for the UK, as presently constituted, the equivalent figure was about 4 million, due to the continued net outflow from Scotland and Northern Ireland to overseas countries as well as to England and Wales. During the 1930s, however, the balance was positive due both to a reduction in emigration and an increase in immigration. The world economic crisis reduced the demand for emigrants to the colonies, whilst many earlier emigrants returned. At the same time, immigration from Eire continued and the UK also accepted thousands of refugees from Europe, including 50,000 Jews between 1933 and 1939. During the Second World War, as in the first, emigration was reduced to a trickle, but both wars resulted in the settlement of thousands of refugees and small numbers of black people who had fought for the mother country.

Population Policy Immediately after the Second World War: Fear of Decline

After the Second World War, the size and quality of the population were issues of concern. Thirty years previously it had been fashionable to believe that overpopulation was a contributory cause of the First World War, and it was also blamed for the mass unemployment that followed. During the 1930s, however, the unprecedented low levels of fertility began to alarm public opinion and depopulation was seen as a serious threat despite net immigration at this time. The increased birth rate during and after the Second World War partially allayed these fears, but closer examination revealed this to be more the result of earlier marriage and the special circumstances of war than of increased family size. Though signs of a turn away from the very small family could be discerned, a future decline of Britain's population was by no means averted.

It was as early as 1944 that a Royal Commission was set up to 'consider what measures, if any, should be taken in the national interest to influence the future trend of population and to make recommendations'.[10] The Commission reported in 1949, preceded a year earlier by an independent report into population policy by Political and Economic Planning.[11] These reports reveal the then current attitudes and concerns regarding the various aspects of population: its size and composition, emigration and immigration. Their policy recommendations lay the foundations and context for immigration in the early post-war period.

Though a smaller population in the UK was not necessarily regarded as undesirable *per se*, the further ageing of the population that would occur with declining numbers was to be avoided. The mortality decline of the last 100 years had contributed to the greater numbers of people at older ages, but the fertility decline of the last 60 years had had by far the greater effect in drastically reducing the numbers in the younger age groups. The continuation of this process was undesirable because of the inevitably increasing dependency ratio as larger numbers of the elderly became a greater burden on the reduced labour force.[12] What was more, the process of ageing was taking place within the labour force, resulting in less mobile labour. This and the rather constant home market due to slower population growth rendered the economy less flexible.

Other factors also pointed to the need to maintain a supply of younger people through adequate levels of fertility. The UK's 'power, security and influence' were at stake.[13] These depended on the young male population of military age, and though the 'importance of mere numbers . . . has probably been declining . . . and . . . may prove to have been radically diminished by the discovery of the atomic bomb . . . numbers must be regarded as an important military factor'.[14] The reduced growth rate in the UK and other countries of western civilisation was seen as a potential danger in the face of the accelerated growth of many oriental populations.

The United Kingdom looked to her Commonwealth both economically and as a means of maintaining her power and influence. This posed a genuine dilemma. If Britain were to maintain her influence in the Commonwealth, a substantial and continuing flow of British emigrants was required. Indeed, Australia and New Zealand in particular had been alerted by the war to the need to populate and were keen to attract even greater numbers of immigrants, especially Britons, than before. Australia planned to absorb at least 70,000 immigrants per year, whilst the Canadian Government wanted more than 100,000. South Africa and Southern Rhodesia had similar policies, whilst the US, Argentina and Brazil also attracted many British emigrants. The dilemma was in the supply of these emigrants. Whilst emigration to the Commonwealth was good for empire and as such was recommended by the Royal Commission,[15] it was not so good for Britain. The departure of young adults from the UK would only add to the process of ageing that was already well advanced. What was more, emigrants tended to be 'men rather than women, . . ., the bright and ambitious rather than the dull and lethargic'.[16]

The possibility of augmenting the population by continuous large scale immigration was not regarded as a desirable solution to this problem. Nevertheless, the case for limited immigration was clear. Economically, some immigration was desirable to relieve the shortage of labour, and in fact the government decided in 1946 to attract at least 100,000 immigrant workers, believing the shortage to be permanent. It soon became evident, however, that temporary labour immigration would be preferable because of expected economic changes. In recognition of the difficulties in enforcing this temporariness, immigrants were to be carefully selected and encouraged to assimilate. In addition to increasing the labour force and improving its mobility and flexibility, immigration could also be used to help redress the demographic deficiencies of the population. The immigration of selected young adults would help to offset such losses due to emigration and would avoid the time lag involved in relying on higher fertility to augment the adult population. Moreover, young adult immigrants could be attracted in sufficient numbers to make up for the shortfall in the population born in the 1920s and 1930s.

Counterbalancing the proposition of immigration were the costs and difficulties that would undoubtedly arise. Immigrants would be costly in capital expenditure on housing, training and other services, and problems of adjustment and assimilation were to be expected. Even if the UK were prepared to meet these difficulties, there would still be the problem of actually securing large numbers of immigrants. In this, the UK looked to Europe, her traditional source of immigration, but since most countries in Western Europe had undergone a similar population transition to the UK and since Eastern Europe was closed as a source of immigrants by national policies, it was unlikely that sufficient numbers could be found. It was true that the UK employed the labour of the European Voluntary Workers, but these were a temporary source and only Holland with her high birth rate, Greece, Italy and Eire were regarded as likely to be significant suppliers of immigrants. The possibility of seeking immigrants from further afield was quickly dismissed, though highly skilled labour was always welcome: white emigration from the Commonwealth was most unlikely at this time and black immigration to the UK would be extremely difficult in terms of their assimilation. It was important that immigrants should be 'of good human stock and were not prevented by their religion or race from intermarrying with the host population and becoming merged in it'.[17] If immigration were on a large scale, these standards would suffer.

Large scale immigration, therefore, was neither a desirable nor a feasible solution to the UK's population problems. Hence, efforts were to be concentrated in encouraging higher fertility to maintain at least a replacement family size. To this end, the Royal Commission on Population recommended that family size should be taken into account in all relevant branches of policy and administration. Natural increase was to continue to be the dominant influence in population growth.

Natural Increase after 1945

The increase in births during and immediately after the Second World War proved to be as short-lived as the Royal Commission had feared, and numbers fell again in the early 1950s, though not so much as to endanger the survival of the population. In 1956, however, births began to increase again and continued to do so until 1964. The reasons for this were complex and included increased numbers of young adults and the greater popularity of marriage, especially at younger ages, as well as a general increase in fertility. In fact, immigration during this period contributed to this upswing in births, not only because it added to the number of young adults but also because of their higher fertility.[18] In 1965, the trend was again reversed and a steady decline in the annual number of births prevailed until 1977. For the three years from 1978 to 1980 a slight upturn occurred but the decline returned in 1981. Figure 1 obscures these fine fluctuations but it does show that births continued after the Second World War to dominate the level of natural increase and population growth. The number of deaths increased slowly after the war as a result of the rise in the number of people in the older age groups, and this effect has been sufficiently great to halt the decline in the death rate. Though natural increase continues to be positive, in 1971–80 it reached its lowest level since records began. The rate of natural increase during this period was only 1.3 per thousand, and fell to about 0.4 during the latter half of the period. The decline of the population may just be beginning.

Fear of overpopulation

Despite the downward trend in births in the late 1960s, pressure groups began to warn of the dangers of continued population growth and of overpopulation.[19] This prompted the Select Committee on Science and Technology to produce a report on the population of the UK concluding that 'the Government must act to prevent the consequences of population growth becoming intolerable for the every day conditions of life'[20] and recommending that a Population Panel be appointed to assess Britain's population growth and its consequences. The panel concluded in 1973 that the 'population will almost certainly go on rising at least until the end of the century'.[21] This increase was not seen as sufficient to 'require immediate policy initiatives designed to reduce dramatically the rate of increase' since the 'not too unstable world situation' meant that 'Britain should be able to find means of accommodating any likely increase in population over the next 40 years'.[22] Nevertheless, emigration on a large scale would involve a substantial loss in terms of the education and productivity of young migrants and would distort the structure of the population and was therefore not to be recommended. Instead, the panel concluded that 'Britain would do better in future with a stationary rather than an increasing population'[23] and efforts to encourage a replacement family size were to be made. Immigration policy, it was noted, had little to do with population size and net migration had every little effect.

International Migration after 1945

Immediately after the Second World War, net migration was negative as the UK resumed her supply of emigrants to the Commonwealth but hesitated to accept such large scale immigration. This dominant trend in British migration was briefly revised from 1958 to 1963 when relatively substantial positive balances occurred. By 1964, however, the balance was again negative and has remained so, with the single exception of 1978–79, until the present.

Prior to 1964 the data collected on international migration flows were deficient, most notably because they did not recognise the invention of the aeroplane and covered only sea ports. There is thus very little useful information on migration for this period, especially on emigration. Some idea of the size of outward flows can be gained from administrative material. In 1947 it was suggested that more than 600,000 people had made definite plans to leave the UK and that the total number who wished to emigrate might have been as high as a million. Certainly, 400,000 people were on the books of the Australian Government in October 1947, and shipping companies had outstanding applications in November 1947 amounting to 95,000 for South Africa, 20,000 for New Zealand and 50,000 for Canada.[24] The peak years of emigration from the UK at this time were 1952 and 1957 when more than 200,000 people a year departed for the Commonwealth. High levels of emigration were maintained throughout the 1960s and 1970s. The number of emigrants rose to 326,000 in 1966–7, but then declined to 187,000 in 1978–9. More recently, emigration has increased again to 234,000 in 1980–1, two thirds of whom were UK citzens.

The Second World War created various sources of immigration to the UK, though they were short-lived and the immigrants themselves often temporary. The Polish Resettlement Corps enrolled thousands of men who had served during the war, the majority under British command. These were either settled in Great Britain with employment or helped to emigrate, either to Poland or elsewhere. About 70,000 had been settled by early 1948 and a further 15,000 had left the country.[25] The European Volunteer Workers provided a second major source of labour. These were recruited from the displaced persons in refugee camps on the continent under the 'Westward Ho' scheme. Only single people were eligible, and they were employed in specific jobs to which they were tied for three years and accommodated in hostels. As cheap labour with severely restricted rights these people were exploited, and many remigrated to the US or Canada. For those that remained, life in the UK improved in the 1950s.

Irish migration to Britain continued after the war, as it had for more than a century, though at the time the Irish Government discouraged the emigration of male workers. The 1950s, however, saw immigration from Ireland in proportions not seen since the last century. From 1951 to 1960 net migration by sea to Britain from Ireland was 30,000 to 46,000 per annum, with annual immigration flows of around 730,000.[26] The 1951 census recorded a total of 538,000 people born in Eire[27] living in Great Britain, and though the Irish population in Scotland was decreasing, this represented a large overall increase since 1931. In contrast to migration norms, females outnumbered males in England, though not in Wales and Scotland. Female migrants were also younger than male migrants and obtained employment in domestic service, catering and nursing. In 1951, 39 per cent of the employed Irish-born[28] females in England and Wales were employed in the personal service sector with a further 22 per cent in the professional sector. In contrast, 18 per cent of employed Irish-born males were in building, 14 per cent were unskilled and 13 per cent in metal manufacture. By 1971, the population born in Eire[29] had grown to 710,000 or 1.3 per cent of the total population of Great Britain, but had decreased by 1981 to 610,000 or 1.1 per cent. In addition, there were 250,000 people in Great Britain in 1971 who were born in Northern Ireland, and 275,000 in 1981. Those born in Northern Ireland, are more likely to live in Scotland than those born in Eire.

Despite the reservations of the Royal Commission on Population and of politicians,[30] black immigration from the Commonwealth began as early as the late 1940s. In 1948 the *Empire Windrush* brought 492 Jamaicans and others soon followed albeit on a small scale. In 1951, of the 1.6 million foreign born residents in Great Britain, 256,000 were from the New Commonwealth[31] including about 8,000 Indians most of whom were students, seamen and professionals. Immigration from the West Indies and later from the Indian sub-continent gathered strength during the 1950s and 1960s. This was in response to various factors including demographic and economic conditions in these newly independent countries (push factors) and economic factors in Great Britain (pull factors). Though there was political pressure on Britain to accept black immigrants in order to relieve political unrest in the New Commonwealth, this was unsuccessful and black immigration was not encouraged at a government level.[32] London Transport and the British Hotels and Restaurants Association directly recruited labour from the New Commonwealth, but the majority came in response to the general demand for labour. By 1955 and 1956, about 30,000 West Indians a year entered Great Britain, falling briefly to 20,000 in 1958 due to recession, but rising again to 75,000 in 1961. The Commonwealth Immigrants Act 1962 was largely responsible for the high level of immigration in 1961, both from the West Indies and from India and Pakistan, as migrants hurried to enter before the introduction of controls. Thereafter, labour immigration from the New Commonwealth declined due as much to economic factors as to legislation.[33] By 1961, there were about 0.5 million New Commonwealth born people living in Great Britain, plus about 100,000 of New Commonwealth origin born in Great Britain.[34] The men were employed in transport, engineering and service industries, whilst the women found jobs in nursing, clothing and footwear and services.

Though black labour migration was restricted by the introduction of a voucher system in 1962, dependants were still free to enter. The nature of immigration from the New Commonwealth thus changed from being mainly young men, though many young single women came from the West Indies, to mainly wives and children. The black population thus continued to grow, both by net migration and natural increase, to reach 0.9 million by 1966 and 1.4 million by 1971. Increasingly restrictive legislation in the form of the Commonwealth Immigrants Act 1968 and the Immigration Act 1971 and subsequent changes in the Immigration Rules, have reduced immigration from the New Commonwealth and Pakistan[35] to a trickle: in 1982, only 30,000 people were accepted for settlement, the lowest annual total since 1962. In 1981, the black population in Great Britain was estimated at 2.1 million, or 3.9 per cent of the total population.

In addition to these major migratory flows to Great Britain, other immigrants have arrived in the post-war years. Many came as refugees including almost 20,000 Hungarians in 1956, Kenyan and Ugandan Asians in the late 1960s and early 1970s, Chileans after the fall of the Allende Government in 1973, Iranians both before and after the revolution of 1978–79, and more than 10,000 boat people from Vietnam. Others came for work, at first from Italy, Greece, Spain and Portugal, and later from the Philippines. Since 1973 many EEC nationals have exercised their right to live in the UK, with 7–8,000 per annum obtaining residence permits, half of them workers.[36] Finally, there has been a large flow of people from the Old Commonwealth, as well as returning British emigrants.

Characteristics of Recent Migrants

In 1964, the collection of data on international migration was improved with the introduction of the International Passenger Survey. Though there are problems concerning the accuracy of the estimates obtained from this survey, it is the only source of data on emigration (as well as immigration) and of the characteristics of migrants.[37]

FIGURE 3
Emigration from the UK by citizenship, 1964/5 to 1981/2

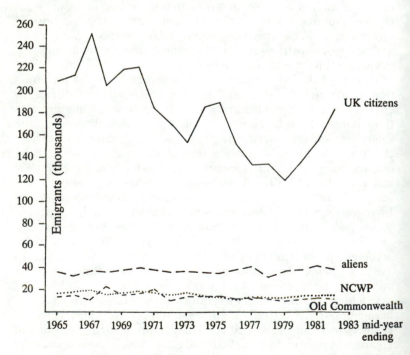

Source: Office of Population Censuses and Surveys, *International Migration*, Series MN.

FIGURE 4
Immigration to the UK by citizenship, 1964/5 to 1981/2

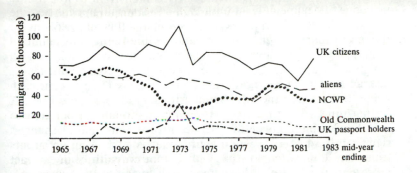

Source: as Figure 3.

FIGURE 5
Net migration with the UK by citizenship, 1964/5 to 1981/2

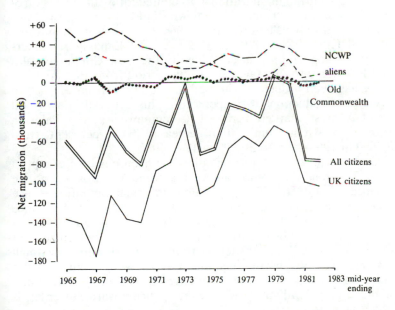

Source: Office of Population Censuses and Surveys, *International Migration*, Series MN.

Figures 3, 4 and 5 show the trend in emigration, immigration and net migration respectively by citizenship. The vast majority of emigrants are UK citizens, though the trend in their numbers has been one of decline at least until 1978–79. It would appear that the British leave Britain in times of recession, and this may account for the recent sharp increase in emigration. Other emigrants maintain remarkably stable levels of migration. Just over half of all emigrants from the UK in 1981 went to foreign countries as distinct from the Commonwealth, with roughly ten per cent each going to the EEC, the US, South Africa and the Middle East. A further third went to the Old Commonwealth and 12 per cent to the New Commonwealth. These proportions have changed significantly since 1974 when approximately half of all emigrants from the UK went to the Old Commonwealth, but in fact represent an increase in this latter proportion since 1978 when only a quarter went to the Old Commonwealth.[38]

Immigration to the UK is on a smaller scale than emigration with less difference between the levels of UK citizens, again the largest group, and other citizenships. Most of the variation in the level of UK citizen immigration is accounted for by the inclusion of the Kenyan and Ugandan Asians who hold UK passports (also shown separately in Figure 4 from 1966–67), most of whom came to the UK in 1968 and 1973. These Asian UK passport holders might be more appropriately added to the New Commonwealth and Pakistan citizens. Over the whole period from 1965 to 1982, there has been a decrease in total immigration, from 223,000 to 177,000, a reduction of 21 per cent. This generally downward trend is most marked for New Commonwealth and Pakistan citizens for whom immigration decreased by 51 per cent, from 73,000 in 1964–1965 to 36,000 in 1981–1982.

On balance, overall net migration has been negative except in 1978–79 when the combination of a trend towards a positive balance and a fluctuating level resulted in a small net inflow. Since then, however, net migration has fallen to its lowest level since 1969–1970, probably due to the recession. Almost all of the net outflow from the UK is attributable to UK citizens, with citizens of Old Commonwealth countries occasionally contributing very small amounts. The positive net migration flows of New Commonwealth and Pakistan citizens and of aliens have both decreased over time, so that until recently there was a convergence towards lower levels of net migration.

In 1981, 46 per cent of all immigrants to the UK were female, while 43 per cent of emigrants were female. On balance, therefore, migration increases the proportion of females in the UK, though the size of the population is reduced. The over-

FIGURE 6
Age and sex structure of migrants, UK, 1981

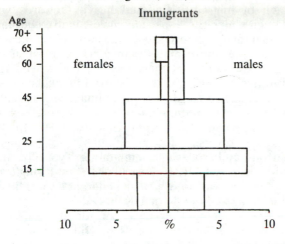

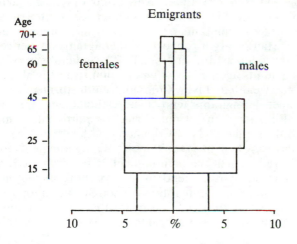

Source: Office of Population Censuses and Surveys, *International Migration 1981*, Series MN, no 8.

representation of males among migrants has persisted since the early 1970s, though females predominated in the late 1960s.[39] The age distribution of migrants is biased heavily towards young adulthood, though emigrants, especially males, tend to be slightly older than immigrants. Figure 6 illustrates these differences. On balance, the UK loses more males than females, most of them aged 25–44. Losses occur at all ages, except females aged 15–24 for whom a positive balance of 2,500 occurred in 1981.

Perhaps surprisingly, given the popular image of migrants as single, married people outnumbered single people in both emigrant and immigrant flows from 1967 to 1980. In 1981, however, this was reversed for immigrants, though married emigrants still outnumbered single emigrants. Typically, therefore, an immigrant to the UK is most likely to be a single male aged 15 to 24 of UK citzenship, whilst an emigrant is most likely to be a married male aged 25 to 44 of UK citizenship.

Of course, these 'averages' conceal considerable differences between citizenships. About two thirds of Old Commonwealth immigrants and emigrants are female, while only about 40 per cent of UK migrants are female. Among New Commonwealth (excluding Pakistan) migrants, 52 per cent of immigrants are female but only 38 per cent of emigrants are female, whilst among aliens (including Pakistan) a larger proportion of emigrants (62 per cent) than immigrants (49 per cent) are female. The general preponderance of young adults aged 15 to 24 among immigrants is also true of Old Commonwealth and New Commonwealth citizens, but UK citizen and alien immigrants tend to be rather older. UK, Old Commonwealth and alien citizens bring proportionately more children with them than do New Commonwealth citizens. Among emigrants, only New Commonwealth citizens are more likely to be aged 15 to 24, rather than the predominant 25 to 44, and UK and Old Commonwealth citizens tend to take proportionately more children with them on emigration. Though migration after retirement does not often occur, it is by far the more common for female Old Commonwealth immigrants and for female UK citizen emigrants.

Within these citizenship categories, further differences occur. In 1981, the small negative balance of migration of Old Commonwealth citizens was due to the net outflow of people to the US, New Zealand and non-EEC Europe, counterbalanced only partially by a net outflow from Canada. Most of the positive net balance of New Commonwealth citizens come from the Indian sub-continent, with most of the small net outflow going to Canada and the US. The balance of New Commonwealth migration with the West Indies was positive but small in 1981, though small negative balances occurred during 1970–74.[40] The net inflow of aliens was about half made up of a net inflow from Pakistan, with others coming from the Middle East and the US. The balance of migration of aliens with the EEC was negative, as was the balance of UK citizens with the EEC. Of the large net outflow of UK citizens, more than half went to the Commonwealth and most of these to the Old Commonwealth. Of the remaining half, most went to South Africa, followed by the Middle East and the US.

Figure 7 shows the occupational distribution of migrants in 1981 Almost a third were professional and managerial, though the volume of manual and clerical emigrants was also high in comparison to immigrants. There has been a marked change in the occupational distribution of migrants since the period 1964 to 1975. At that time, the largest category was manual and clerical occupations, but even so such occupations were under-represented amongst migrants in comparison to the working population of the UK, whilst the second largest category, professional and managerial, was over-represented in comparison to the working population.[41] The fact that professional and managerial occupations have now become the more prevalent among migrants only increases their over-representation, while clerical and manual occupations are correspondingly under-represented to a greater extent. In fact, professional and managerial immigrants outnumbered manual and clerical immigrants for the first time in 1974, while the decrease in manual and clerical emigrants stems from late 1974 when more selective immigration policies were introduced by the main countries which receive emigrants from the UK.[42] Examination of the 1981 data by citizenship reveals that Old Commonwealth immigrants are over-represented both in the professional and managerial occupations, at the expense of New Commonwealth immigrants, and in the manual and clerical occupations, at the expense of New Commonwealth and alien immigrants. In compensation, there are very few Old Commonwealth student immigrants. Emigrants' occupations are more evenly distributed by citizenship, except that manual and clerical emigrants are under-represented among New Commonwealth citizens and aliens, both of which have relatively large proportions of student emigrants.

In 1964 to 1975 approximately 30,000 students per annum entered the UK, whilst less than half that many left. By 1981, roughly equal numbers of students left as entered, though their numbers were reduced to about 20,000. Student immigrants are more likely to be New Commonwealth citizens or aliens, but this is even more true of student emigrants. It appears that student immigration from the New Commonwealth, in particular, and

FIGURE 7
Occupational distribution of migrants, UK, 1981

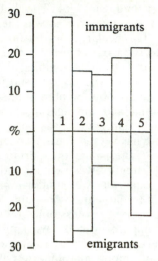

1. professional & managerial
2. manual & clerical
3. students
4. housewives & others
5. children

Note: These are percentages of immigrants and percentages of emigrants, and do not compare absolute numbers of emigrants and immigrants.

Source: Office of Population Censuses and Surveys, *International Migration 1981*, Series MN, no 8.

from other countries has declined substantially in recent years, most probably the result of increased student fees. The emigration of students with New Commonwealth citizenships accounts for almost half of the total New Commonwealth outflow. On balance, almost half of the net loss of people from the UK in 1981 were manual and clerical workers but large losses also occurred in the professional and managerial occupations. Students were the only group to gain by migration, mostly due to the net inflow of UK citizens.

Indirect Effects of Migration

Even if net migration were nil, the differing demographic characteristics of emigrants and immigrants would have an effect on the structure and characteristics, and hence the growth, of the population of the UK. It has been seen above that migration tends to increase the proportion of females in the population, to increase the proportion of people aged 15 to 24 and to increase the proportion of single people. To these can be added differential nuptiality, fertility and mortality. All of these factors change the dynamics of population growth, albeit by small amounts dependent on the magnitude of both the migrant flows and the demographic differences between immigrants and emigrants. These effects are additional to the direct effect of migration on population size and structure through net flows.

The estimation of these indirect effects is not easy, not least because information on emigrants is lacking. Nor are these effects straightforward. Age, for example, leads to somewhat paradoxical conclusions: though the effect of migration in any one year is to increase the proportion in the age group 15 to 24, thereby reducing the average age of the total population, its cumulative effect has been to *increase* the average age of the population. Since immigration was higher in the past than at present, most immigrants to the UK are now considerably older than 15 to 24, and continue to age with time. By 1971 the median age of immigrants living in England and Wales was over 36 years, with further increases occurring in the past 12 years such that the average age of immigrants is now much older than the average age of the total population. Thus, one effect of immigration has been to increase the average age of the total population. However, this will have been offset by emigration which will have had the opposite effect, despite the slightly older age of emigrants, of decreasing the average age of the population.[43]

These effects take no account of children born to migrant parents gained by immigration and lost by emigration. To measure these full effects in combination with the effects on the population of other characteristics such as marital status, fertility and mortality, it is necessary to make population projections.[44] Using this technique, it has been estimated that the indirect effect of migration over the period 1951 to 1976 was to augment natural increase in the population by some 330,000. In other words, the natural increase of the immigrant population was 330,000 greater than the lost natural increase of the emigrant population. Since net migration over this period was an estimated 280,000, the indirect effect of migration was greater than the direct effect.[45] Even so, this was small in comparison to the total natural increase for the period of more than 4.7 million.

The attention paid to one particular section of immigrants to the UK, namely those from the New Commonwealth and Pakistan, allows comparison of the development of this population with that of the total population. The demography of the population of New Commonwealth and Pakistani ethnic origin has been well documented[46] and the progress of its growth since 1966 is shown in Table 2. It is seen that net migration has constituted a higher

TABLE 1
The components of population growth, England and Wales, 1801–1981

Period	Population at beginning of period	Change over period	Births during period	Deaths during period	Natural increase	Net Migration
	(1)	(2)	(3)	(4)	(5)=(3)−(4)	(6)=(2)−(5)
1801–1810	8,892,536	1,271,720				
1811–1820	10,164,256	1,835,980				
1821–1830	12,000,236	1,896,561				
1831–1840	13,896,797	2,017,351				
1841–1850	15,914,148	2,013,461	5,488,735	3,769,396	1,719,339	+ 294,122
1851–1860	17,927,609	2,138,615	6,471,650	4,210,715	2,260,935	− 122,320
1861–1870	20,066,224	2,646,042	7,500,095	4,794,498	2,705,597	− 59,555
1871–1880	22,712,266	3,262,173	8,588,780	5,178,311	3,410,469	− 148,296
1881–1890	25,974,439	3,028,086	8,890,240	5,244,770	3,645,470	− 617,384
1891–1900	29,002,525	3,525,318	9,155,150	5,575,375	3,579,775	− 54,457
1901–1910	32,527,843	3,542,649	9,298,210	5,248,774	4,049,436	− 506,787
1911–1920	36,070,492	1,816,207	8,096,220	5,188,052	2,908,168	−1,091,961
1921–1930	37,886,699	2,065,678	7,129,070	4,722,991	2,406,079	− 340,401
1931–1940	39,952,377	2,297,888	6,064,515	4,992,208	1,072,307	−1,027,776
1941–1950	—		7,251,010	4,997,653	2,253,357	
1951–1960	43,757,888	2,346,660	7,075,035	5,188,116	1,886,919	+ 459,741
1961–1970	46,104,548	2,645,027	8,326,055	5,603,838	2,722,217	− 77,190
1971–1980	48,749,575	405,112	6,472,080	5,849,489	622,591	− 217,479
1981	49,154,687					

Note: These are de facto population counts. Until 1911 the census did not distinguish between residents and visitors.

Source: 1801–1961: R. K. Kelsall, *Population* (Longmans, 1967); 1971 and 1981 censuses.

proportion of growth in the past than at present, though fluctuations in migration still have a marked effect. This is, of course, expected, not only because immigration has been drastically reduced but also because of the more recent arrival of women. Very recently natural increase has accounted for as much as two thirds of growth, and increases in this proportion are expected to continue.

In comparison with the total population of the UK, the population of New Commonwealth and Pakistani origin is growing rapidly though at a much slower rate than previously. This is seen in the increasing proportion of the population comprised of people of New Commonwealth and Pakistani origin. Part of this increase is due to the differential impact of migration on the two populations: the black population gains by migration, by 1.3 per cent in 1980, whilst the total population loses. In addition, the black population is growing by natural increase at a greater rate than the total population, due to the differential demographic characteristics of

TABLE 2

Estimated size and growth of population of New Commonwealth and Pakistani ethnic origin, Great Britain

Mid-year to mid-year	Population at beginning of year (thousands)	Growth over year (thousands)	% due to natural increase	% due to net migration	Growth per thousand	% of total GB population at beginning of year
1966–67	886	+87	–	–	98	1.7
1967–68	973	+114	–	–	111	1.8
1968–69	1087	+103	–	–	95	2.0
1969–70	1190	+91	–	–	76	2.2
1970–71	1281	+90	–	–	70	2.4
1971–72	1371	+82	55	45	60	2.5
1972–73	1453	+94	45	55	65	2.7
1973–74	1547	+68	57	43	44	2.8
1974–75	1615	+76	51	49	47	3.0
1975–76	1691	+80	50	50	47	3.1
1976–77	1771	+75	56	44	42	3.3
1977–78	1846	+74	59	41	40	3.4
1978–79	1920	+93	54	46	48	3.5
1979–80	2013	+91	59	41	45	3.7
1980–81	2104	+80	67	33	38	3.9

Source: Office of Population Censuses and Surveys Immigrant Statistics Unit (1966–1971 figures); OPCS Monitor PP1 81/6, mid-1980 estimates of the population of New Commonwealth and Pakistani ethnic origin; Office of Population Censuses and Surveys Monitor PP1 83/2, mid-1981 estimates of the population of New Commonwealth and Pakistani ethnic origin.

the two populations. Not only is fertility higher in the black population,[47] but the relatively young age structure of the population means that a larger proportion are in the reproductive age groups. Indeed, this latter factor can be sufficient to outweigh the effects of falling fertility. Other factors such as lower death rates also contribute to the greater rate of increase of the black population. As these demographic differences diminish, the two populations will become similar in structure and growth.[48]

Conclusions and Expectations

Historically, it is emigration rather than immigration that has contributed to the development of the population. With only brief exception, the UK has been a net exporter of people, with very moderately sized net flows. Net migration has, in fact, been an insignificant factor in the development of the UK's population compared to the much greater contribution of natural increase. Similarly, the components of migration have been much less significant than the components of natural increase: emigration and immigration pale into insignificance alongside the volume of births and deaths. In fact, it is births rather than deaths that have dominated the level and trend of natural increase. Births have been the major factor in the development of the population. This is borne out in the reports of the two inquiries into population, the Royal Commission on Population in 1949 and the Population Panel in 1973, both of which dealt in the main with questions of fertility.

Today, immigration is lower than it has been for more than 25 years, and there are signs of a trend towards lower levels of net migration. At the same time, trends in the numbers of births and deaths have reduced natural increase to very low levels indeed. Population growth in the UK was only one per 1000 in 1980–81, and was negative during the 1970s, due mainly to negative net migration but also in the late 1970s to the excess of deaths over births. Current projections for England and Wales suggest that the population will in fact continue to grow at a very slow rate for the next few decades, stabilising towards the middle of the next century.[49]

It would seem, then, that the UK is well on the way to achieving the Population Panel's recommendation of zero growth. Such an equilibrium can only be maintained by very low levels of migration, a condition which is not hard to meet or justify. Certainly, there is no need for large scale labour immigration at a time of high unemployment and technological change: the possibility of a labour shortage now seems unthinkable. By the same token, emigration is not expected to be high because most countries now operate strict immigration controls even on the highly trained.

With different economic conditions, such as those which we are currently told to expect, the idea of labour immigration might seem an attractive proposition from a demographic standpoint because it would help to alleviate the problems of ageing and increasing dependency ratios. The proportion of the elderly in the population is now higher than ever before and continues to increase, while projections show that the proportion of working age is expected to decrease, especially in the younger age groups. This situation is much the same as that faced by the Royal Commission on Population after the Second World War and some of their concerns remain relevant today. However, the UK no longer relies on the emigration of her citizens to maintain her influence in the world, so that emigration could now freely be discouraged because of its detrimental effect on the age structure of the population. In this context, immigration could only be allowed at the expense of an increase in the size of the population, a cost which would probably be unacceptable for what would amount to a temporary decrease in the dependency ratio.

Hence, from a purely demographic point of view, large-scale immigration would by no means be advantageous to the development of the population. But as has been shown, demographic considerations have had very little bearing on past migration. Instead, political and economic criteria have dominated as, for example, in emigration to the Colonies or in immigration after the Second World War. Though in demographic terms, a low level of migration would be necessary to maintain zero or very low growth, there is little reason to suppose that demographic criteria will assume any greater importance in the future than they have in the past.

Notes

1 N. File and C. Power, *Black Settlers in Britain 1555–1958*, (Heinemann Educational Books, 1981), p. 6.
2 W. Cunningham, *Alien Immigrants in England* (Swan Sonnenschein, 1897).
3 Natural increase = births *minus* deaths; net migration = immigration *minus* emigration; and growth = natural increase *plus* net migration.
4 G. M. Trevelyan, *A Shortened History of England*, (Penguin, 1959).
5 Most other estimates are for the UK and as such are not comparable because of the large migratory flows from Ireland and Scotland. UK estimates reported by Milos Macura ('Population in Europe 1920–1970', *The Fontana Economic History of Europe*, Vol. V, Ch. 1) indicate balances of −65,000, +24,000, −4,000 and +46,000 for the periods 1920s, 1930s, 1950–60 and 1960–66 respectively. It should be noted that errors in the census and in birth and death registration, especially in earlier years, are all implicitly included in the estimates of net migration presented here, though some may cancel out others. In addition, it is clear from the numbers of registered deaths that casualties of the First and Second World Wars are not included, and these are therefore represented as emigrants, leading to very large negative balances for the periods 1911–1920 and 1931–1950. As there was no census in 1941, because of the war, this latter period cannot be divided further, thus concealing a positive migration balance during the 1930s.
6 The true numbers of births and deaths at this time were probably higher than these data suggest because full coverage of vital events by registration was not legally enforced until 1874.
7 Those reported here are taken from R. K. Kelsall, *Population* (Longmans, 1967); Andre Armengaud, 'Population in Europe 1700–1914', *Fontana Economic History of Europe*, Vol. III, Ch. 1; Milos Macura, 'Population in Europe 1920–1970', *Fontana Economic History of Europe*, Vol. V, Ch. 1; Colin Holmes, 'The Promised Land? Immigration into Britain 1870–1980' in D. A. Coleman (ed) *Demography of Immigrants and Minority Groups in the United Kingdom* (Academic Press, 1982); D. V. Glass, *Population Policies and Movements in Europe* (Cassells, 1940); and *Report of the Royal Commission on Population*, (1949), (Cmnd 7695).
8 Since 1841 the census has included a question on place of birth, and it is this that

is used to identify foreigners. These figures therefore omit immigrants' children born in Britain. In addition, the 1871 Census identified 71,000 people in England and Wales, and 10,000 in Scotland, who were born in the British Colonies and the East Indies, most of whom would have been white people whose parents served in the Empire.

9 In fact, this estimate is roughly in line with the estimate of 2.8 million, including some First World War deaths, given in Table 1.

10 *Royal Commission on Population, op. cit.*, p. iii.

11 Political and Economic Planning, *Population Policy in Great Britain*, (PEP, 1948).

12 Though increased fertility would also increase the dependency ratio in the short run by increasing the school age population, it would in the longer term improve matters.

13 *Royal Commission on Population, op cit.*, p. 133.

14 *Ibid.*, p. 134.

15 *Ibid.*, p. 135. This endorsed the earlier recommendation of the Committee on Empire Migration of the Economic Advisory Council which reported in 1932 (Cmnd 4075).

16 Quoted in Political and Economic Planning, *op. cit.*, p. 101 from the Report of the Committee on Empire Migration. The British Government reserved the right in 1948 to restrict the emigration of too many highly skilled workers.

17 *Royal Commission on Population, op. cit.*, p. 124.

18 Evidence from the 1961 census shows that the fertility of immigrants was less than the average in the countries from which they came. Immigrants would not necessarily increase fertility permanently. See Select Committee on Science and Technology, *First Report, Population of the United Kingdom*, (1971), (379), p. 29.

19 Among them was the Population Stabilisation Group which sent in a report to the Population Panel: *Population Stabilisation, A Policy for Britain*, (July 1972) and later published *Decline or Fall – A Case for a Decrease in Britain's Numbers* (August 1974). Others maintained that there was no pressing need for a population policy in the UK, except that birth control facilities should be improved: see G. Hawthorn, *Population Policy: A Modern Delusion* (Fabian Society, 1973). The idea of an 'optimum' population was also raised again for discussion at this time: see, for example, L. R. Taylor (ed) *The optimum population for Britain* (Academic Press, 1970).

20 Select Committee on Science and Technology, *op. cit.*, p. x.

21 *Report of the Population Panel*, (1973), (Cmnd 5258), p. 1.

22 *Ibid.*, p. 6.

23 *Ibid.*, p. 6.

24 *Hansard*, 24 November 1947.

25 Political and Economic Planning, *op. cit.*, p. 113.

26 J. A. Jackson, *The Irish in Britain* (Routledge and Kegan Paul, 1963), pp. 14–15 and Appendix Table XIII.

27 Including 20,000 born in Ireland, part not stated.

28 Including Northern Ireland.

29 Including 93,000 born in Ireland, part not stated. The 1981 figure includes only 577 people who did not state in which part of Ireland they were born.

30 Cabinet Office files for 1951 show that the control of black immigration was considered as early as 1950. See *The Times*, 2 January 1982.

31 In the last 20 years or so, the Commonwealth has been divided for statistical and other purposes into the Old Commonwealth and the New Commonwealth, a division on implicit racial grounds following immigration law. The Old Commonwealth comprises Australia, New Zealand and Canada whose citizens are mostly white. The New Commonwealth comprises the remainder of the

Commonwealth, including the Caribbean countries, India, Bangladesh and certain African countries, most of whose citizens are black. Until 1 September 1973, the New Commonwealth also included Pakistan.

32 For an elaboration of these push and pull factors, see C. Peach, *West Indian Migration to Britain: A Social Geography* (OUP, 1968), and C. Peach, 'The Growth and Distribution of the Black Population in Britain 1945–1980' in D. A. Coleman (ed) *op. cit.* Evidence of political pressures is documented by M. R. Duffield, 'Racism and counter-revolution in the era of imperialism: a critique of the political economy of migration' (Unpublished paper, 1981; SSRC Research Unit on Ethnic Relations, University of Aston, Birmingham).

33 C. Peach (1968), *op. cit.*

34 C. Peach (1968), *op. cit.*, shows that the 1961 census probably under-estimated the West Indian born population by about 20 per cent. This estimate is therefore too low. It also includes white people born in the New Commonwealth.

35 When Pakistan left the Commonwealth, it became necessary to refer to the New Commonwealth and Pakistan so as to maintain the same grouping for social and political purposes.

36 The number of EEC nationals coming to Britain is greater than this, since permits are not required for the first six months. In 1981, 5.5 million EEC nationals entered the UK but many of these were tourists. These figures do not include the Irish.

37 The levels of migration estimated by the International Passenger Survey are irreconcilable with those obtained from Home Office immigration control statistics. For details of this problem, see Office of Population Censuses and Surveys and Home Office, *Immigration statistics: sources and definitions*, Office of Population Censuses and Surveys Occasional Paper 15 (1979). The main problem with the International Passenger Survey data is their large standard errors arising from the very small samples employed, but they are also deficient in that they omit migration with Eire. For a critique of the International Passenger Survey, see Runnymede Trust and Radical Statistics Race Group, *Britain's Black Population* (Heinemann Educational Books, 1980), Chapters 1 and 7. International Passenger Survey data appear annually in Office of Population Censuses and Surveys, *International Migration*, Series MN.

38 Office of Population Censuses and Surveys, 'International migration: recent trends', *Population Trends*, 18, (1980).

39 C. Walker, 'Demographic characteristics of migrants 1964–75', *Population Trends*, 8, (1977).

40 Contrary to the impression given in recent articles in *New Society* (David Selbourne, 'The new exodus: blacks who have their eyes set on home', *New Society* 19 May, (1983) and 26 May, (1983)) only 500 people of New Commonwealth citizenship and 2,100 of UK citizenship left the UK for the Caribbean in 1981.

41 C. Walker, *op. cit.*

42 C. Walker, *op. cit.* and Office of Population Censuses and Surveys (1980), *op. cit.*

43 C. Walker and M. Gee, 'Migration: the impact on the population', *Population Trends*, 9, (1977).

44 The projection is actually made assuming no migration and this is compared with reality to assess the effects of migration.

45 C. Walker and M. Gee (*op. cit.*) also show that most of this effect arises from the net inflow in the 1950s.

46 See, for example, H. Booth and D. Drew, 'Britain's Black Population', in Runnymede Trust and Radical Statistics Group, *op. cit.*

47 The fertility of all New Commonwealth and Pakistan born women has decreased, and for those born in the West Indies is almost as low as for England and Wales. See H. Booth and D. Drew, *op. cit.*

48 See H. Booth and D. Drew, *op. cit.*; and W. Brass, 'The Future Population of New Commonwealth Immigrant Descent: Numbers and Demographic Implications' in D. A. Coleman (ed) *op. cit.*

49 Office of Population Censuses and Surveys Monitor PP2 83/1, Population projections: mid-1981 based; key features for England and Wales.

Further Reading

N. H. Carrier and J. R. Jeffery, *External Migration: A study of the available statistics 1815–1950*, General Register Office: Studies on Medical and Population Subjects, No 6 (HMSO, 1953).

C. Holmes, 'The Promised Land? Immigration into Britain 1870–1980' in D. A. Coleman (ed) *Demography of Immigrants and Minority Groups in the United Kingdom* (Academic Press, 1982).

J. Isaac, *British Post-War Migration* (CUP, 1954).

J. A. Jackson, *The Irish in Britain* (Routledge and Kegan Paul, 1963).

C. Peach, *West Indian Migration to Britain: A Social Geography* (OUP, 1968).

Runnymede Trust and Radical Statistics Race Group, *Britain's Black Population* (Heinemann Educational Books, 1980).

T. E. Smith, *Commonwealth Migration: Flows and Policies* (Macmillan, 1981).

Immigration and the Economy

KEN MAYHEW

Fellow of Pembroke College, Oxford

[This chapter is a collection of reflections on the reasons why relatively few economists have attempted, over the last 25 years, to study the effects of immigration on the economy of the UK. Éric-Jean Thomas's chapter has shown that in most continental countries economic considerations have been paramount and immigrants have been seen, until recently, primarily as units of the labour force. In the UK, on the other hand, Ken Mayhew's remarks show up a completely different pre-occupation: that immigrants are black settlers. So, where other countries have collected data about alien workers, the UK has collected data about ethnic minorities.

In the 1950s and 1960s, when significant numbers of Commonwealth and Colonial citizens were arriving to work or settle, most adult non-Europeans in the country were also immigrants in the proper sense of the word. By now, the majority of the ethnic minority residents is British-born. But even in the 1950s and 1960s, immigrants who were not white were not the whole set of immigrants: over half the entrants were Irish, white alien or white Commonwealth. An investigation of black people's role in the economy has therefore never been an investigation of immigrants' role in the economy, properly speaking. We therefore lack information on the economic effects of immigration as a whole. Ken Mayhew argues that this might be just as well: there are many dangers in attempting a cost-benefit analysis. The following remarks are based on proceedings at the AGIN conference (see p. 216).   *Editor*]

May I start with a disclaimer. I am not an expert on immigration problems, nor am I about to attempt a comprehensive analysis or survey of the economics of immigration. Rather, I intend to make some observations about what I believe the economist can or cannot contribute to the debate.

Fifteen to 20 years ago, an economist would have put positive and negative arguments concerning immigration. On the positive side, immigrants often filled shortages in specific occupations in particular areas of the country. This was the case with some of the early West Indian arrivals. On the negative side, it was argued that immigration might create an over-supply of labour and thus cause or exacerbate unemployment problems.

Ram Kaushal has commented (see p. 153) how sad it is that economists have not done enough to try to work out immigrants' positive contribution to the economy of the host country. I agree very much that some researchers' preconceptions have precluded this, but not, I think, because they are racialists. Rather the conditioning they have had and what they have read outside their own sphere of economics, has led them to assume there is a 'problem' – a problem of discrimination and disadvantage. I am not sure I agree with the accompanying argument which was 'please let's measure the contribution'. This could be positively undesirable. Going too finely into the economic calculus carries dangers, including the possibility that too much cost-benefit consideration might lead us to think in terms of a guest worker scheme. Such a scheme might be mutually beneficial if the guest workers themselves wish to be seasonal workers and have somewhere to return to for six months of the year or for longer periods every so often, as we plunge into yet another economic depression and we act to protect the jobs of the indigenous population. So, if by awareness of an economic function of migration one actually starts to speculate along these lines, then I am rather glad that we have been lacking in awareness.

Though there was, 15 years or so ago, some direct 'cost- benefit' analysis concerned with such issues, more often economists examined the fortunes of particular groups of immigrants, leaving the reader to draw his own conclusions about the implications for entry policy. Commonly a picture was painted of unrelieved misery and gloom, of economic failure relative to the rest of the population. An examination of the 1971 Census modifies this. The information there relates to ethnic groups, but for many such groups the majority were in fact immigrants. Some of the groups, like the Pakistanis, West Indians and Irish, present the archetypal picture of immigrant disadvantage. They experienced higher unemployment rates than the indigenous population. They were crowded into a relatively small number of occupations, and by and large these were unskilled manual jobs. However, there were a number of groups who did much better than this – African Asians are a case in point. They, like the West Indians and Pakistanis, were crowded into a narrow range of occupations as compared with the white labour force. The occupations involved, however, tended to be superior ones. To a lesser extent, this was also true of the Indians. So, if one examines the 1971 data – and whatever one can pick up since then – the first lesson the economist has to learn is that the fortunes of immigrants in the labour market may vary greatly from group to group.

What explains these varying fortunes? Primarily two factors. First, levels of education. There is a strong correlation between the latter and economic success. In other words, the East African Asians and the Indians were on average better educated than the white indigenous population. By contrast the West Indians, Pakistanis and Irish were much less educated. The second important influence is the date of entry. As a broad generalisation, it is those groups who entered after the extension of immigration controls in the 1960s which have done best; hardly surprising, given the nature of those controls. As they were exercised, they tended to be biased in favour of the better educated, in favour of the sort of people who were liable to be more successful.

As a qualifier to the above, there is little doubt that most immigrant groups – even the ones who do well occupationally – get less well paid than a white British-born male within any occupation. One obvious example of this would be in the medical profession. For groups like the West Indians, to this type of earnings disadvantage is added the further disadvantage of being crowded into poor occupations. Of late economists have concentrated on measuring this earnings disadvantage. That proportion of it which they have been unable to 'explain' by the characteristics of the immigrants themselves generally has been defined to be the consequence of discrimination. In this context it would be interesting to have more information which gave us greater separation between racial minorities who are immigrants and those who are second-generation to see if there are differences in patterns between the two groups.

On characteristics of racial prejudice and how far there is an economic basis for such prejudice, I was very interested in Christopher Husbands' suggestion that the economic seems to be relatively minor compared with other aspects. His research has indicated that the highly prejudiced (including some National Front supporters) are less concerned with the effect of immigration on jobs than its effects on housing and on cultural change. I make just two points. What evidence we have indicates that discrimination on the labour market is significant, and that partially at least it stems from desire to derive economic advantage. Secondly, it is very often difficult to disentangle the motives for discrimination. The answers obtained from asking people or studying their behaviour are not necessarily reliable. There is much potential for economic discrimination which may find its expression in other forms of discrimination; so I wouldn't want to underplay the importance of racial discrimination in economic life.

Unfortunately, whatever its other merits, work on racial prejudice and discrimination does not make a major contribution to the debate on how much immigration there should be. Rather, with some trepidation we have to move back closer to the cost-benefit approach mentioned at the beginning of this chapter.

The argument that immigrants might be used to fill shortages in specific occupations and jobs seems to be an extremely weak one today. We have high unemployment. Where there are skill shortages, it would be difficult to fill them with immigrant labour. Undoubtedly if the economy picks up, skill shortages will emerge rapidly and they could severely prejudice the recovery. But again they are unlikely to be the sort of shortages which could be closed by any relaxation of immigration controls. Further many of the subsidiary arguments which accompanied this main justification would be regarded as unacceptable for a whole variety of practical and ethical reasons. Such arguments include the fact that immigrants are willing to accept low status, low skill jobs thus improving vertical mobility for nationals of the host country; that their acceptance of piecework and automation permits the full utilisation of capital and assists the successful harnessing of technical progress; that the acceptance of low wages helps the host country's international competitiveness.

It used to be said that a burden on the state was relieved because other countries bore the educational costs of the host country's labour force, whilst immigrants helped to finance the social security system. However, of late these possible advantages would seem to be insignificant compared to a large potential negative effect.

The standard argument against immigration is that social costs are incurred to the extent that immigrant groups suffer disproportionately high unemployment rates. Even if the immigrant is not jobless, in an era of high unemployment he is likely to be depriving an indigenous worker of a job. Clearly a burden is imposed on the state. But if one thinks in terms of percentages, then the higher the national level of unemployment, the less significant the burden appears for any absolute level of immigration. If one looks at the numbers of people coming into the country annually and postulates the likely addition if immigration controls were somewhat relaxed, then immigration is likely to make only a small percentage contribution to our unemployment problems. Thus although the positive argument for immigration may have disappeared, in a strange sense the negative one has become relatively insignificant, assuming that the current debate is about only marginal changes in entry controls.

So far I have outlined the arguments in a very parochial or nationalistic way. Often they are put in more internationalist terms. Examined in terms of aggregate international welfare, mobility of labour would appear to be 'a good thing' as would the mobility of any other factor of production. The play of market forces would ensure that factors are attracted to wherever they can make their biggest economic contribution. Yet even this more internationalist stance in practice often boiled down to a parochial one. Even in the context of a belief in the international mobility of labour, the acid test was generally whether this provided a net advantage for Britain and not for the world community as a whole.

In this light, you will remember the 'brain drain' debate of the 1960s. I was very interested in Heather Booth's paper which implied an occupational 'balance' between the types who went out and the types who came in. Certainly a popular non-professional presumption has been to the contrary, i.e., that there was a net social cost. In fact the occupational breakdown is too broad to permit any firm conclusions. Indeed the data on emigrants are still probably insufficient for analytical purposes. I agree with David Coleman that the statistics we have on workers entering and workers leaving are seriously defective: not only are the IPCS categories too crude to be useful, but the numbers – a few thousands each way – are too small for reliable analysis to be made. But the great problem is that one really wants to work from stock statistics rather than flow statistics, and the former are very inadequate.

A common specific argument is that in one respect occupational categories can be misleading – they do not allow for entrepreneurial talent. There is a time-honoured thesis here, going back to the Hugenots and before, suggesting that Britain has been the beneficiary from imported entrepreneurial talent. Again the problem with this approach in the modern context, is that it is impossible to quantify the net benefit or loss.

These, then, are the sorts of issues to which economists have addressed themselves. Either, generally thinking in terms of a national cost-benefit analysis, or specifically analysing the economic fortunes of immigrant or minority groups. It seems to me that the outstanding conclusion is that it is very hard to believe that the economic issues raised by the present immigration debate are of massive importance in the context of our other economic problems. If the debate is to be decided, it should be on grounds other than economic ones, unless it is believed that the sort of economic disadvantages immigrants suffer create vast social problems in the broader sense.

In a wider context, however, Sarah Leigh and Andrew Nicol have suggested that the economic effects, not on the UK but on Third World countries, should be taken into account in forming policy.

There are many studies concerning the effect of immigration on Third World countries. Those which I know tend to be partial, in that they take one particular problem, one particular occupational group, and one particular country. And so it is very difficult to generalise. An occupation which is often written about is the medical profession. And in this case, there does seem to have been a cost imposed upon some Third World countries, in terms of taking talent out of the country and keeping it in Britain. There has been a second cost, which is that even when the talent has gone back, it has often been trained in a manner which is totally inappropriate for the way the country of origin runs its health system. But that is more than just a problem of migration, it is also one of where people get their training. On the other hand, there is some evidence that immigration has a very positive effect on the donor countries. First, and most obviously, it allows them to export excess labour supply. Secondly, immigrants send remittances home. Thirdly, where more highly qualified manpower is concerned there is a feedback. Such workers may go back home after 10 or 15 years residence in the developed country, and return with knowledge and skills and technology, which are actually useful. On balance, the evidence is so scattered, so specific to individual countries and individual occupations that it is difficult to come to general conclusions but it is something that ought to be considered.

The main message, however, that should come across very strongly is not only that economists have not actually made much contribution to analysing the immigration problem. They probably should not. And I think if we get too much into the area of fine economic calculus, then we are probably making – on balance – a negative contribution. In other words, for once I am not an economist who is going in for job creation – at least for other economists.

Nationality and Immigration Status

ANN DUMMETT

Research Worker, Joint Council for the Welfare of Immigrants

Introduction

In international law, a state has a duty to admit to its territory its own nationals, even if they are ill, mad, criminal or subversive (characteristics generally disliked by governments, not because they are all on one moral level, for they are not, but because they give trouble and expense to the authorities). The nationals of other states, on the other hand, have weaker claims to admission, resting on several possible grounds, and it is generally accepted that a state may refuse a non-national on grounds of public health or national security. The purpose of this article is not to examine the distinctions made by international law between nationals and non-nationals, but to take them for granted and then to ask what are the implications for UK immigration law and policy.

Until 1948, the UK followed the customary practice of states in admitting its own nationals to the UK: the people concerned were British subjects, including not only persons born, or naturalised, or with a male ancestor born, in the UK, but all those who had become British subjects by connection with a Colony or self-governing Dominion. However, there was no freedom of movement for all British subjects between all the territories for which the British Government was internationally responsible, nor throughout the Commonwealth. Since the first decade of the twentieth century, the self-governing Dominions of Canada, Australia, New Zealand and South Africa had imposed immigration restrictions on British subjects of Indian and Chinese descent. And all the Colonies had Immigration Ordinances governing the entry not only of aliens but of British subjects (and Irish citizens) from outside the Colony concerned. Someone born in Britain had no right to enter Bermuda, though someone born in Bermuda had the right to enter Britain. Laurie Lee, in *As I walked out one midsummer morning* describes vividly how much easier he found it to enter Spain than to get into Gibraltar, and how disconcerted he was not to get a welcome, but to be received with hostility and suspicion, where the Union Jack flew over the Rock.

Thus, if one regards British subjecthood as the nationality of the Commonwealth in 1948, there was not full internal freedom of movement between the territories on which the nationality was based. However, every British subject had the right to enter the UK, and those connected with other territories had, in general, each the right to enter their own territory of origin – with some exceptions: a few of the Colonial Ordinances were so restrictive that birth on the territory did not confer the right of re-entry on an individual who left.

The quality of being a British subject arose from allegiance to the Crown. British Subjecthood served, in practice, as a nationality, since a subject could apply for a British passport and seek diplomatic or consular protection from the British Government, but, as a status, it did not have the same rights attached to it as nationality, or citizenship, in many other states. Nor was British subjecthood the only form of British nationality so far as other states were concerned: the status of British Protected Person was, in international law, indistinguishable from that of Subject, although UK domestic law differentiated between them, and regarded British Protected Persons as aliens under British protection. The people concerned were, for the most part, persons born in protectorates, protected states or mandated territories, though a few had had the status conferred on them individually. Even in 1948, then, the character of British nationality was not simple to understand or easy to define precisely, and the relationship between British nationality and freedom from immigration control into countries under British rule was complicated.

Commonwealth Immigration

From 1949, when the British Nationality Act 1948 came into force, British subjecthood was a secondary status acquired by persons whose primary status was citizenship of a self-governing Commonwealth country. Canadian citizens, were still British subjects though they held Canadian passports. British subjects, even with other countries' passports, remained exempt from UK immigration control alongside citizens of the UK and Colonies. This was not regarded as anomalous: there was a very strong sense of unity with the rest of the Commonwealth in the late 1940s and still in the 1950s. It did not matter much, for practical purposes, that definitions were vague or complex. It was the agitation which began in the late 1950s against 'coloured' immigration from the Commonwealth which breached this unity, and which succeeded, by 1962, in pushing through the Commonwealth Immigrants Act 1962. The arguments on that measure were concerned, openly or thinly veiled, with race: some of them dealt with the character of the Commonwealth as a whole; there was little or no attention for the significance of a distinction between British nationals, with British passports, and citizens of other countries. Those who wanted racial exclusiveness wanted to keep out British passport-holders who were black and brown, together with Commonwealth country citizens with other passports who were black or brown: it was essential to their argument to ignore the significance of UK and Colonies citizenship. Those who opposed the measure were passionately concerned with the Commonwealth as a whole and with preventing racial distinction in immigration control: they wanted rights for Indian citizens to come to Britain as freely as they wanted UK and Colonies citizens from Montserrat to come, and so for them too the issue of citizenship was beside the point. Unhappily, however, once the principle of excluding British passport holders from right of entry had been established in 1962, it was followed through in a series of measures for the next 20 years. The Commonwealth Immigrants Act 1968 imposed entry control on British passport holders who had no colonial territory to go to and so were left without right of entry anywhere at all. The Immigration Act 1971 re-affirmed their exclusion under a new set of definitions: the distinction between patrial and non-patrial. The British Nationality Act 1981 took the final logical step in the illogical series, and re-named the then existing categories of British nationals under five headings, making those who were already free of entry control 'British citizens', still free from entry control, and explicitly denying right of entry to all other categories of British passport-holder.

Basis of British Nationality Law

British nationality law has now been established on the basis of British immigration law. This is precisely the opposite of the practice of other states. In all other cases (except that of Israel, whose nationality law is based on the Law of Return) a state defines its own nationality, takes for granted that its own nationals have right of entry to its territory, and then proceeds to devise a regime for the control of non-nationals. And Israel, of course, admits its own nationals. The UK is unique in refusing entry to its own nationals. Some states may expel their own citizens and deny them return, but the process is preceded or accompanied by deprivation of citizenship: however deplorable the practice may be, at least the principle is observed that an individual who is a national of a state has the right to enter that state. The UK not only flouts this universally accepted principle: it has drawn the lines in such a way that the vast majority of British citizens, free from immigration control, are white people (at a rough estimate, 54 million out of a total 57 million) while over 95 per cent of the people in the four categories of British without right of entry are of non-European descent. This distinction has been made even sharper than the Bill originally provided, in that the Act was successfully amended to give all Gibraltarians the right to register as British citizens, and in 1983 the Falkland Islanders were made full British citizens without needing to register.

Reform of British Nationality and Immigration Law

Against this background, it would be foolish to consider any reform of British immigration law which ignored the need to reform British nationality law first. The first essential step in policy must be to lay the foundation: all British nationals should have right of entry to the UK and/or to a British dependency before a system of control for non-nationals is devised. This first step requires amendment of the British Nationality Acts 1981–83.

Such amendment must be preceded by detailed consideration and discussions, whose scope lies outside the subject of this book. Here, one can only indicate the problems that would need to be tackled. Taking for granted that all British citizens would remain British citizens, one would have to decide how best to deal with each of the other four categories of national. There are about 3 million British Dependent Territories' Citizens, of whom about $2\frac{1}{2}$ million, or more, are in Hong Kong. Their national status will almost certainly change when sovereignty is formally transferred to the People's Republic of China, whose law regards them already as Chinese nationals if they are of Chinese ethnic origin. The remaining citizens of other dependencies, numbering less than half a million, could either become British citizens with right of entry to the UK or receive a citizenship attached to their respective territories, with right of entry to their own. There are various possible options open for the other categories: British Overseas Citizen, British Protected Person, British subject. These options would have to take account of the situation, and the wishes, of the people concerned, some of whom are resident overseas and wish to remain so, but all of whom lack an effective nationality except for those British Overseas Citizens who are dual nationals – most of this group are in Malaysia and a few in Argentina or other states around the world. Here it must suffice to say that, at least for those British nationals outside dependencies who have no other nationality (a group numbering perhaps 300,000 but probably under 200,000) British citizenship offers the only just and feasible solution to *de facto* statelessness.

How would this affect immigration to the UK? Already, for many years past it has been the case that a sizeable fraction of those who enter and settle each year are British citizens who have been residing abroad. Most of these have been white people. But of course the majority of the British citizens resident outside the UK (the last government estimate, admittedly rough, of their numbers, was about three million) do not return to settle but stay overseas. Information available suggests that the same would be true for the majority of those British nationals who are now barred from entry: the reason they want British citzenship is not so much that they want to live in Britain, though of course there are some with relatives here who do, but that they want passports that will enable them to travel elsewhere, they want the sense of security which an effective nationality gives as an insurance for possible moments of crisis, and they want justice from the country that conferred its nationality on them in the past, and which some of them have fought or worked for. The impact on entry figures would probably be comparatively small.

There are of course several million Commonwealth citizens who have right of abode in the UK under the British Nationality Act 1981 (by reason of having had a parent born there) or who can, under paragraph 29 of the 1983 Immigration Rules, enter, settle and take work freely (by reason of having had a grandparent born in the UK). This anomaly in immigration control, under which a very large number of other countries' nationals can enter without any restriction whatever, could be maintained or abandoned when the Act was amended. So far as crude numbers are concerned, it is far more significant for potential entry to the UK than the extension of full citizenship to all existing British nationals would be.

Conclusion

But the argument for amending nationality law does not rest on deductions drawn from crude numbers: it rests on legal and moral assumptions and, arguably, on political good sense, independently. Few people in Britain realise what a bad name our combined nationality and immigration policies have given us in the outside world in recent years, or how obvious to outsiders is their racism, or how great a contrast they afford to other countries' laws, or how silly it looks to enact a system that establishes white British superiority over lesser breeds in the present world of superpower political dominance, Asian economic growth and British backwardness. As the foundation for a new and reformed system of immigration control, a revised nationality law would, therefore, not only have the function of simplifying and clarifying the basis of control: it would be a political gesture, domestically and internationally, of great significance. It would show that the UK had, at last, realistically come to terms with its post-imperial role, abandoned racism, and learned to look ahead.

Immigration and Nationality – Caribbean Families: An Inside View

YVONNE COLLYMORE

Freelance writer

If my father had not been wounded fighting in the British army during the Second World War, I should not be in Britain today. Out of what later proved to be a misguided sense of British nationalism, he was one of thousands of British subjects of the UK and Colonies who volunteered to serve what they believed was their country, and for which they were prepared to give their lives. Whilst lying wounded in the English hospital to which he had been transferred from Egypt, he used his time to study. On his release, he sent for his family whilst he continued his studies at his own expense. Hence, I came as a child in 1948 on my mother's passport.

When my father's country of birth became independent he had already left the UK for more than 10 years so was no longer eligible on grounds of residency for a UK passport. He had automatically become a citizen of the land of his birth. Because of British immigration laws and rules he now has to apply for a visa to come and visit his children who are resident here, or to attend an ex-servicemen's reunion.

Every single member of my family now has a different nationality! I had to apply for British citizenship and pay £50 after having held a British passport for more than 20 years when the country of my birth became independent. This took two years and meanwhile I could only travel by applying for a Vincentian passport. I am one of the lucky ones who can hold dual nationality; but not so fortunate is my niece. She would have to renounce her Trinidadian citizenship to apply for British citizenship. Yet, if she were to have another child and did not have British citizenship the child would not be eligible for British nationality for 10 years, and then it would still be discretionary.

If the British nursing organisations had not been actively

recruiting nurses in Trinidad in the 1960s, my niece would not have come here in the first place.

My brother was born in Britain so he does not have these complications. What is more, being male, he can bring his wife to Britain to settle and take his nationality. Being female, I could not do the same if I met a man I wished to marry who was resident outside the UK. My sister also has right of abode though not through birth, but by marriage to a British patrial. Presently, she has an automatic right to register, but once the grace period has expired or if her husband dies she will lose that.

What is the point of all this family history? Only to underline the complications which the various changes in immigration and nationality Acts and Rules have posed for individuals and for families. Whilst one must accept the right of every country to impose restrictions of entry, residence and the right to work, such restrictions should not discriminate on the grounds of race or sex without justification. (Such justification might be, for example, restrictions on the entry of nationals from a country with which there is a war or territorial dispute.) In drafting such legislation, therefore, governments should take account of the effects on those families and individuals already resident if restrictions are applied to members of their families. Two further examples may serve to illustrate the difficulties that can arise.

In the first case, a mother of three children was referred for literacy help by a social worker. The family had many problems including the fact that the father was in hospital following a nervous breakdown. The mother was thus forced to work full-time leaving the children unattended after school. One of the children attended a Special School and had particular difficulties. The grandmother was brought over from the West Indies to help with the care of the children. One day, the literacy tutor called to discover that mother was down at the police station because 'The police came and took granny away'. Appeals lodged by the social workers had failed to reverse the Home Office decision to deport the grandmother. The chances of that mother coping with the children alone were slight; the likelihood was that the children would be taken into care at great cost to the state whereas the grandmother had provided care, stability and love at little cost whilst maintaining the independence and dignity of the family.

In the second example, a trainee teacher who had come to Britain on a student visa met a British patrial who asked her to marry him. Living some distance apart whilst she studied, the relationship was already under strain without the opposition of his family to him marrying a black girl. With the cutbacks in education and the falling school population, the trainee was not certain to get a teaching job for her probationary year in order to achieve her status as a qualified teacher. Whilst awaiting her examination results to see whether she would be able to go on to the degree course, she obtained a part-time, temporary post where the employers would apply for a work permit. Suddenly, she received a telephone call that her mother was dying in the West Indies. She was aware that if she went to her mother, she might not be admitted back into the country. The period of her student visa was up, she had no proof of a place on another course for the next term, neither did she have a permit to work. Because she had intended to marry, she had not applied for an extension at the appropriate time; now her relationship was shaky and the marriage might not take place.

These examples might not be typical, but they have one thing in common – all of those people had something to offer this country in the way of service and/or skills. Changes in their circumstances prompted a situation which they could not have anticipated when coming to this country – whether as a serviceman, nurse, teacher or supportive relative. I believe that any immigration and nationality laws should not be so rigid in drafting, or in application, that they cannot respond flexibly to such changes in family needs and circumstances. Further, the costs of citizenship should not be so high that they cause hardship to families already settled before the change in legislation or rules. The present cost of £70 per person and £35 for a child (these charges were altered in early 1983, to £55 and £55 respectively) is prohibitive for a family where the breadwinner is unemployed or threatened with redundancy; where for three successive years there is a child transferring to secondary school and needing expensive uniform; or where there are elderly relatives to support in the Caribbean. In such situations, the family are likely to postpone the formalities of registration until too late; when their automatic right to register may have been lost. Meanwhile, the government has made a massive profit of £1,200,000 on the whole process of registration and the misery of families.

The Continuing Paradigm of Immigration Control: Institutional Racism British Style. Can We End It? (A Black Viewpoint)

RAM KAUSHAL

Member, North West England and Scotland Campaign Group on Immigration and Nationality

Immigration control of black people has now firmly become an 'internalised norm' of British white majority thinking. It is often expressed in the media-celebrated widely held myth 'There are too many blacks in Britain'. Recently I had a bit of 'culture shock' while teaching race relations to college students and running 'race awareness' seminars for different professional groups. I tended to ask the question, 'How many black people do you think live in Britain? On every such occasion, estimates given varied from 3 million to over 20 million. Individuals who believed in the 'exaggerated numbers' displayed a marked degree of confidence in their respective estimates.

All public and private efforts to establish a sensible view of the black population seem to have had very little effect on eroding the myth of large numbers. This tendency is a reflection of the dominant view that black people are essentially a 'problem' and a 'burden' in British society. The paradigm of immigration control in Britain has both developed and sustained the white 'folk-mythology' about the 'negative and racially motivated' stereotypes about black people.

Black Commonwealth immigrants like myself who came here just before the Commonwealth Immigrants Act 1962 have witnessed and experienced the bipartisan consensus of Labour and Conservative Governments on the question of immigration control. Our social, economic and psychological survival was so painful that our lack of 'sufficient protest' was and is seen as a sign of 'political apathy' or 'passivity'. There are many studies on the 'problematic aspects' of the black communities in Britain – many white social scientists have thrived on them – but it is rather sad that there is no well-documented research to indicate the contributions of black Commonwealth immigrants to economic and social life of Britain. For example, it is arguable whether the textile industry in the North West of England would have survived without the cheap labour supply of Asian Immigrants. Some imaginative and statesman-like undertaking by the British Governments in 1960s and 1970s would have led to counter-arguments against the Powellite dogma that hideously flourished 'unbated' in this period.

The growth of what is now pejoratively called the race-relations industry took place in the grim shadow of a one-sided immigration debate. It is no wonder that the seven-year operation of the Race Relations Act 1976 has produced so little in terms of 'racial equality or justice'. Hence it is my view that the continuing obsession with immigration control has hindered any rational debate on the positive role of the black community in Britain. Therefore the development of any venture that seeks to repair the psycho-social damage done to black people should receive a wide pattern of support. It is in this sense that the movement to reform the existing immigration laws is crucially required.

Britain can ill afford the pretence of 'equal rights' for all its citizens when the administration and practice of immigration law continue to legitimise racist thinking, and heap misery on black families who are lawfully settled here. The wide gap between the government statements on immigration control and on their desire for a truly multi-racial society cannot help win trust and co-operation of black people. What is being asked of them is a sort of schizophrenic behaviour. They should believe that they live in a fair and democratic society and at the same time continue to suffer the humiliations and injustices of the immigration service. Let me demonstrate this tendency by quoting two statements made on behalf of the last Conservative Government:

Firm immigration control is a pre-requisite of good community relations. When there is not firm control, honest decent people become frightened about their jobs, their futures and may find it difficult to accept new-comers.
(Speech by Mr David Waddington, QC, MP, Minister of State, Home Office, in Blackburn on 28 January 1983 and released by *News Service*, Conservative Control Office).

How reassuring it must be for the black people living in

Blackburn! This *firm* and *unfair* policy on immigration is sold to them as a panacea for the ills of multi-racial society.

> Members of the ethnic minority communities who were born here or are settled here are part of this country and part of its future. They are entitled to the same respect as any other citizen. The Government believes that recognition and accept-ance of this fact by all members of society are essential not only to the development and maintenance of good race relations but also to the future well-being of this country. Members of the ethnic minority communities undoubtedly have an important role to play in shaping the Britain of the future. They represent an important source of talent but their full potential will only be realised within a society free from prejudice and discrimination. (*Racial Disadvantage* paragraph 4. The Government Reply to the Fifth Report from the Home Affairs Committee session 1980–1981 HC 424 1982, Cmnd 8476).

These two statements highlight the nature of 'double-think' in British politics. The negative impact of the first statement can hardly contribute to the positive pretentions of the second. This logical irrationality has been the mainstay of those arguments that have frequently indulged in the case for 'forced' or 'induced' repatriation. This paradox also reveals the nature of British-style institutional racism. If the black people were to believe the pious intentions of the second statement, the government concerned will have to examine the incongruency of their arguments on immigra-tion control in the name of good race relations.

In 1967, the 'Kerner Commission Report on Civil Disorders' pointed to the American Nation the central fact, 'What white Americans have never fully understood but what the Negro can never forget is that white society is deeply implicated in the Ghetto. White institutions created it, white institutions maintain it and white institutions condone it.' There is here a very relevant message for British white institutions to ponder over their attitude to black people in Britain. In Britain, there is a general assumption that the practice of public administration operates fairly impar-tially and possesses a fair amount of goodwill towards ordinary people, whatever their background, yet there is plentiful evidence on how black people suffer arrogance, indifference, antipathy and even hostility from officials in public service and authority. Nowhere is it better exemplified than in the administration of Immigration Rules and Immigration Service.

I would like to know how a British white citizen would feel if he or she had to wait three long years before his or her widowed ailing mother can join the family in Britain. The cases of divided or separated black families are far too numerous to be mentioned here. They certainly display the iniquitous rigidity and hypocrisy of an arbitrarily devised system that subjects individuals to long delays, inhuman interrogation and demands for many documents. This multiple experience of harrassment and oppression has left a deep scar on the psyche of black people. To redress the balance, the least any government can do is to remove the 'unfairness' of its rules which disproportionately apply to them.

Therefore a plea for reform, as far as immigration laws are concerned, is not so much 'begging mercy' for black people. It is an opportunity for the government in particular and British society in general to make a fresh start in creating a genuine climate for immigration issues to be discussed and resolved fairly. It would be grossly unjust for the present government to justify its present stand on immigration policy with the force of its comfortable majority in Parliament.

It is interesting to note that while the Police Bill was being debated in the last Parliament, it was due to the pressure of the articulate lobby of clergymen, doctors and lawyers that the Home Secretary became ready to introduce changes in the provisions of the Bill. To bring about changes in immigration law, one would hope such a powerful lobby would emerge to educate various political interests about their desirability and feasibility. The efforts of JCWI alone cannot deliver it – although one has to admire its powerful opposition to both immigration and nationality laws. I am also not suggesting that other groups and organisations have not also played their part. What is needed is a strategy for combined and concerted endeavour to gather support for mobilising public opinion against the present state of affairs.

Finally, since it is the black community that is so much afflicted with the presence of such laws, it must put up a united and vigorous fight. Its members, whatever reasons they may have had in the past for their lukewarm attitudes to resist this injustice, must now undertake positive action. Their resolve and determination for a non-racist immigration policy will hopefully attract other sympathetic voluntary groups to increase pressure on the government to rethink.

Their initiative and self-direction are desperately needed. The days of passive acceptance are over. Those individuals in the black community that enjoy trust and leadership of their members must play their part in giving this issue the priority it deserves. The continuity of the present position will perpetuate Anglo-centric narrow thinking and will adversely affect the cause of good race relations. The investment of political effort in achieving substantial reform in immigration law is an opportunity that ought not to be missed.

III. The United Kingdom: changing the law

In the light of the wider considerations and international comparisons described in earlier parts of this book, this section goes on to look at specific problems arising out of the present law, and asks what changes need to be made. It is impossible to consider here every detailed aspect of the Acts and Rules, and their administration in practice, but the chapters below give some indication of the range of questions to be considered: legal process; administrative discretion and rights of appeal; procedures for entry clearance overseas and the use of immigration status to determine certain important rights within the UK; the relationship of entry by refugees to other categories of entry, and the influence of immigration policy as a whole on the admission of students from overseas for temporary study.

It would have been possible to compile a much longer list of practical questions about possible changes. But these chapters move on from the general accounts above to specific problems which can be understood in terms of the personal fate of individuals and families, and the importance of the wording of particular regulations and of the practices that have grown up around them. They are included not only because they are important in their own right – and they raise some urgent and disturbing questions – but because they illustrate the link between general and particular. Also, they deal with practices that are little known to the public, even to that part of the public which takes a close interest in politics and social affairs.

Refugees and Asylum-seekers: Proposals for Policy Changes

MAUREEN CONNELLY

Refugee Unit, United Kingdom Immigrants' Advisory Service

Introduction

Britain has a generous tradition of granting asylum to those who are the victims of persecution: often beyond the terms of the 1951 Convention on the Status of Refugees. Various governments have recognised the need to protect victims of mass persecution, where it is difficult to show an individual fear of persecution, by taking policy decisions which permit those people to stay. As far as individual asylum-seekers are concerned Home Office statistics for 1982 show that 3,585 cases were resolved: of these 2,368 were granted asylum (with or without refugee status) – 61 per cent (some of these were reversals of previously negative decisions). Of the 1,217 refused asylum, a considerable number have been granted exceptional leave to remain and a further number are still pursuing their claims by appeal or further representation. The Home Office cannot be criticised for its general asylum policy. The problems which arise within the current procedures arise for those who for one reason or another are unable to express their fears; have language difficulties; have no idea of the procedures or access to advice and, who, in immigration terms, have a dubious history. It is to prevent these problems that an adjustment of current procedures is required.

Present Policy[1]

The 1951 Convention on the Status of Refugees and the 1967 Protocol are incorporated into domestic law through the 1980 and

159

1983 Immigration Rules, which provide that 'where a person is a refugee full account is to be taken of the provisions of the Convention and Protocol relating to the Status of Refugees'.[2]

Article 1A of the Convention states that a refugee is a person who owing to a well-founded fear of persecution on the grounds of race, religion, nationality, membership of a particular social group or political opinion cannot return to his country of nationality. This definition is reflected in paragraphs 73, 134 and 165 of the Immigration Rules.

The Convention lays down, in broad terms, the principles for the treatment of refugees. Each country signatory to the Convention is free to set up whichever mechanism is considered most suitable to fulfil its obligations under the Convention.

In the UK the authority competent to determine asylum and refugee status is the Home Secretary. Applications for asylum, wherever made, are dealt with by the Refugee Section of the Home Office's Immigration and Nationality Division. If a person has a valid visa or entry clearance and is refused entry, or if he is refused asylum having made an application while he still had permission to remain in the UK, he has a right of appeal against refusal of asylum prior to any action to remove him from the country.

If a person does not have a valid visa or entry clearance or is an alleged illegal entrant he does not have the right of appeal whilst still in the UK. When an application for asylum is made after the expiry of permission to remain and is refused there is no right of appeal until deportation proceedings begin. In such instances further representations may be put to the Home Office for reconsideration of their decision.

Problems of the Present Policy

'Fear' is a subjective emotion: which is why the UN Convention contains the objective element of requiring fear to be 'well-founded'. However it must be recognised that genuine fear leads people to act in ways which often appear illogical.

By the nature of events which produce refugees, asylum-seekers do not normally arrive in the UK in nice tidy immigration parcels – legally and with firm evidence that they will be persecuted if returned to their country of origin. Instead they arrive in any way possible – on false passports, by totally evading immigration control, or by lying on entry due to fear of authority (as it is normally fear of their own authorities which has caused their flight). For those already in the UK who have become refugees *sur place* or who being refugees have obtained entry in another category of the Rules there is often a tendency to delay applying for asylum either through fear of authority, fear of stating one's case and the information finding its way back to one's own authorities, an ignorance of asylum procedures, or in the hope that 'things will change at home'. For all these reasons, very valid reasons for individual asylum-seekers, refugees fall, at the time of their application, under many different categories of the Immigration Act 1971 – illegal entrants, overstayers, detained pending removal, as well as those who have valid permission to be in the UK.

As soon as a person applies for asylum the claim takes precedence over current immigration status. If however the application is refused, and there is no right of appeal against refusal of asylum, he reverts to his previous immigration category. This means that while the person may have an appeal against a previous Home Office refusal under another category of the Rules, an overstayer has no right of appeal, an illegal can be removed. The only recourse in these cases is further representations to the Home Office.

A system which after initial Home Office refusal of an asylum claim then treats people differently according to their immigration status at the time of application and denies all asylum seekers equal treatment to present their case is a violation of natural justice and is unacceptable.

It is suggested that asylum seekers should either be separated from the present Immigration Rules or the present system should be amended, both legally and administratively, to provide all asylum seekers with equal rights in the processing of their claim and in their treatment during the pre-asylum period. The following proposals, if implemented, would go a considerable way to ensuring that all asylum seekers are treated equally and reduce the possibility of error and undue stress on the asylum seeker.

Proposals for Policy Changes

Access to Advice

Recommendation R(81) 16 (Harmonisation of National Procedures relating to asylum) of the Committee of Ministers of the Council of Europe (November 1981) recommends, amongst other things:

The applicant shall receive the necessary guidance as to procedures to be followed and shall be informed of his rights. He shall enjoy the guarantees necessary for presenting his case to the authorities concerned and shall have the right to be heard . . . as well as the possibility to communicate freely with the office of the UNHCR and to approach a voluntary agency working for refugees.

This is also reflected in Conclusion (XXVII) 'Determination of Refugee Status' adopted by the Executive Committee of the United Nations High Commissioner for Refugees.

Access to advice/assistance should be a basic right of an asylum seeker. At present access to advice is a matter of chance rather than right and the people least likely to have access, e.g., the non-English speaking alleged illegal entrant in detention, are often the people who most need advice. In a recent parliamentary reply[3] the Minister of State at the Home Office stated that in future where the Home Office intended to refuse an asylum seeker and where it appeared the person had not received advice the Home Office would inform UKIAS. This statement is welcomed, however, in view of the time it often takes to reach a decision it is important that this information is given to the individual or agency immediately after the Home Office substantive interview is completed. This is particularly important in cases where the individual is detained. In such cases not only can the person receive advice but also, where appropriate, accommodation arrangements can be made thus enabling the asylum seeker in most instances to live within the community pending the Home Office decision on his claim.

It is recommended that all asylum seekers are informed in writing (with verbal translation where necessary) of where they can seek advice at the time they are interviewed by the Home Office on their application for asylum and, in instances where the person is detained, an appropriate agency should be informed of their presence at that time.

Reasons for Refusal

Resolution (77) 31 (Protection of the individual in relation to the acts of administrative authorities) of the Committee of Ministers of the Council of Europe (September 1977), whilst not dealing directly with refugees and asylum seekers, includes amongst its provision:

where an administrative act is of such a nature as adversely to affect his rights, liberties or interest the person concerned is informed of the reasons on which it is based.

Although the principles of natural justice do not, as yet, include the requirement that reasons should be given for decisions, there is a strong case to be made for the giving of reasons as an important element in administrative justice. Indeed in several areas of the law the principle of reasoned decisions is virtually recognised, especially where a right of appeal exists.

The Home Office decision-making process is an administrative act: it is normal practice within the Home Office to give statements of reasons for refusal prior to an appeal against refusal of asylum or when an MP has become involved and rarely in other instances. Often the reasons when they are given are inadequate, and it is obviously difficult for an asylum seeker or his representative to re-state an asylum case when the reasons for refusal are not known. Equally, a statement of reasons could allow an individual to approach other countries or to accept the Home Office decision. It is also likely that a full statement of reasons would both prevent future confusion and ultimately save time for all concerned.

It is recommended that in all instances of refusal of asylum a detailed statement of reasons for refusal is given at that time.

Right of Appeal

Whether or not an asylum-seeker whose application is refused has a right of appeal depends on his immigration status at the time he made the application. There are therefore many people who fall outside this safeguard e.g., illegal entrants, overstayers, those recommended for deportation, those who have been refused an extension of stay in another capacity and who then apply for asylum, and people who arrive at a port of entry without entry clearance.

This is perhaps the area of greatest discrepancy of treatment between asylum seekers. As pointed out earlier, asylum seekers are not always able to fall within the Immigration Rules and the right of appeal should not depend on them so doing. Whether or not a person is a genuine student or businessman is normally a matter of fact. Whether or not a person is a refugee is a matter of assessing what might happen to the person if returned to their country of origin. Agencies dealing with refugees believe it is the right of every asylum seeker to have an independent hearing of an asylum claim when the Home Office do not agree with the individual that he has a well-founded fear of persecution.

It is recommended that measures are taken to institute substantive rights of appeal for all asylum seekers where an application is refused by the Home Office.

Length of time between applications and decision

In many cases the length of time taken by the Home Office to reach decisions is excessive. One solution is for the Home Office to speed up procedures: but this cannot be guaranteed. However if all asylum seekers are to be treated equally, given rights of appeal and detailed reasons for refusal, other arrangements are possible. A time limit of six months could be made for deciding on asylum applications and if no decision is reached within that time the individual could then be given interim permission to remain, without restriction on employment, for six months periods. In this way straightforward, strong asylum cases, and also spurious applications, could be dealt with quickly. In those cases where there are genuine difficulties facing the Home Office in reaching a decision, for whatever reason, the delay would not be of such detriment to the individual. This latter point is important, as the lengthy asylum procedure and the lack of control over their own lives can often have very serious effects on asylum seekers who are already living with the trauma which caused them to become refugees.

It is recommended that any asylum seeker who does not receive a Home Office decision within six months is given formal permission to take employment pending resolution of the application.

Immigration Service interviews with asylum seekers

Asylum seekers are interviewed by the Home Office on their claims to asylum either at Lunar House, Croydon, or through the Immigration Service at ports of entry or for applications from outside London, and occasionally by the police.

Interviews at Lunar House give little cause for complaint. Although there are sometimes complaints about interpreters it is rare to hear complaints against interviewers at Lunar House. However this is not the case with asylum seekers interviewed by Immigration Officers. Whilst it is not claimed that every Immigration Officer is unsympathetic to asylum seekers, there have been sufficient complaints to indicate that the system is not satisfactory. Complaints are normally about the attitude and gratuitously offensive/sarcastic remarks made during the course of interview. The asylum seeker often becomes even more nervous or appears aggressive and does not answer questions fully or offer, often vital, further information.

Immigration Officers appear, in most instances, to have no background information on the countries which produce refugees and, as they have little experience of interviewing asylum seekers, it is easy to see why the interviews are sometimes misdirected and the right supplementary questions are not asked, even in instances where good will is not lacking.

It is recommended that if Immigration Officers have to interview asylum seekers they should be experienced officers of CIO level, who have benefited from basic training on refugee law and the situations which produce refugees as well as receiving background country information prior to individual interviews.

Home Office Acknowledgement of Applications for Asylum

In view of the need of asylum seekers to approach the DHSS for social security and since the introduction of health charges, it is important that all asylum seekers have proof that an asylum application has been lodged with the Home Office. Without this proof there are often lengthy delays in obtaining welfare benefits, causing great difficulty to individual asylum seekers.

It is recommended that anyone who applies for asylum is provided with a formal Home Office letter acknowledging receipt of an asylum application.

Instructions to Immigration Officers

It is believed that secret instructions to Immigration Officers regarding asylum lead to, perhaps unwarranted, suspicion. Publication of these instructions can only lead to better communication and understanding between the Home Office, asylum seekers and their representatives.

It is recommended that all instructions to Immigration Officers concerning asylum are published.

Acquisition of British Nationality

(a) Registration/Naturalisation charges
Naturalisation is seen by the UNHCR as one of the solutions to the refugee problem. Article 34 of the 1951 Convention states that:

> The Contracting States shall as far as possible facilitate the assimilation and naturalisation of refugees. They shall in particular make every effort to expedite naturalisation proceedings and to reduce as far as possible the charges and cost of such proceedings.

It is recommended that all persons granted asylum who, at the time of application for naturalisation are in receipt of unemployment benefit, supplementary benefit, family income supplement, etc.

165

should either pay no fee whatever, or if this is not possible that a purely nominal sum is charged.

(b) Children born to refugee parents
It is recommended that all children born in the UK to those granted permission to remain as the result of an asylum claim should be entitled to British Nationality from birth or as soon as the parent(s) has been given such permission to remain.

Access to the DHSS when an asylum claim is pending

The reasons why asylum seekers appear in many different ways and why they often find themselves for valid reasons in conflict with the provisions of the Immigration Act have already been discussed.

Recently the DHSS have interpreted more strictly the Urgent Cases Regulations with dire consequences for asylum seekers.

In March 1983 in a letter to Lord Avebury the DHSS set out the following position:

> People who are illegal entrants, who are subject to a deportation order or who have overstayed their limited leave to stay in the UK are normally entitled neither to supplementary benefit, nor to child benefit; under existing regulations . . . A person whose leave to remain in this country has expired is no longer lawfully present here. He may subsequently apply for permission to remain, but this is treated as a new application, not as a variation of the conditions which have expired.

It is recommended that the DHSS regulations are amended to make full provisions for the welfare of all refugees during the pre-asylum period.[4]

Statelessness

People who are granted asylum do not lose their nationality. If conditions in their country of origin change they have a country to which they can go and are therefore not stateless. A stateless person is someone who is not recognised as a national of any country under its law.

Britain is a signatory of the 1954 Convention on the Status of Stateless Persons. Whilst it is rare to find a person in the UK who is stateless with residency rights in no other country, it is not impossible for this to happen. Unfortunately nowhere within domestic law is this Convention mentioned and there is therefore no recourse in law to argue that a person is Stateless.

It is recommended that provision is made, legally and administratively to enable stateless persons who have no country which will admit them as residents, and who apply to be recognised as Stateless persons in the UK, to benefit from the same legal and welfare rights as asylum seekers.

Exceptional Leave to Remain

It is within the discretion of the Home Office to grant exceptional leave to remain i.e. outside the Immigration Rules. This form of discretion can be applied in a number of ways: either as a decision to permit a specific number of a particular group entry to the UK, e.g. Ugandan Asians; as a decision to permit nationals of a particular country to remain on a temporary humanitarian basis because of events in their country of origin, e.g. Poles; or to permit individuals to remain because of their particular circumstances. Perhaps the main concern for those granted permission to remain exceptionally and where it is not leading to settlement is the question: how long should their stay be considered temporary and at what stage does it become permanent? It would seem just that if chaos, war or repression prevented a person from returning to their country for a number of years that they should be granted residency here and that when (if) the situation in their own country changes the choice of whether to go or stay is that of the individual.

Provisions under the Immigration Rules

Much of the administrative treatment of refugees is not specifically provided for under the Immigration Rules. (For example nowhere in the Rules is provision made for those granted asylum to obtain indefinite leave after four years.) As the Convention lays down the principles for the treatment of refugees but does not cover administrative detail there is valid reason for incorporating within the Rules administrative practice to be applied to refugees.

Notes

1 A paper 'Legal Status of Refugees' detailing current procedures prepared by WUS and UKIAS is available from the UKIAS Refugee Unit.
2 HC 169, paras. 16, 96, 153.
3 *Hansard*, 31 March 1983, col. 524.

4 The British Refugee Council has prepared a detailed report 'Asylum seekers and the DHSS Regulations' which sets out the problems and makes clear recommendations for improving the situation. This document is available from the British Refugee Council.

Family Settlement Problems

SARAH LEIGH

Solicitor in private practice

Introduction

The fundamental principle of present UK immigration control is that persons not born in the UK are to be excluded from living and working here unless they can establish entitlement under certain very restrictive categories, which are set out in the Immigration Rules. The most important category of people so qualifying are the close relatives of people settled in the UK, and the purpose of this article is to examine the principles on which such qualifications are based, their relationship to the people affected, and how the system works in practice.

The Limits of the Family

The family for this purpose includes the following relatives of a person settled here.
(1) The wife of a man who is a Commonwealth citizen who was settled in Britain before January 1983.
(2) The spouse of all other settlers, subject to certain rigorous restrictions and obstacles.
(3) Children under 18 where both parents are or will be settled in the UK (there are great difficulties in the way of settling a child only one of whose parents live here).
(4) In special circumstances, fully dependant and unmarried daughters over 18 and under 21.
(5) Dependent parents and other close relatives subject to restrictions and qualifications so rigorous that only a fraction of such dependent relatives can qualify.

It is not citizenship which determines the right to settlement in most cases, but the settled status of the 'sponsor'. 'Settled' means ordinarily resident in the UK without any restriction on one's stay.

All such family members must have entry clearances obtained

at a British post abroad before they set out; (see the section on entry clearance problems below).

Men who come to work, run a business or study here can bring their wives and families with them; there is no corresponding right for women. This effectively prevents women from establishing themselves here, unless they happen to be single.

These rules would seem to be based on the following ideas:—

(1) A man has more of a right to take his wife to live with him in the country where he lives and works than does a woman to take her husband.

(2) An arranged marriage is automatically under suspicion of being for immigration purposes which would disqualify a spouse from entry. It is up to the couple to prove otherwise, even where the marriage is acknowledged to be genuine and designed to last.

(3) Young children should be with their parents, but only if both parents are here; immigration control may be the deciding factor where only one parent is here.

(4) A close relative who is a dependent financially or otherwise of a person settled here has a much greater claim to live with her or him than does a similarly close relative who is not dependent.

(5) Children over 18, parents, grandparents and other relatives are not generally to be allowed to join members of the family settled here unless they can conform to the rigorous and rarely found conditions. Interestingly, such relationship is a qualification if the applicant is very rich; the presence of a close relative here constitutes a close connection with the UK which will qualify a person of independent means – who must have more than £150,000 in capital – to admission where they would not otherwise qualify.

The family model the rules fit, is, then, that of a male-dominated middle class, British nuclear family, where other relatives apart from mother, father and young children are of little importance. Who is it that this model fits? It looks like the model of a society which has probably never existed at all but perhaps seemed, in the early 1960s, to be just around the corner for a certain section of middle-class British society; the society from which civil servants and MPs are mainly drawn. For most people even in the UK grand-parents and other relatives have always been important in the lives of most children, and grandchildren have always been of vital importance to grandparents. Grown-up children are frequently deeply attached to their parents and vice versa. Above all, children in their twenties are still closely dependent on their parents, emotionally if not financially and often both. It should be emphasised that we are not talking here

170

about whether members of the same family should live together in the same house, but simply whether they may be allowed to live in the same country. No one can maintain an effective relationship with a grandchild if they live many thousands of miles away.

At this point it may be of interest to speculate about just who it is who decides on the content of the Immigration Rules. It might be assumed that they were the result of careful consultation and sociological study. But this does not appear to be so. The rules are produced by a system of vetoes; the civil service seems to invent the details of them normally without any consultation and produces either a set of rules to lay before the House of Commons or (occasionally) a White Paper. Representations made by pressure groups are normally ignored and it is rarely possible at this stage to modify the scheme in any significant way. Once the rules have been laid before Parliament they can be disapproved but this debate always centres on at most two or three very controversial points, usually connected with the rules concerning spouses. The fundamental scheme of the rules is never properly debated and never challenged, and details relating to peripheral relatives are never given proper attention. They may be examined in various aspects later by the Home Affairs Select Committee, but the creative act of writing the rules is done by nameless civil servants without any intervention of the democratic process and usually they get through almost unchanged.

This is of course true of much of our rule making. It usually happens when the subject is one to which the main body of articulate opinion in the country is indifferent (as here) or is thought to be too difficult or complex (as here) though really few subjects are simpler.

This seems a strange way to arrive at the principles which cause so much misery and distress. One would at least expect that some careful consideration was given to them by our elected representatives.

Whom do the rules fit?

The family model adumbrated by the rules is a sort of caricature of a male-dominated middle class British family. But are the Immigration Rules there primarily to control the immigration of such families?

Immigration control is there to prevent the immigration of anyone considered undesirable. For the last few years it has been frankly admitted (at least by Conservative politicians) that it is there to prevent the 'indigenous' population being 'swamped' by people from the Indian sub-continent. In fact of course people come to the UK from every country in the world and the picture of people affected by the Rules is infinitely more complex. At present, however, the largest numbers do come from the Indian sub-continent.

If the Rules are there to cope with the Indian sub-continent surely they ought to conform to its family models. For what is the point of having a model to protect family life (if this is the purpose) if it operates to separate the families to which it is applied?

At the risk of being obvious it must be pointed out here that the family in the Indian sub-continent is still one in which the oldest male is dominant and the head of the family until his death. His sons and daughters of whatever age regard themselves as members of his family until his death (in the case of the sons) or their marriage (in the case of the daughters). Mothers expect their sons to live in the same family house or at least the same compound all their lives, and their daughters to make long visits to the family home. They expect that their grandchildren will grow up under their eye. The health and welfare of elderly parents are of the most vital importance to their grown-up children; these elderly parents are naturally the head and centre of the family until their death. This is a matter of age-old tradition; as a client from Bangladesh wrote to his wife: 'I heard that mother and father are ill. Always take care of them. Because their days are ending. If they are not pleased with us now and curse us then we will be the sufferers.'

There will obviously be many other pressures keeping families apart; many old people find this country unbearably cold, lonely or unsociable, compared to the life of the village. In my experience no grandparents from the Sylhet district of Bangladesh (from which most Bengalis here come) will come and join the family here. These grandparents expect that their children will bring all the grandchildren back to see them every few years (despite the enormous drain this is on the family's financial resources) and in the meantime or where circumstances do not permit this, they concentrate their attention on the children of other sons and daughters who have not left the home country. Again and again one finds that a sponsor who is bringing his family here is prevailed upon by his parents, usually by his mother, to leave one or two children behind so that she does not lose all her grandchildren at once.

To summarise, then, the Rules do not keep intact the sub-continental families for which they were apparently intended, and nor do they cater for ordinary British families, where the woman may be the breadwinner, or where the child may wish to live with the parent settled in this country rather than the other parent at home.

EEC families

It has been a remarkable feature of our law on this subject since 1972 that the Rules for the admission of members of the family of other EEC nationals are very much more liberal than those for the admission of the families of people settled here, even when these are British citizens. The rules for EEC nationals follow, of course, the penumbra of the family as laid down in the EEC legislation. For some years the Home Office tried to shield the ordinary relative in the street from full appreciation of this situation by actually misrepresenting the European legislation in the summary which appeared in the Immigration Rules under the section applying to EEC nationals. This stated that the family of an EEC national 'should be regarded as consisting of his *wife*, their children under 21, their other children if still dependent, and their dependent parents and grandparents.' After protest Home Office changed this in the 1980 rules (HC 394) to read 'a person's spouse' instead of 'his wife'.

Now if it is hard to explain to a woman whose home is in this country, who may have lived here since she was a small child that she cannot bring her foreign husband to live here, how much harder is it to explain that a French or Irish woman can bring *her* husband (no matter what his nationality) and immediately procure for him a five-year residence permit and thereafter settlement? There will be no back-breaking process of application for entry clearance, intrusive interviewing and years of delay; no period of probation followed by further interviews. The happy couple can simply present themselves at a port armed with evidence of the wife's employment and valid identity documents. One example of this I remember which amused me very much was that of a Polish woman who had come here as an au-pair two or three years before, contracted a marriage with an Irish citizen which had been speedily dissolved and then came to me for advice on getting in her Polish fiancé. As she was an Irish citizen and had a job this was automatic. At this time, however, I was dealing with the cases of a number of young women who had either been born here or had lived here since they were small children and were encountering great difficulties in getting permission for their Indian husbands to join them.

These husbands had to prove a negative – that they did not marry in order to obtain entry to Britain – to sceptical entry clearance officers who tend to assume that men from third world countries only want to come here to work and that arranged marriages are synonymous with marriages of convenience. In 1984 46% of husbands and fiancés applying in the Indian sub-continent were refused entry clearance, 89% of these on primary purpose grounds.

New immigration rules, in force since August 1985, extend the 'primary purpose' requirement to the entry of some wives and provide that couples must be able to support and accommodate themselves – most husbands will therefore have to obtain employment before entry, putting themselves at greater risk of being excluded because the 'primary purpose' of their marriage is to come to Britain and find work.

On other relatives, the contrast with the EEC rules is even more marked. Any 'dependent' parent or grandparent is to be admitted, with no requirement for entry clearance, and no oppressive restrictions. A parent of a British citizen, by contrast, must fulfil very detailed criteria relating to dependants, must also show they are 'without other close relatives in their own country to turn to', and must normally be over 65. If they are not over 65 they must 'have a standard of living substantially below that of their own country' or 'be living alone in the most exceptional compassionate circumstances'. So if an elderly person in India wishes to settle in the UK her best method would be to marry her daughter to a West German citizen and then persuade the son-in-law to get a job in the UK.

The same observations apply to children over 18; children of EEC nationals under 21 do not even have to be dependent (whereas normally children of British nationals have to be under 18). Under the EEC rules, dependent children of any age are admitted.

Now if the UK agrees with other European governments that these outlines adequately cover the family members of a person working in the UK who should be allowed to accompany them, why has it never been prepared to extend them to relatives of other residents, even its own nationals?

Problems in Practice

These are in three main classes; non-entitlement (where the Rules do not cover a family member but the family is desperately anxious for the person's admission), verification (where the authorities will not accept either the identity or the other qualifications of the applicant) and entry clearance procedures.

It will be obvious that there must be many non-entitlement problems. Elderly parents (usually one parent only) who have relatives in the country of origin but desperately want to be with the child here, and older children left alone in the country of origin while all their family settles here are the two most problematic categories.

Verification and entry clearance problems are usually two aspects of the same thing.

Verification and Entry Clearance

Everyone coming here to settle must have an entry clearance obtained at a post abroad before that person sets out. This is supposed to make it easier to verify their claim. In practice at present the majority of such problems arise in Dhaka, where the applications of the dependants of Sylheti men who settled here in the mid 1950s and early 1960s are processed. Overwhelmingly problems are arising because entry clearance officers don't believe that the wife or child in question (and they are almost all wives or children) is related as claimed. The uselessness of documentation and the prevalence of the practice of claiming tax relief for wives and children one had not in fact got have contributed to a nightmare situation in which immigration officers see themselves as fighting a war against a tide of people not entitled to enter the UK. It is against that background that the horror stories of that war have to be judged; the bullying and long interrogations, the ludicrous x-ray estimations of age, the interminable detailed questions, the incompetent village investigations and above all the incredible delays. It takes two years to get to first interview, and in most cases where the marriage is an old one the case is then deferred for further enquiries which may take years, then one or more further interviews, and the result can be interminable delay. I am at present engaged on a case where the application was made in April 1974 and which has only now reached the Immigration Appeal Tribunal.

Conclusion

Clearly, if the purpose of the Immigration Rules is to protect the family, it is not doing its job; it protects only the well-documented, Northern nuclear family. As a result much suffering is caused which could mainly be avoided if the EEC system which Britain applies to relatives of the nationals of EEC states applied also to citizens of Britain.

175

Immigration Appeals – The Need for Reform

CHARLES BLAKE

School of Law and Social Science, Ealing College of Higher Education

Introduction

In recent years disquiet has been expressed about the system of immigration appeals. It has not been subjected to detailed scrutiny since it began to operate some 13 years ago, although other areas of tribunal jurisdiction (notably Social Security) have come under close examination and have been substantially reformed. Immigrant organisations and appellants criticise the system for its failure to follow accepted legal norms. The absence of the appellant in appeals from abroad and the low success rate overall are the most notable criticisms although a more detailed survey of existing attacks on the system is made below. The Home Office is not happy with the system either. It is seen as too expensive and too slow and too favourable to appellants already here, though the suggestions put forward in 1981 have not been acted upon.[1]

It is worth remembering that no amount of changes to the appeal system will satisfy those who consider the structure of control unfair, unjust and racialist in character. But such a critique should not be allowed to obscure the fact that even an unjust system needs to operate according to its own criteria and to be seen as so operating. Therefore the general standard of decision-making, the basis on which decisions on disputed matters of fact are reached and the abilities and qualifications of those appointed to make decisions should be examined with care. Even the low success rate has its own significance – it is not so low as to enable or entitle critics to write off the system entirely.[2]

The Origins of the System

The report of the Wilson Committee[3] is the basis of the present system. The report makes curious reading. The focus was upon reassurance of immigrants and their families, not upon the possibility that errors, bias, even prejudice could enter into the decision-making process. The establishment of the Committee is itself curious. In 1965 the debate on the Queen's Speech produced a proposal by the government (having by then abandoned its opposition to the 1962 Act) for an inquiry into the administration of controls.[4] Quite how this became transformed into a proposal to establish an inquiry into an appellate structure is a mystery and will remain so until papers are released in due course. One product of this happening had been to remove the primary decision-making process from all scrutiny. Even the Commission for Racial Equality has had great difficulty in observing the civil service at work as part of its investigation.

Whatever the reasoning of and reasons for creating the Wilson Committee, its firm proposal for an independent appellate structure must be seen as a positive step. But the committee made several errors.

(1) It failed to foresee how technical and complex the corpus of immigration law would become.
(2) It imagined that most appeals would be 'instant' in nature following a refusal at a port. This was partly because it would have allowed immigrants to remain, in order to contest such decisions and partly because entry certificates were to be voluntary only. In the event the former proposal was part of the Immigration Appeals Act 1969 but was never implemented (one suspects because of Home Office dilatoriness). The latter proposal was not followed, the government introducing compulsory certification at a late stage of the passage of the 1969 Act.
(3) It underestimated the difficulty of determining disputed factual matters in the absence of the appellant.
(4) It did not foresee (perhaps it would not have welcomed) the growth of representations to the Minister, often in cases which had already been before the appellate authorities. This alternative appeals system is given further attention below.

Some Problems of the System

In this part I try to set out all the criticisms of the appeals systems known to me. In the final part I try to evaluate these criticisms.

(1) The system has always operated with little public scrutiny or even interest. The work of adjudicators and Tribunal Chairmen is seen as low grade by many lawyers. By contrast

the work of social security and industrial tribunals is seen as much more significant, both legally and socially.

(2) Access to decisions of the Tribunal and the courts (on judicial review) is very difficult. The annual Immigration Appeal Reports appear on a far from annual basis. (Compare the speed with which Industrial and Social Security reports are produced). Decisions of the courts are even less accessible. Few seem to attract the interest of the law reporters.

(3) The other personnel involved within the system are also open to criticism. There is no legal aid available. The government has preferred to put its financial resources into funding UKIAS. But its staff are mostly underpaid and the overall level of support for the service is not high. It cannot always devote the time needed to detailed preparation of complex cases. Its staff inevitably vary in quality and competence. It must be an open question whether substitution of legal aid and existing legal services for the Service would produce a better standard of representation. Presenting officers also vary in quality. Few can cope with complex legal arguments. They too have inadequate opportunities for preparing their cases. Often they do not follow their own internal instructions in failing to draw attention to all relevant Tribunal and High Court determinations. The point that emerges here is that good quality work on individual cases can only be done with adequate resources. The best work done recently by UKIAS has been its painstaking investigation of many family cases in the Indian sub-continent. It seems that further funds for such work will not be provided. Yet without such back up many individual cases will be lost for want of proof. This is a matter of great importance and seriousness.

(4) The selection of adjudicators is in the hands of the Home Office. This is often criticised as diminishing the independence of the appellate authorities. But it does not follow that a Home Office appointee will be a puppet or a cypher. What seems equally important is *who* gets appointed in terms of quality and competence. Clearly this is linked to the issue of who makes the appointment. But there is no evidence to show that any other body or person is able to carry out the work of appointment any more successfully. A possibly more important criticism is that the normal pattern of a three person first-tier body with an appeal to a further three (one in Social Security) person body is reversed. Lay members sit on the Tribunal although it is primarily concerned with legal issues. Adjudicators sit alone and carry a heavy burden of

resolving disputed issues of fact and discretion. It has been suggested that juries (or their equivalent) should decide disputed issues of fact and of merit in deportation cases. This is an argument worth considering.

(5) The speed at which the appeal proceeds and the presentation of the official case is entirely in the hands of the Home Office. The appellate authorities have no control over the length of time taken to prepare explanatory statements. Whilst the giving of notice of appeal to the Home Office generates an internal review and, in some cases, a change of decision by the authorities, the inability to control its own cases is a mark of weakness on the part of the appeals system.

(6) The explanatory statement itself is an extraordinary document. Hardly ever tested by cross-examination (often because representatives do not ask for it) it contains a mixture of facts, assertion, law, hearsay, conclusion and inference. Paradoxically the evidence is often of a higher quality in port appeals because there has been insufficient time to prepare an explanatory statement. Further, those who prepare the statements (not always those who took the decision) have little or no knowledge of the case law of the Tribunal or of the courts. These problems are coupled with the lack of control over the conduct of interviews and village visits abroad. The Tribunal has heard many family appeals but has failed to give any worthwhile guidance on the standard of proof, the relevance of documentary evidence and of alleged discrepancies between the version of the family relationship given by one interviewee and another.

In this connection the tape-recording of interviews would only be a partial solution.[5] It would be equally important to know the guidance given to Entry Clearance Officers and the manner in which family members ought to be interviewed – assuming, of course, that lengthy inquiries are to continue to be made in each case. Little work seems to have been done in this area. (A separate note is given below on family cases.)

(7) It is frequently impossible to come to sensible agreements about pending appeals. The Home Office cannot easily be contacted by telephone. Presenting officers have no authority to act without reference back to the Home Office. Ian Macdonald explains this on the basis that one party is saying 'you should not be here' whilst the other is saying 'I am entitled to enter or to remain.'[6] According to him the differences between the parties are very great.

(8) Some recent decisions of the Tribunal and of the courts have shown some confusion about the exact basis of the appellate

authorities' functions. Can an adjudicator exercise a discretion where it has not been exercised by the Home Office?[7] Can an adjudicator receive fresh evidence of a matter not before the Home Office?[8] What is the distinction between true fresh evidence and new evidence of an existing fact?[9] Connected with this is the dismal failure of the Tribunal to establish any criteria for the exercise of broad discretions in such areas as deportation, returning residents, foreign husbands (especially the nature of a 'marriage of convenience').[10] A weak judicial body will, in effect, never do more than rubber-stamp previously taken official decisions without making clear why it approves that decision.

(9) The appellate authorities have no control over the exercise of discretion by the Home Office outside the Rules. There are several areas where the Rules are very tightly drawn yet the Home Office on a more or less regular basis (sometimes published) departs from the Rules in favour of some class of persons or individual.[11] The legality of this is very much in doubt[12] but it is a practice which has not been challenged for fear of the withdrawal of 'concessions'. It is a thoroughly bad basis for openness in immigration control, even if it benefits some immigrants.

(10) The role of the Tribunal within the system has never been clear. It must grant leave to appeal (as must an adjudicator) when an arguable point of law is involved, when entry clearance is held up and in one or two other cases.[13] It may do so in other cases and its jurisdiction in this regard is quite arbitrary and unpredictable. It can receive new evidence but it cannot, strictly speaking, hear appeals on fact alone. Whilst this is a characteristic of other branches of civil law it is different in e.g., appeals from magistrates to the Crown Court. The issues are no less important.

(11) There is no appeal on a point of law to the High Court – only judicial review is available. Whilst this is less significant than it used to be (because of reforms to judicial review procedures) it is anomalous in relation to other tribunals.

(12) Appeals by dependants need a fuller analysis – a start on this is made below.

Dependants: Wives and children

Introduction

Under paragraph 44 of HC 394: "The wife of a person who is settled in the United Kingdom or is on the same occasion being admitted for settlement if the requirements of paragraphs 42 and 43 are satisfied." Under paragraph 42 the husband must be able and willing to maintain and accommodate the wife, and paragraph 43 imposes the holding of a current entry clearance as a condition of admission.

The admission of children is governed by paragraph 46:
". . . children under 18, provided that they are unmarried, are to be admitted for settlement

(a) if both parents are settled in the United Kingdom, or
(b) if both parents are on the same occasion admitted for settlement, or
(c) if one parent is settled in the United Kingdom and the other is on the same occasion admitted for settlement, or
(d) if one parent is dead and the other parent is settled in the United Kingdom or is on the same occasion admitted for settlement."

The other circumstances in which children are eligible for admission as dependants, for example where it has to be proven that there had been sole responsibility or that exclusion is undesirable are dealt with elsewhere as quite different considerations apply in such cases.

The issues in dispute in the appeals of wives and children rarely involve points of law. The interpretation of the relevant paragraphs of the immigration rules is seldom questioned. Typically, the appellants will have been refused entry clearance on the ground that the Entry Clearance Officer was not satisfied that they were related to their sponsor in the United Kingdom as claimed. The questions at issue therefore in appeals against refusals of entry clearance are often exclusively of a factual and evidential nature. The question to be answered is: was the evidence such that the Entry Clearance Officer should have been satisfied that the appellants were related to the sponsor?

There is, therefore, only limited scope for examining the extent to which the interpretation of the rules has imposed additional burdens upon particular ethnic groups. Nonetheless, the approach of the Tribunal even to factual and evidential questions may be relevant in so far as it endorses or allows the use of unfair practices and procedures in the processing of applications, thus putting applicants at a disadvantage.

The Burden of Proof

The burden of proving that the claimed relationship exists is upon the applicants. The onus is upon the applicants to produce the evidence which supports their claim to be eligible for admission.

181

The standard of Proof

The existence of the claimed relationship must be proved on the balance of probabilities. In *Syed Bashar Hussain* (Divisional Court 19.9.72, unreported) the court agreed with the Tribunal's view that this was the proper standard of proof to apply: "this is essentially a civil matter and proof on the balance of probabilities is in my judgment the right test to apply in those circumstances . . ."

In practice most difficulties arise over the application of the standard of proof, the matter at issue being whether the standard of proof has been satisfied by the appellants.

Entry Clearance Procedure

Understanding the significance of Tribunal decisions in this area will be facilitated by a brief description of the procedure followed in the processing of applications for entry clearance from wives and children. The procedure described is that typically used in the Indian sub-continent (in particular Bangladesh), from which the vast majority of such applications originate. Applications from other countries are both few in number and rarely the subject of dispute as the production of documentary evidence of the claimed relationship will generally suffice to satisfy the Entry Clearance Officer.

Once an application is made the applicants will some time later be called for interview (at present the waiting period for interviews in Dacca is about 15 months). They will be expected to produce documentary evidence that they are related to the sponsor as claimed and will be questioned in depth about their family tree and other details of their family life.

The sponsor may also be interviewed, either at the High Commission or in the United Kingdom. Depending on his assessment of the evidence the Entry Clearance Officer will either grant entry clearance or refuse to do so on the ground that he is not satisfied that the applicants are related to the sponsor as claimed. In general the refusal is based on alleged discrepancies in statements made during interviews with the Entry Clearance Officer.

The Tribunal and the standard of Proof

From an examination of the Tribunal's decision in this area, it is difficult if not impossible to derive any principles of general application regarding the standard of proof. Each case is treated as being decided entirely according to its own particular facts. No comparison is made with the facts of previous cases and precedent is not relied upon one way or another. It is difficult to discover the principles according to which one appeal fails and another succeeds. The reasons why the evidence in one case is accepted as meeting the standard of proof but the evidence in another is not, are rarely made explicit. The Tribunal's written determinations in such cases appear to follow a regular pattern. Typically the evidence, both oral and documentary, is described at length, often with no comment on its strength. This is followed by a statement to the effect that the Tribunal is (or is not, as the case may be) satisfied that the Adjudicator's decision was correct. The reasons for this decision may amount to no more than this. The following is a typical example:

"We have carefully considered all the facts of this case but in view of the multitude of unexplained discrepancies no reasonable person could be satisfied on the balance of probabilities that the appellants are related to the sponsor as claimed." (*Abr. Hassain (1201)*)

One explanation for the reluctance of the Tribunal to lay down any principles as to what evidence meets the standard of proof may be the importance generally attached to oral evidence by adjudicators. Where an adjudication has been based by the adjudicator largely upon the sponsor's evidence and his assessment of its credibility, the Tribunal is usually reluctant to interfere with his decision. The Tribunal's approach has been summed up in this way:

"The Tribunal has on many previous occasions indicated the manner in which they approach appeals when they involve simply matters of fact. It will not interfere with the adjudicator's findings of fact, unless it is considered that no reasonable adjudicator properly directing himself could have come to the conclusions reached. The reason for this is that in most cases the adjudicator has seen and heard witnesses examined and has been able to form a view as to their veracity. . . ." (*Karima Bibi (1281)*)

Thus in Abdul Haque (1972) the Tribunal concluded that:

"In our opinion the outcome of this appeal which depended entirely upon the determination of matters of fact, rested to a very great extent upon the sponsor's credibility. The adjudicator who heard the sponsor giving evidence (an advantage which we have not enjoyed) found that he could give little credence to his evidence . . . we are unable to find that the findings of fact were so unreasonable that we should upset them."

The Tribunal has also shown deference to what is perceived as the more advantageous position of the Entry Clearance Officer:

"In cases like the instant one the decision of an entry clearance officer is not lightly to be overturned. He is the man on the spot with particular knowledge of the local people and conditions, and actually interviews those seeking entry to the United Kingdom . . . it cannot be stated that there are no grounds, or insufficient grounds upon which the Entry Clearance Officer could have reached the conclusion which he did reach." (*Dorud Miah (1297)*)

The effect of the Tribunal's approach, the typical reliance by adjudicators on the oral evidence and the Tribunal's reluctance to interfere with the findings of fact made by adjudicators, is that success or failure of an appeal will depend to a very large extent on the ability of the sponsor to convince the adjudicator of his honesty and truthfulness.

The Tribunal has endorsed the importance of the sponsor's oral evidence in such cases, and indeed of the oral evidence given to the Entry Clearance Officer. This evidence will comprise discrepancies in statements about the family tree of the applicants and in details provided about family life, such discrepancies being treated as evidence that the applicants and sponsor are not related.

The Tribunal has indicated that while every single discrepancy need not be explained it is expected that the sponsor should provide an explanation for the major discrepancies.

"In the absence of a credible explanation together with reliable documentary evidence the adjudicator should not be satisfied of the existence of the claimed relationship." (*Mohd. Iqbal (87)*). Hence the importance normally attached to the oral evidence of the sponsor.

Where there are few or no discrepancies in accounts of family details, this need not of itself be regarded as adequate proof of the claimed relationship. The Tribunal has said that:

"Consistency in family trees given by a sponsor and an applicant for entry clearance could indicate rehearsal by the parties of inaccurate details to be put forward."

Documentary Evidence

Documentary evidence presented in support of applications may include marriage certificates, birth certificates, affidavits, details of the sponsor's tax claims and correspondence between family members. Entry Clearance Officers regard documentary evidence originating from the Indian sub-continent as being easily obtainable and therefore of poor evidential value. Little can be said about the approach of the Tribunal as no general principles have been laid down as to the acceptability of various forms of documentary evidence.

Evidence accepted in one case as being of probative value may

184

not be accepted in another. In general the Tribunal has shared the views of Entry Clearance Officers and adjudicators regarding the value of documentation originating in the Indian sub-continent. Again this has the effect of placing particular importance on the oral evidence and the resolution of alleged discrepancies.

Legal Evidence

As indicated, points of law seldom arise in cases of this nature. It is instructive however to look at three aspects of the Tribunal's interpretation of the rules applicable to dependants.

(a) It may happen that the sponsor does not wish to bring all his children to the United Kingdom at once. The personal or family reasons why this may be so can be readily appreciated. However, the children he wishes to come are only eligible for admission if their mother is at the same time being admitted for settlement. In such circumstances the sponsor's wife may apply to come to the United Kingdom at the same time in order to ensure the admission of the children. It may be the intention of the family that the wife should return to her own country in order to look after young children, or, say, elderly parents. The Tribunal has held that where this is also the case, the applicant's children are not eligible for admission as their mother is not "being admitted for settlement" within the meaning of the relevant rule. The wife's application for settlement could not succeed as it was not a "genuine application for settlement". Rather, according to the Tribunal, the arrangement described above was "simply a device to circumvent the requirements of paragraph 38 relating to children who would otherwise be inadmissible to join one parent only for settlement". (*Anavat Bibi (1994)*)

The Tribunal rejected the argument that the wife should be admitted for settlement if the criterion laid down in the rules are satisfied.

Such families (and given the nature and pattern of immigration from the Indian sub-continent there are many) are thus prevented from organising their family affairs in the way that is both most desirable and most convenient for the whole family.

(b) Some applicants may apply in a name other than their own. This may be because the sponsor has previously made false tax claims for a wife and/or children which at the time he did not have, a not wholly uncommon practice in the case of men arriving from Bangladesh in the early sixties. It is then felt

185

desirable that the sponsor's wife and children should use the names previously sent to the tax authorities.

In *Sabura Khatum* (2276) the Tribunal held that where the applicant's children (which the Tribunal accepted as related to the sponsor) had impersonated other sons of the sponsor, they were not applicants or indeed appellants at all. Neither their applications nor their appeals could therefore succeed.

In *Khanom* (2381) this rule was extended to cover those cases where no impersonation had taken place but where the applicants had merely used names different from the ones they were normally known by. The Tribunal based its decision on the "practical view" that entry clearance could not be stamped on a passport that did not bear the holder's true name.

In *Hasreen Akhtar* (2460) the Tribunal affirmed the above principle. The submission that the issue was one of relationship and that the practical problems could be resolved was rejected. Instead the Tribunal found that the appellant was a figment of the sponsor's imagination and that "she did not in reality exist". In order for entry clearance to be granted the appellant would have to apply again in her real name, even in those cases where the real name has been revealed to the Entry Clearance Officer before the decision.

The effect of this ruling is that at the very least genuine applicants will have to wait a further 18 months (which is the current delay in processing applications in Dacca) to be issued with entry clearance, while in some cases their eligibility for entry clearance will have lapsed by reason, for example, of having exceeded the age-limit while waiting for an appeal to be heard.

(c) As indicated, there are long waiting lists for applications from dependants to be processed in the Indian sub-continent, particularly in Bangladesh. The tribunal has held that where the applicant has ceased to be eligible for admission by the time a decision is made on his application he is no longer entitled to entry clearance: *Abdur Rashid* (1947) where the applicant's son had become over-age by the time his application was decided. The current immigration rules (H.C. 394 paragraph 12) reverse the above decision to the extent that an applicant does not now cease to be eligible for entry clearance by reason of having passed the age-limit between applying and having his case decided. However it remains the case that an applicant may cease to be eligible for reasons other than age, for example because he is no longer a dependant or is no longer unmarried.

186

Conclusions

The rules relating to the admission of wives and children may be regarded as having been interpreted and applied so as to impose a higher burden on certain ethnic groups for the following reasons.

1. The great majority of applications originate from the Indian sub-continent, particularly Bangladesh. Documentary evidence originating in these countries is regarded in general as suspect and therefore of little probative value by entry clearance officers, who therefore determine applications on the basis of lengthy interviews with applicants and sponsors. This approach, regarded by many as inherently unfair and discriminatory, has been endorsed and encouraged by the Tribunal, which typically gives primary weight to the oral evidence and is reluctant to interfere with assessments of the credibility of witnesses by adjudicators or entry clearance officers, and normally avoids coming to different conclusions on factual questions.

2. The Tribunal has failed to lay down clear guidelines as to what evidence can be accepted as meeting the standard of proof. Instead, each case is treated as bearing entirely upon its own particular facts. Applicants cannot therefore be aware of what evidence should be produced in order to prove their case. Once again, therefore, emphasis is put on a subjective assessment of credibility, and consistency in decision-making cannot be guaranteed.

3. The Tribunal's ruling regarding "courier" wives prevents families from arranging their affairs in the way they choose. It discriminates against families from the Indian sub-continent as the situation to which the rule applies will in practice be likely to occur only among families from there.

4. The Tribunal's ruling that applicants who apply in a different name are not applicants at all may result in the separation of genuine applicants from their father/husband. It discriminates against families from the Indian sub-continent to the extent that, once again, the situation to which the ruling is applicable is only likely to arise there, particularly in Bangladesh.

5. The ruling that the eligibility for entry clearance is to be determined in the light of the applicant's circumstances at the time of decision discriminates against applicants from the Indian sub-continent, where the queues for entry clearance are longest.

Conclusions and Recommendations

I am pessimistic about achieving major changes to and within the present appeals system. It is not realistic to believe that appellants will be enabled to be present at the hearing of appeals from abroad.

Any reforms must start from the position that there will never be a full appeal with all parties present and the procedure to be adopted must reflect this fact. Certain improvements to the right of appeal are needed. Thus refugees, returning residents, those returning during the currency of an existing leave all need fuller rights of appeal than they now have. Equally the position of work permit and special voucher applicants, late applicants, those refused on medical grounds and those arriving without entry clearance for a short-term purpose could all be assimilated to the better rights of appeal of other appellants.[14]

Better quality personnel are badly needed within the appeals system and considerable thought needs to be given to:

(1) The existing practice about evidence of family relationships.[15]
(2) Changing the basis for the appointment of adjudicators.
(3) Allowing adjudicators to exercise discretion outside the Rules (now prohibited).
(4) Dissolving UKIAS in favour of legal aid but restricting the grant of it to certificated practitioners (as is the case with Mental Health Review Tribunals).
(5) Opening up the procedures used for investigating applicants at ports and abroad.
(6) Introducing cross-examination into appeals wherever possible. Again it is unlikely that entry clearance officers will frequently be present.
(7) Allowing appeals to be lodged with the appellate authorities and not with the Home Office.
(8) At the same time introducing a Registrar of appeals to administer such a system. The function of that office would be to receive notice of appeal, to impose a time limit on the Home Office for preparation of the case and to deal with procedural applications for discovery of documents, cross-examination of Home Office officials and whether late appeals should be allowed to proceed. There might be a summary procedure for dealing with plainly misconceived appeals.
(9) Granting a right of appeal to the courts on a point of law.
(10) Introducing a lay element at the level of adjudicator.
(11) Spending much more money on advice and investigative agencies overseas. The question of cost is often ignored. An appeal system cannot be operated cheaply if, as is essential, appellants are given the means to challenge Home Office factual conclusions. Yet the system of entry clearance officers whilst not expensive in terms of personnel is very lavish in the time allocated to interviews and inquiries. How does this compare with the time spent in investigating, say, tax evasion?

(12) Introducing some kind of appeal on the facts against an adjudicator's decision.
(13) Giving alleged illegal entrants a full right of appeal before removal. Above all the Home Office needs to be persuaded (as the DHSS was in the case of Supplementary Benefit Appeal Tribunals) that matters are seriously amiss. It is the inertia within that department that leads me to my deepest pessimism.

Notes

The section on dependants' appeals was originally prepared by Jim Gillespie, legal worker with JCWI. I am grateful to him for this work and for many discussions on the immigration appeals system.
1 In 1981 the Home Office issued a discussion document entitled, *Review of Appeals under the Immigration Act 1971* which proposed a reduction in appeal rights. In early 1984 it seemed that some more limited changes might be introduced by amending the existing rules of procedure. This was done later that year.
2 The overall success rate is about 15 per cent but is higher in family appeals (about 23 per cent) and lower in deportation appeals (about 3 per cent). There are about 18,000 appeals each year about half of which concern family cases.
3 *Report of the Committee on Immigration Appeals* (1967), (Cmnd 3387).
4 See *Hansard*, November 1965, *passim*.
5 Recently the Foreign Office has announced that an experiment in recording interviews has not been a success and will not be continued.
6 Ian A. Macdonald *Immigration Law and Practice*, (Butterworths, 1983), p. 297, note 15.
7 See *R.* v. *Immigration Appeal Tribunal*, ex parte *Kwok On Tong* [1981] Imm AR 214.
8 See *R.* v. *Immigration Appeal Tribunal*, ex parte *Weerasuriya* [1983] IALLER 195 and Macdonald, *op. cit.*, pp. 301–5.
9 See *R.* v. *Immigration Appeal Tribunal*, ex parte *Taj* (Court of Appeal, unreported, 30 June 1982).
10 See the criticism made by the Court of Appeal in *Mahmud Khan* [1983] 2WLR 759 of a decision of the Tribunal on an alleged marriage of convenience.
11 Numerous examples exist. See for example the practices described in Macdonald, *op. cit.*, pp. 228 and 232.
12 The Immigration Act 1971, s. 3(2) requires the Home Secretary to lay before Parliament statements of the rules laid down by him as to the practice to be followed in the administration of [the] Act. This, it is submitted, means *all* the rules and not merely some of them. For a fuller discussion of this point see C. Harlow and R. Rawlings, *Law and Administration*, (Weidenfeld and Nicolson, 1984) especially Ch. 17.
13 See The Immigration Act, 1971, s. 22(5) and Immigration Appeals (Procedure) Rules 1972 S.I. 1972/1684, r. 14.
14 Essentially, in all the cases mentioned there is either no right of appeal or its exercise is seriously limited.
15 In addition to the issues discussed in the text see, *Report of Immigration and Race Relations Sub-Committee of Home Affairs Committee of House of Commons* (1981–1982) (HC 90) and government reply (Cmnd 8725).

United Kingdom Immigration Controls and the Welfare State

HUGO STOREY

Harehills & Chapeltown Law Centre, Leeds

Introduction

Until the mid-1970s it was broadly true that immigration law impinged hardly at all on the provision of benefits and services in the UK. The post-war welfare state doctrine of Beveridge, Bevan and Butler was one of equal access to benefits and services for all those in need regardless of immigration status,[1] and this held fast. Today however there is a close tie-up at various points between immigration status and welfare entitlement. Those who are settled in the UK continue to enjoy equal access under the law, but they increasingly face checks and scrutiny, and other categories increasingly face disentitlement and exclusion. As a result welfare law advisers require knowledge of immigration law in a growing number of cases. There is now a recently published book[2] which provides a detailed practical guide for dealing with such cases, but in this chapter I wish to analyse the broader implications of such changes for social policy. Because the spread of immigration controls into the welfare state has arisen in an ad hoc way with little public debate and apparent lack of thought for the wider consequences, I begin by a brief description.

How These Controls Operate

To hear talk about immigration controls within the welfare state still surprises many people who assume the classic post-war doctrine still prevails in practice.[3] Such controls have two 'arms', one formed by immigration officials, the other by welfare state officials.

The immigration 'arm' of these controls is not new, although 1980 changes in the Immigration Rules[4] and computerisation have made it a growing cause of concern. A number of categories of people under the Rules are only allowed to stay further if they can show that they can maintain and accommodate themselves 'without recourse to public funds'. Such people are mainly those who can only stay temporarily, for example visitors and students; but they also include those who can hope to have limits on their stay removed after a period, for example fiancés after 12 months of marriage and most employment categories after four years of working.[4] The requirement that such persons be able to show that they can live here 'without recourse to public funds' involves immigration officials in checking not only whether people are *likely* to become a charge on public funds but also whether they have a *history* of using services or claiming certain benefits.

The welfare state 'arm' consists of a growing number of officials within welfare state agencies performing immigration control functions: benefit officers when dealing with claims for supplementary benefit by claimants who appear to have come from abroad; other DHSS staff when checking eligibility for certain national insurance benefits (including child benefit); staff at unemployment benefit offices when handling claims for unemployment benefit by people whom they suspect of being under a Home Office ban on work; administrative staff in hospitals when checking whether patients are eligible for free NHS treatment; deputy registrars when determining whether fiancé(e)s are able to marry in accordance with the Immigration Rules; Department of Employment staff when deciding whether to admit candidates to certain government training courses; various local authority housing officials when deciding whether to re-house persons or treat them as homeless or grant them housing benefit; school heads or their secretaries when deciding whether to enrol a child; local authority education administrators when assessing students for awards.

How often and how extensively such officials investigate people's immigration status varies from service to service and benefit to benefit. For DHSS staff who administer national insurance benefits, for example it arises infrequently and rarely goes further than a passport check. Whereas for DHSS staff who administer supplementary benefits for example, it arises frequently and often leads to liaison (via DHSS HQ) with the Home Office. There is also a great deal of variation in the contents of codes instructing them to perform such functions. Supplementary benefit staff are given mandatory instructions as part of a published 'S' manual;[5] local authority housing officials are merely encouraged to make checks on immigration status by Department of Environment 'guidance'.[6] Some welfare state officials seem to take on such functions without either orders or encouragement – in apparent response to a growing climate of opinion that this is part of their job.

Legal and Institutional Basis

Although passport checks of this last kind do seem to be occurring more often in fact,[7] it is important to note that very often they have a legal basis. They derive from legislation and jurisprudence which require welfare state officials to satisfy themselves that claimants or service-users have an appropriate immigration status. Sometimes this basis in law is direct and explicit, for example as in the supplementary benefit regulations which bid special treatment for 'persons from abroad'.[8] Sometimes it is direct but implicit, as in the Social Security Act 1975 and regulations on 'availability for work' into which Commissioners have read a requirement that claimants must be lawfully present and legally permitted to work by the Home Office.[9] Sometimes it is indirect but explicit, as in the October 1982 NHS regulations on charges for 'overseas visitors' which are amplified by a Manual which exempts from charges only specific immigration categories amongst those who lack ordinary residence.[10] Sometimes it is indirect and implicit (but none the less effective for that), as in the new regulation laid down for deciding whether students fulfil *both* a 'three years ordinary residence' test and a 'no educational purpose' test (I stress 'both' because the House of Lords ruling in the *Shah* (or *Akbarali*) case[11] did *not* sever entirely the link between residence and immigration status: it still excluded from 'ordinarily resident' those who reside here unlawfully. The 'no educational purpose' test, introduced in April 1983 (in respect of awards)[12] and May and July 1983 (in respect of fees and discretionary awards)[13] to nullify the effect of *Shah* on awards and fees, plainly entails that administrators check whether overseas applicants are here in accordance with the Immigration Rules on students).

Because of this legal framework, it would be folly to suppose that problems can be solved simply by ending 'passport checks'. As long as eligibility tests bringing in immigration status go on, so will some form of checks. Indeed, insisting on alternative evidence of date of entry and so on can often impose more on people than do passport checks, since it may lead to their having to swear affidavits or sign written statements.[14] It is perhaps for this reason that NHS administrators appear in some parts of the country at least to be ignoring Manual instructions not to ask for passports.

The Tie-Up

Out of immigration officials concerning themselves with welfare questions, and welfare officials concerning themselves with immigration questions, a system of liaison has developed between the Home Office (and sometimes immigration police) on the one hand and a variety of government offices on the other. The degree of transfer of information about immigrants' status varies, ranging from the Home Office at one extreme (which not only seeks and receives most personal information on immigration status but supplies it to other departments in a wide variety of circumstances)[15] to the Inland Revenue at the other extreme (which does not disclose such information except with claimant authorisation or a court order).[16] Approaches to liaison can vary within the same department. For example DHSS staff on the NHS side make contact with the Home Office but subject to safeguards including disciplinary action for infringements of the same;[17] whereas a special unit at DHSS HQ liaises freely with the Home Office over many cases referred to it by regional or local supplementary benefit offices. The trend seems towards more, not less transfer of information.[18] The specific exemption from protection of crime and security data given in the Data Protection Act is likely to make matters worse, and to lead to a further erosion in the respect for privacy and in the observance of confidentiality at present shown by government departments when it comes to immigrants.

Another factor fuelling this trend is the introduction of computerised information systems. For example since 1980 the Immigration Service Intelligence Unit has had a computer system for tracing overstayers. Also since 1980 the Immigration Service has been using a system called INDECS (Immigration and Nationality Department Electronic Computer System) for matching landing and embarkation cards. Both systems have links with the national Illegal Immigration Intelligence Unit based at New Scotland Yard which in turn has access to the Police National Computer's Wanted and Missing Persons Index. In addition the Home Office is about to computerise the Suspect Index (SI) used by immigration officers, so as to double its capacity to 36,000 names compiled and amended annually.[19] Computerisation of this kind has increased the technical capacity for regular and instant liaison between the two 'arms' of these internal controls, and the planned phasing in of machine-readable passports[20] will continue this process further over the remaining years of this decade and beyond.

Obviously, such developments raise questions about the wisdom of continuing a policy of criminalising those who breach the immigration laws at a time when many observers are saying that the immigration issue which dominated British politics for the last 15 years is now over. But what is at issue here is the spread of such a system into unrelated areas of government administration concerned with need, care, health and so on. Here the primary context is not controls applied *before* or *on* entry, but *after* entry. This context makes a qualitative difference. For example, there are obviously immigration policy arguments for and against making it a requirement for certain categories of people wishing to *enter* the UK that they support and accommodate themselves without recourse to some types of 'public funds'. Policy in recent times has increasingly moved towards making such requirements necessary for more and more categories.[21] But when such requirements are set for people *already here* an extra dimension is added which radically alters the nature of the issues at stake. Serious problems arise in limiting the powers of immigration authorities so that they do not encroach on civil liberties. Serious problems also arise over the implications for such a system of controls with respect to non-discriminatory provision of benefits and services. Immigration officials are increasingly making inquiries or receiving information about immigrants' use of benefits and services. And although we lack hard empirical research in this area, it is agreed by most people working on the ground in ethnic minority communities that the knowledge that such tie-ups exist deters certain people from using the welfare state when they need to, even where in fact they do have an entitlement.[22] Common perceptions of this tie-up by ethnic minorities and their advisers have not been helped by the vagueness of Home Office policy and the uncertainty of case-law on the phrase 'recourse to public funds'.[23]

Switching focus to the role played by welfare officials in this system of controls, it is important to note that it is not simply an 'outreach' one of *reporting* suspected offenders against immigration law to the Home Office or police, although this is a significant part of it. Increasingly they have to make a decision on immigration status for their own purposes, since eligibility can hinge on this factor. Alongside *means-tests* and other eligibility tests, we now have *status-tests*. The clearest example is in the field of supplementary benefits where the regulations refer directly to categories defined in the Immigration Act 1971.[24] But other examples arise, even where the tests are apparently unconnected to immigration status, as with most residence tests. Thus the *Shah*[25] case imported a 'lawfully resident' condition into the phrase 'ordinarily resident', thereby renewing the licence for welfare state officials to vet residents for possible offences of overstaying or illegal entry.

Nor must it be forgotten that our immigration law is far from clear about who falls into what category, 'illegal entrant' being a classic example. The courts, the Home Office and leading practitioners have struggled with this term for over a decade and the latest House of Lords case[26] has still left scope for confusion and uncertainty. Anybody conversant with immigrant law generally will know that ascertaining a person's correct immigration status by reading passports frequently requires a high degree of expertise as well as experience. Some of the efforts by welfare state officials to decipher immigration status from passport stamps would be ideal material for TV comedy were they not so damaging in their consequences for those concerned, as well as for the sense of security of ethnic minorities generally.

The increase in tie-ups also leads in practice to an increase in people caught up in bureaucratic confusion, sometimes of kafka-esque proportions. For example, a welfare official may doubt whether someone is observing immigration rules and so check with the Home Office: whereupon the Home Office may in turn treat the information thus obtained as evidence of 'recourse to public funds' in breach of Immigration Rules. This process can also be started from the Home Office end, although this is less common. They may want to check whether someone they consider an overstayer is known to the local DHSS; the local DHSS may in turn decide that the 'culprit' should not have had supplementary benefit after all, and may go on to refuse current benefit – and stick by that decision – even if subsequently the Home Office decide that the 'culprit' should be allowed to remain, for example on political asylum grounds. The people who get caught up in such confusions are a mixture of those who are innocent and those who are guilty of breaches of immigration control. But in either case they have only become entangled because they were in need and sought help from the welfare state system.

History

It is beyond my scope here to attempt a history of the growth of these controls except for a few comments which may help to give some perspective.

Certainly there are elements in this system of interlocking

controls that are not new. For instance, the practice of deputy registrars in checking immigration status and/or reporting on suspected marriages of convenience is long-standing.[27] And the 'availability for work' test for unemployment benefit has been tied to immigration law at least since 1957.[28] But key elements are new. It is quite misleading, for example, of the DHSS to say that the introduction of regulations in 1980 requiring special treatment of supplementary benefit claims by 'persons from abroad' simply put previous policy into statutory form. Before November 1980 the only legal basis for excluding those in need on the grounds of immigration status was the general discretionary power to deny benefit in individual cases;[29] and exclusions could be successfully overturned upon appeal. Neither was there previously any legal power to make sponsors liable to maintain dependants.[30] But even those elements that are not new have taken on an entirely different hue under the weight of tighter Immigration Rules and the growing numbers categorised as overstayers or illegal entrants between 1973 and 1982.[31] Against such a background, long-standing and apparently benign provisions (such as the 'availability for work' provision) are suddenly commandeered to exclude from benefit whole categories of people who have enjoyed an entitlement for decades.[32]

Any history of the rise of this type of control would have to record that despite the outcry by certain politicians and the media in the early and mid 1970s about '5-star Asians' etc., economists seem agreed that immigrants as a category make comparatively smaller demands on public funds than non-immigrants.[33] It would also need to emphasise that these controls have been mounted in the context of a welfare state system where immigrants generally face extra difficulties in getting access to benefits and services, because of language problems and greater problems in being able to verify particulars such as date of birth;[34] so that for ethnic minorities they are often seen as adding insult to injury.

Many a historian would doubtless find it ironic also that such controls began to gain a grip just around the same time that the UK Government had fought off EEC pressure to extend internal controls to the *place of work* – professedly for the reason that ethnic minorities would see such an extension as oppressive.[35] Yet no such concern was expressed when such controls began to extend to a far more personal sphere – *the point of need*!

Mismatch between Ideology and Practice

Despite their *ad hoc* growth, the official account given in

196

justification of extending such controls to the welfare state has been explicit and consistent. It will be most familiar to readers from the debates which preceded the ushering in of new NHS regulations for charging 'overseas visitors' in October 1982. I shall call it the 'permanent inhabitant' ideology after the phrase employed by ex-Home Office Minister Timothy Raison in a letter which continues to reflect current policy:[36]

> There is . . . a general principle running through the Rules that those who come here for temporary purposes are expected to be self-sufficient both as to maintenance and accommodation without calling for assistance or making use of services provided for what may loosely be called the permanent inhabitants.

Raison was talking about the requirement not to have 'recourse to public funds' which crops up in various Immigration Rules; but the same general principle has been invoked to justify exclusion of certain immigrants from supplementary benefit and free NHS treatment.

The problem about this justification is that the controls that have come to operate in welfare state territory do not discriminate only against so-called 'temporary inhabitants' (elsewhere referred to as 'gatecrashers', 'birds of passage', 'tourists', 'short-stay-visitors'). They apply much more extensively. Several Immigration Rules embracing a significant number of immigrants contemplate that people will come here for permanent residence but first undergo a 'probationary period' during which their permission to stay is limited in time (and sometimes subject to a ban on work and on recourse to public funds). Examples are fiancés, fiancées, work permit holders, business categories, and some refugees.[37] Such categories can find themselves denied even 'safety-net' benefits and services along with tourists and visitors. Work permit holders who become unemployed and cannot claim unemployment benefit are denied[38]; fiancés and husbands claiming unemployment benefit or supplementary benefit between marriage and receipt of a Home Office letter varying their three months leave to a 12 months leave which is no longer subject to work or public funds restrictions.[39]

There is a much more fundamental reason why the 'permanent inhabitant' ideology misrepresents reality. The immigration authorities take it for granted that the 'temporary inhabitants' most likely to become a charge on benefits and services will often be black people from third world countries. At the same time the bulk of post-war United Kingdom immigration has been permanent settler immigration and we now have a multi-racial society, in which over three million 'permanents' have either been born here to immigrant parents or have roots here several decades deep. They are predominantly the same colour – black – as are the 'temporaries' who are presumed to be among the most likely users of benefits and services. It follows inevitably from the racial composition of contemporary Britain that internal controls will frequently mistake 'permanents' for 'temporaries'. It will remain impossible to devise non-discriminatory tests which deny benefits and services only to short-stay visitors. Any such test must interfere in the enjoyment of equal rights of access to the welfare state by black Britons born or settled here.

It is sometimes suggested that this reality of discrimination could be solved by the introduction of a universal system of pass or identity cards verifying immigration status. Practices in some countries in western Europe are cited to placate fears that such a system might mean a lurch towards South African style apartheid. Apart from the fact that in a United Kingdom context it would subject the entire population to a considerable reduction in personal freedom, it is difficult to envisage how such a system could avoid selective enforcement in practice so that it once again bore most heavily against – and so discriminated against – black people in this country.

As intimated earlier, the inability of any system of tests to avoid netting 'permanents' along with 'temporaries' has not been solved by the change in some fields from direct and/or explicit tests to indirect and/or implicit ones. Thus most residence tests, even if purged of the implied 'lawfulness' test left intact by the *Shah* decision,[40] still discriminate against 'permanent inhabitant' immigrants – because as a group such people are less able to fulfill residence conditions:[41] significant numbers of them have not been here long enough[42] or they have had to be absent abroad for family reasons.

The various tests in operation at present also in practice discriminate more than they would against certain groupings of 'permanent inhabitants' because of the foothold of racism. The perceived increase in the incidence of passports checks cannot be explained in terms of legal changes alone. The 1980 supplementary benefit regulations, for example, barely affect 'permanent inhabitant' immigrants at all. Nevertheless it is they who often experience difficulties under the guise of these regulations. It seems that when regulations bid DHSS staff in local offices to 'watch out' for immigrant claimants in certain contexts, some staff interpret this as a licence to 'watch out' for them in others. There is also a knock-on effect. Regulations which specify nothing about immigrants are interpreted or applied in new ways largely with immigrants in mind. An example is the use of threats of prosecution for failure to maintain a liable spouse against husbands who go abroad, even where such trips are accepted as being genuinely urgent and for compassionate reasons, such as the sudden death of a parent, or the serious illness of a child. This new attitude even comes to be reflected in Commissioners' decisions, for example in *R(SB) 12/82*, supplementary benefit was denied to an Asian woman on the basis that she was a 'member of the same household' as her husband who had never set foot in the United Kingdom and had been unable to hitherto because of the immigration rules. Such a decision would have been unthinkable a decade ago. And it is only by virtue of United Kingdom obligations under European Community law to introduce equal treatment between the sexes, that some women with husbands stuck abroad can now (since November 21, 1983) claim, despite this decision.[43]

The Need for Reform

In my view a number of aspects of our present system of internal immigration controls should be reformed, but in this chapter I wish to confine my attention to those involving the welfare state. Two questions are in order here: first, 'Are internal controls of this type necessary to achieve their functional purpose?' and secondly, 'Are they defensible?'. It would take a great deal of space and a very close scrutiny of facts and figures to deal adequately with the first. Of relevance would be the fact that Immigration Rules over the past decade have become progressively tighter; that recent immigration statistics show that the numbers coming to the UK for settlement are lower than they have been for a very considerable period and that the UK is now a country of net emigration;[44] that economists no longer assert in unqualified terms that the UK has an 'over-supply of labour';[45] that the UK does not have a geographical land-border problem as, say, the USA does with the dramatically poorer country of Mexico; that the Law Lords have recently acknowledged[44] that the working definitions used over the past decade for 'illegal entrants' were too broad and sweeping. For such reasons it now seems very open to question whether such a tight system of controls is necessary to achieve the continuing level of overall immigration control still called for by policymakers.

Even if policymakers insist on keeping this first question closed, there is still the second question as to whether these controls are defensible.

There would be broad agreement that our immigration system should be compatible with democratic principles. All major political parties are also expressly committed to the tenet that black

Britons and other settled people should be able to enjoy equal rights and opportunities, non-discrimination in the provision of benefits and services, and genuine security.[46] In consequence, no system of internal controls can be accepted solely because it 'works' in its functional purpose of discriminating against those subject to immigration control. A pure 'pass law' society has no qualms in achieving such a purpose, but it entails gross violation of democratic principles and human rights. The question therefore is whether the extension of controls into welfare state spheres is justifiable in a democratic Britain. Having sketched the problems which exist in this area, I will now summarise my reasons for believing that we require a radical change of direction by policymakers.

Such a system of internal controls undermines a central principle of our welfare state, the principle that benefits and services should be available to all on the basis of need. The welfare state exists to secure provision for social need and adequate care for those who require it without regard to their ability to pay nor to their immigration status. Much of it works as a safety net to rescue people from the effects of poverty, ill-health, old age, homelessness and so on. Meeting such needs should not be subject to vetting on status grounds. This has been the philosophy put into policy by Beveridge, Bevan and Butler.[47] It is still thought to be current by most people in this country. Any system of restricting access to those who can show that they hold a correct immigration status is wholly alien to such a philosophy.

Such a system must undoubtedly deter potential users who are in need. On this topic no hard research has yet been done. But the overwhelming experience of people working on the ground in ethnic minority communities is that, first, some people who are entitled are being deterred from use of services and benefits, and secondly, some entitled people who do seek access are experiencing checks and obstacles to which their white English-speaking counterparts are not subjected. Many advisers in this field find that they are having to spend more and more time allaying misconceptions born of rumours and fears which have exaggerated the extent and scope of the problems. It is now seen as a priority to get across the message of reassurance that the vast majority of black people in this country need have no fear about using benefits and services. This state of affairs is often blamed by Government on troublemakers stirring up fears. It would be better to remove these fears at source, by dismantling the growing system of interconnected controls which leads to actual cases of black people experiencing such things as passport checks. Nor must it be forgotten that the relatively rapid changes analysed here are becoming known in ethnic minority communities at a period of history when their sense of security has been shaken by a number of changes in immigration legislation over a relatively short period,[48] by a new Nationality Act,[49] and when there is considerable confusion even amongst Home Office officials as well as judges as to exactly who is an 'illegal entrant', 'returning resident', 'visitor', etc. Against this wider background[50] much more is required than bland pledges about equality and nondiscrimination.

Such a system embroils welfare state personnel in performing functions which are supposed to be confined to the immigration service and to have nothing to do with the aims and ethics of the caring and welfare professions. Performing such functions not only undermines the trust at present placed in these professions by the ethnic minority communities; it also diverts those concerned from devoting their full attention to dealing with social need. Moreover, if the experience in the supplementary benefits field is anything to go by, the existence of regulations sanctioning the performance of such functions in some instances, seems to lead at least some welfare officials into thinking it is legitimate to perform such functions in other instances.

As part of this process, such a system increases welfare state bureaucracy, since it inevitably requires officials to undertake extra paperwork and extra inquiries to ascertain whether someone's immigration status permits them to obtain free treatment or qualifies them for benefit. Added up throughout all sections of the welfare state where such inquiries now arise, such duties must consume thousands upon thousands of hours of time which could otherwise be spent on directly assisting social need. Bearing in mind the present crisis in our welfare state and its financing, this consideration would seem particularly germane.

Such a system involves extensive violation of the right to privacy and confidentiality, in that it lends sanction to immigration officials intruding into separate areas of state administration which are not their concern and results overall in both immigration and welfare officials using personal information for purposes other than those for which they were sought. The normal rule adopted by government departments is that information they hold relating to individuals is confidential, held for a specific purpose and not to be passed on by them to any other department or third party without express consent from the individual concerned or upon order of a court.[51] However the exceptions made have come to include not only security and crime but also anything relating to immigration control.[52] As outlined earlier, several government departments now wholly or partially disregard confidentiality principles in relation to immigration matters. Now that the Data Protection Act

1983 is law, it is likely that the statutory exemption it affords to data relating to crime and security from protection will further erode the guarded assurances given by other government departments to respect confidentiality in the transfer of data about immigration status.

Perhaps most serious of all, such a system institutionalises discrimination in the provision of benefits and services. There is no escaping the fact that the system of controls which has sprung up possesses in the main a legal and institutional basis, and that its operation discriminates against 'permanent inhabitant' immigrants, that is, most black and most foreign-looking-or-sounding people settled in the UK. It is impossible to devise nondiscriminatory tests in the UK context, by virtue of overlaps (of colour, race, language, nationality and religion) between entitled and non-entitled categories. The only tests which could function without discrimination would be those based on the principle of 'universal challenge'. But if the experience within the NHS since October 1982 is anything to go by, this principle is not practised: many white English-speaking patients are not challenged. If such a principle were introduced more widely – and actually practised – it would severely curtail the freedom at present enjoyed by people in this country.

The reason that discriminatory tests remain legal in the UK can be traced to the Race Relations Act 1976 s. 41, which exempts from unlawfulness any acts done under statutory authority. Although the courts have held that public bodies providing facilities and services can nevertheless be held to discriminate unlawfully under section 20, section 41 largely renders UK legislation immune from scrutiny under any domestic anti-discrimination law.

The only clear justification given for spreading internal immigration controls into the welfare state sphere concerns possible 'abuse' by visitors and others who would otherwise be free to 'scrounge' unchecked on benefits and services intended for genuine inhabitants. It is noteworthy that the only empirical study attempted on this subject to date – within the NHS – found that the problem of abuse was insignificant.[53] But it does not follow that one can dismiss outright concerns about *potential* abuse, even if they are sometimes stated in lurid language. Nonetheless, existing controls before and on entry would seem to be more than sufficient to prevent such abuse materialising to any significant degree. And neither can policymakers sensibly afford to examine the problem of abuse – actual or potential – in isolation from other considerations, in particular the damage done by such controls to the causes of racial equality and harmonious race relations. Finally, it is surely possible for policymakers to devise an alternative system of internal controls which deters abuse without at the same time compromising basic principles.

A Programme for Reform

If, as the former Home Secretary Leon Brittan said in Bradford recently, 'it is no longer appropriate to speak of the ethnic minorities in this country as immigrants,'[54] then it can no longer be appropriate to sponsor a system of internal controls which brands them as such. Reform in the area examined in this paper is possible without any substantial change in present immigration policy, a policy which tightly regulates admission to the UK and ensures prompt departure by temporary categories upon expiry of their leave to stay. Rather than 'reform', what is called for is a halt to a dangerous drift which conflicts with basic principles of social policy.

How could this halt be put into effect? I would propose the following as an outline programme. It requires concerted action on both immigration and welfare 'fronts'.

In the sphere of immigration law and practice, there should be a review of after-entry requirements on support, accommodation and 'no recourse to public funds'. For certain categories under present immigration rules such requirements are superfluous to ensuring that their leave is limited and that they are here in accordance with the purpose for which they were admitted (an example is work permit holders). As part of such a review, the meaning and scope of application of the term 'public funds' should be clarified so that those who are subject to this requirement know where they stand. Stricter guidelines are also required for the immigration service and police in cases where they seek information from welfare state departments, either at central government or local authority level. The need for stricter guidelines has been made even more urgent by the Data Protection Act's exemption for crime and security matters.

In the sphere of welfare law and practice, there must be changes in legislation and administration to remove all statutory and/or administrative sanction for making welfare entitlement dependent on immigration status. This would require repeal or amendment, not only of direct links but of indirect links which at present result from residence tests requiring lawful as well as factual residence in the UK.

There would also be a need for a thoroughgoing review of the use of residence and related tests[55] for eligibility to benefits and services. The trend appears to be away from contribution tests and towards residence tests,[56] and it is surprising therefore that such a review has not been undertaken previously. To ensure that such tests do not operate as surrogate immigration checks, more than purely factual definitions are required. One would also need to standardise a number of exemption categories to prevent indirect discrimination against those who are less able to fulfil such tests by virtue of their immigration history, such as recently arrived dependants and spouses, or returning residents. The need for exempt categories has been recognised in recent NHS and education regulations.[57] This proposal is therefore a call for policymakers to make their criteria more explicit and comprehensive and to apply them across the whole of the Welfare State.

Alongside such steps, it would also be essential to revise present verification procedures, to ensure, once again, that immigration status is not resurrected as an issue by insistence on passport checks. There should be clearer criteria for the acceptability of alternative evidence to passports. There should be proper disciplinary sanctions against welfare officials who seek to transfer or obtain information for a purpose other than that for which it was given. Wherever strict proof is required of the claimant or service-user, so should strict discipline be kept of benefit or service administrators. Additionally, consideration should be given to replacing strict proof criteria by self-certification procedures wherever there is no valid reason to expect abuse. Operation of such procedures could be implemented, if necessary, with reserve powers to revert to strict proof criteria if and when abuse was established as a significant problem.

My outline programme is certainly no charter for 'immigrant scroungers'. It assumes that before and on entry controls will continue to screen various categories of entrants in the light of their ability to support and accommodate themselves without recourse to public funds. All those in the country with limited leave would continue to be subject to control by the immigration service and the police, albeit with more adequate safeguards on the proper parameters of that control.

Conclusion

No doubt this outline programme could be much improved upon once the nettle is grasped. But no-one should forget what is at stake. It is not simply the realisation of a more just society or the ensuring of an equitable distribution of public funds. The present system of internal controls undermines the security of black people in this country and of other ethnic minorities here. By undermining their security it undermines the concept of a multiracial society. Whatever foundation can be given to the theory that strict immigration controls overall improve race relations, this theory cannot stand in relation to after-entry controls which have spread to areas of the state dealing with social need. The ideology of the 'permanent inhabitant' is in direct conflict with a central idea of our welfare state, as well as being unworkable in practice. What we find today is a system of internal controls which (*pace* Lord Scarman[58]) permits institutional racism. Its present scope is limited but it appears to be spreading in relatively rapid fashion. To tolerate laws and practices which either bar some immigrants entirely or (as in the NHS) require payment for welfare services may well assist in paving the way for a general shift towards a welfare state in which selectivism and privatisation figure more prominently. But it is unjustifiable and dangerous to single out black people and other ethnic minorities to use in this way.

Notes

1 See e.g. E. Bevan, *In Place of Fear* (1954).
2 *Immigrants and the Welfare State* by Wendy Collins and Hugo Storey. Published by NACAB (National Association of Citizens Advice Bureaux). December 1983.
3 Statement of Changes in Immigration Rules, February 1980, House of Commons (hereafter HC) 394. Since replaced in December 1982 by HC 66 and, from February 1983, by HC 169.
4 HC 169, paras. 102–4, 106–110, 12–6, 116–122.
5 S Manual. Now published through HMSO (August 1983).
6 Department of Environment letter to Association of Metropolitan Authorities dated 19 October 1979.
7 1983 nationwide survey conducted mainly through C.R.C.s by 'No Pass Laws in the North West Campaign', c/o 593 Stockport Road, Manchester 12. For further background see Paul Gordon. *Passport Raids and Checks.* (Runnymede Trust, 1981). Steve Cohen, *From Ill-Treatment to No Treatment*, Manchester Law Centre Immigration Handbook No. 6 (1982); Vijay Sharma, 'Second-Class Claimants: A Report on Ethnic Minorities and Social Security', Leicester CPAG, 40 Sanderson Rd., Leicester; David Pearl, 'Social Security and Ethnic Minorities', [1978–79]; Stephen Jones and Hugo Storey, 'Immigrants and Supplementary Benefit' [1982] *LAG Bull.*, April and June; John Douglas, 'Supplementary Benefit and Race', *Poverty*, April 1982; all issues of *No Pass Laws Here Bulletin* and most issues of *ICWI Bulletin*, both available from 44 Theobald's Rd., London WC1; *Welfare Rights Bulletin* issues of April, June, August 1982 and April 1983; and most issues of *Runnymede Trust Bulletin*, available from 37A Gray's Inn Rd., London WC1.
8 Supplementary Benefit (Requirements) Regulations, reg. 10(4a) and Sched. 2, para. 9A.
9 Social Security Act 1975, s. 17; Social Security (Unemployment, Sickness and Invalidity Benefit) Regulations 1975, S.I. 1975 No. 564 reg. 7; *R(U) 13/57* and *R(U) 1/82*

10 NHS Charges to Overseas Visitors: Manual of Guidance for Hospital Staff, Annex 2 (HC(82)(15)), amended by Health Service Development: NHS Treatment of Overseas Visitors (HC(83)10), April 1983 Circular. See also H. Carty, 'Overseas Visitors and the NHS' [1983] *JSWL* 258.

11 *Shah* v. *Barnet LBC* [1983] 1 All ER 226.

12 S.I. 1983 No. 477 (see note 56).

13 Education (Fees and Discretionary Awards) Act 1983 and regulations made thereunder (see note 56).

14 As happens under NHS Manual of Guidance (n. 10), paras. 2, 14–2, 16 and 6.5; for supplementary benefit procedure see also S Manual (August 1983).

15 Hansard, Vol. 20, No. 76, col. 65 (March 16, 1982).

16 Letter from Inland Revenue to NACAB, March 22, 1982.

17 NHS Manual of Guidance (note 10) para. 2.13; Lindrop Committee; *Report of the Committee on Data Protection*, Cmnd. 734 (1978), para. 7.09.

18 S Manual (August 1983).

19 See article in February 1983 issue of *Computing*, also discussed in *No Pass Laws Here, Bulletin* No. 6, April 1983.

20 *Rights*, vol. 7, No. 2 Summer 1983 (Report of NCCL evidence to House of Lords committee scrutinising European legislation).

21 *Cf.* HC 394 (introduced in February 1980) with previous Immigration Rules.

22 See note 6. The 'deterrent effect' was acknowledged in relation to NHS users by Gerald Vaughan when a minister at the DHSS, *Hansard* 25 June, 1981.

23 The Home Office has persistently refused to define it and the Divisional Court case *Ex parte Ved, The Times* (12 May, 1981) only clearly establishes that use of NHS and state education does not constitute 'recourse to public funds'. See further Wendy Collins and Hugo Storey, *Immigrants and The Welfare State*.

24 See note 7 and for fuller analysis, Stephen Jones and Hugo Storey, 'Immigrants and Supplementary Benefit' article.

25 *Shah* v. *Barnet LBC* [1983] 1 All ER 226.

26 *Khawaja* v. *Secretary of State for the Home Department* [1983] 1 All ER 765, and Ian Macdonald, 'Illegal Entry by Deception in Immigration Law' (1983) 133 NLI 475.

27 Letters from General Register Office to JCWI, 26 June, 1978 and 29 January, 1980.

28 *R(U)13/57.*

29 Supplementary Act 1976, Sch 1 para. 4 (1) (b) (now repealed).

30 Supplementary Benefit Act 1976 as amended by Social Security Act 1980, s. 17.

31 E.g. figures given for 'Deportations under Immigration Act 1971' increased from 465 in 1973 to 2, 195 in 1981. See Home Office *Control of Immigration Statistics 1981*: Cmnd. 8533 (1982).

32 E.g. 82/031 82 disentitled work permit holders from unemployment benefit.

33 Certainly in relation to social cost measured in terms of the average lifetime cost of an individual. See K. Jones and A. Smith. *The Economic Impact of Immigration* (1970); Department of Employment Unit of Manpower Studies. *The Role of Immigrants in the Labour Market* (1976).

34 *Savjani* v. *Inland Revenue Commissioners* [1981] 1 All ER 1121. For fuller treatment see Wendy Collins and Hugo Storey, *Immigrants and the Welfare State*.

35 Statement by John Grant when Employment minister in June 1977, as quoted on p. 59 of Paul Gordon, *Passport Raids & Checks* (*op. cit.*). This booklet contains an excellent discussion and analysis of EEC moves and United Kingdom responses. Gordon rightly attributes much of the responsibility for United Kingdom pre-occupation with internal controls generally to the one-sided study of illegal immigration conducted by the Select Committee on Race Relations and Immigration, 1977–78 Session (H.C. 303–1) 1978 HMSO.

36 Letter dated 30 August, 1980.

37 HC 169, paras. 41, 44, 46 and 116, 35–37, 16. On refugees see Larry Grant and Ian Martin, *Immigration Law and Practice*, Cobden Trust 1982, pp. 145–146.

38 *R(U)1/82.*

39 *R(U)13/57, R(U)1/82* exclude them from unemployment benefit. Those not required to be available for work as a condition for claiming supplementary benefit might in certain instances be able to claim normal benefit (e.g. fiancés after marriage) or urgent need benefit. New choice-of-claimant provisions will also help some couples: see S.I. 1983 No. 1004.

40 *Shah* v. *Barnet LBC* [1983] 1 All ER 226.

41 This objection has less force in respect of short residence tests, but even these can involve unequal access to needed benefits and services, by for example, newly arrived settlers (see note 42). And in any case the residence tests that now apply to most benefits and services specify periods longer than a year. It is interesting to note that a three-year residence test in the education sphere has been recognised as 'covert discrimination' by the Divisional Court, as least against 'workers' from European Community countries: see *MacMahon* v. *Department of Education and Science, The Times*, 21 July, 1982.

42 For a recent House of Lords decision on a combined 'normally residing' and 'local connection' test under the Homeless Person legislation, see *R.* v. *Eastleigh Borough Council ex parte Betts* [1982] 2 All ER 481.

43 See S.I. 1983 No. 1004.

44 Home Office, *Control of Immigration Statistics 1981*, Cmnd. 8533 (1982).

45 See chapters by economist Kenneth Mayhew and demographer Heather Booth in this book.

46 For outline of political party positions in 1983 see *Runnymede Trust Bulletin* No. 156, June 1983.

47 But for a critical analysis of Bevan's underlying views and indeed the whole subject see Steve Cohen, *From Ill Treatment to No Treatment (op. cit.).*

48 Since the 1979 change of government there have been three different sets of immigration rules, see note 3.

49 British Nationality Act 1981. For analysis see Ian Macdonald and Nicholas Blake. *The New Nationality Law*, (1982).

50 Also acknowledged in recent Select Committee on Home Affairs, 3rd Report Session 1982–3, on 'British Nationality Fees', HC 248, paras. 4, 35.

51 See Lindop Committee (*op. cit.*) Chaps. 6, 7, 8, 9, 11 and on links between government departments, see Wendy Collins and Hugo Storey, *Immigrants and the Welfare State.*

52 See Wendy Collins and Hugo Storey, (*op. cit.*).

53 The Central Management Services pilot survey of 10 hospitals in 1981 was commissioned by the DHSS Working Party set up by the Minister, Norman Fowler, in the same year. It found abuse to be virtually nonexistent.

54 *Yorkshire Evening Post*, 7 July, 1983.

55 See note 41.

56 See e.g. recent changes in maternity grant criteria, described in detail in Wendy Collins and Hugo Storey, (*op. cit.*).

57 The National Health Service (Charges to Overseas Visitors) (No. 2) Regulations 1982, S.I. 1982 No. 863, reg. 4, NHS Manual of Guidance (*op. cit.*), paras. 13, 7, 14; The Education (Mandatory Awards) Regulations 1983, S.I. 1983 No. 1183, and The Education (Fees Awards) Regulations 1983, S.I. 1983 No. 973.

58 *The Scarman Report: The Brixton Disorders 10–12 April 1981* (1982).

Admission of Overseas Students

ALISON BARTY

United Kingdom Council for Overseas Student Affairs

The Present Requirements

In order to be admitted as a student a person has to produce evidence that:
(1) they have been accepted for a course of study at a University, Polytechnic or further education establishment, an independent school or any *bona fide* private education institution;
(2) the course will occupy the whole or a substantial part of their time;
(3) they can, without working and without recourse to public funds, meet the cost of the course, the cost of their own maintenance and accommodation and that of any dependants during the course;
(4) that they are able and intend to follow the proposed course of study and intend to leave the country on completion of the course.

Entry clearance is not a requirement but is advisable to enable the person to appeal from within the UK if refused entry.

A full-time course is defined as a course of not less than 15 hours per week of organised daytime study of a single subject or related subjects.

Problems Areas

The major problems faced by people seeking entry or leave to remain as students are:
(1) establishing their intention to leave the country on completion of their studies;
(2) establishing that they have sufficient funds to support and accommodate themselves;

208

(3) the definition of a full-time course;
(4) changing status from visitor to student;
(5) changing courses, particularly after exam failure or mid-course.

Intention to Remain

Casual remarks made in the course of questioning which suggest that a student might like to remain in the UK, or enquiries about the possibility of applying for permanent residence or refugee status have been taken as evidence that a student does not intend to leave; also a period of several years spent on a succession of courses, whether or not these follow on obviously logical succession. Students from countries where there is 'pressure to emigrate' for financial and career motives are particularly likely to have doubts cast on their intentions.

Funding

Frequently foreign exchange restrictions and political upheavals make it difficult for students to have sufficient funds to meet the full cost of their course on arrival or to pay instalments on time.

Full-time Courses

Although many university courses do not require a student to be 'in class' for 15 hours per week, but include long periods of library study and individual research, particularly at post-graduate level, this flexibility in interpreting 'full-time' is not extended to courses of further education or professional courses where the 15 hour rule is rigidly maintained.

Changing Status from Visitor to Student

It is extremely difficult to change status if admitted as a visitor even where there has been a genuine change of intention after arrival. Where a person has not declared an intention to study because they were unsure and had made no firm arrangements, they are likely to be refused an extension of stay, on the grounds of making false representations.

Changing Courses

Changing courses tends to be seen as an attempt to prolong stay. Factors such as fear of loss of face if a student returns home without a qualification or pressure to take a course unsuited to the student's ability and inclination either from the home Government or the student's family are often not taken into account.

Recommendations for Reform

1. The administration of the Immigration Rules should be less subject to discretion and individual interpretation on the part of immigration officers and entry clearance officers.
2. A student's ability to pay fees should be determined by the institution rather than by the immigration service.
3. Students hit by a sudden financial crisis which is beyond their control should be able to apply to have employment restrictions lifted on a temporary basis and should be allowed to remain temporarily without having to fulfil normal student conditions if they are unable to do so because of the financial crisis.
4. The burden of proof on establishing a person's intention should be with the immigration service, rather than the student.
5. The definition of 'full time' course should be more flexible.
6. Immigration officers and entry clearance officers should be provided with sufficient training and background information on overseas students, their educational, social and cultural background, their reasons for coming to the UK and the benefits to the UK of their presence, for their decisions on student applications to be made on the basis of a full understanding of the circumstances and not on impressions and prejudices.
7. Attempts should be made to cut down on delays in processing student applications so that students do not have to relinquish their passports for three to six months.

Legal Education and the Law of Immigration and Nationality

J. HUTTON MA BCL(Oxon)

Lecturer, Newcastle Polytechnic

The study of law at universities and polytechnics in the UK has traditionally been concerned with the imparting of techniques of legal critique and the steady acquisition of skills which will be of lasting benefit to the student in his or her professional life. These skills include the abilities to master a large amount of information, to be highly selective when it comes to identifying relevant material, and to understand and apply complicated rules to practical situations.

This process of legal education has however concentrated on a rather limited range of subjects which, although perfectly capable of achieving the above objectives, often suffers from the criticism of lacking social relevance. 'New' subjects such as labour law and welfare law, have been added to many law courses over the last few years, which to some extent has met this criticism. One subject however which has been almost completely excluded from legal education has been immigration and nationality law. This exclusion is particularly surprising for two main reasons. First, the questions of immigration and nationality have consistently been one of the most politically controversial areas of post-war legislation. Given this controversy and the resulting interest generated, it would have been reasonable to expect a demand on the part of 'law course consumers' for the subject to be offered by polytechnics and universities. This has not happened. Secondly, as a subject itself, immigration and nationality law offers an almost perfect vehicle by which traditional legal skills can be inculcated in the student. The subject provides a delicate combination of statutory and non-statutory rules together with a burgeoning volume of judicial precedent. In addition the student will be

211

required to master a highly complicated legal framework and eventually the ability to operate these rules in courts and in tribunals. So quite apart from the social relevance standpoint, the subject ought to fit easily within, and complement, the more traditional of our law courses. These arguments have clearly failed to impress those responsible for legal education in the UK.

Admittedly, immigration and nationality law does make a 'token' appearance in courses currently on offer. Courses concerned with human rights, civil liberties, family law and administrative/constitutional law might make some reference to immigration and nationality issues. But only at one polytechnic (Newcastle-upon-Tyne) does the subject merit consideration on its own. No British University offers this as a separate subject. This failure to recognise the social and legal significance of the subject is a major defect in British legal education at the present time, and one which must be corrected in the near future.

Legal education is not, of course, confined exclusively to academic courses but covers professional 'conversion' courses run by the Law Society (for solicitors) and the Council for Legal Education (for the Bar). But here again, immigration and nationality law forms no part of these courses. The whole subject has, therefore, slipped almost entirely through the net. What are the consequences of the failure to incorporate immigration and nationality law into mainstream legal education?

The principal consequence has been that legal advisers have been thrown on to their own resources. They have to teach themselves the law. How serious is this? Obviously, immigration and nationality work is not spread evenly throughout the country and many solicitors will never undertake such work during their professional lives. But many other lawyers who work in this field will have had no basic training whatsoever. There are no other professions which permit their members to practice in fields where they are not qualified. Why should law be any exception?

It is submitted that the omission of this subject from legal education in the UK is glaring and undesirable. However the Law Society is, at last, seriously considering the necessity of continuing post-qualification legal education for solicitors and it is to be hoped that the opportunity to attempt some partial remedy to the situation will be taken.

At the same time, two final observations can be made. First, there can be no disguising the fact that adding on some reference to immigration and nationality in a package designed to update solicitors on the law will not solve the basic weakness in our system. There needs to be a solid academic basis for the study of the subject, a study which can introduce the student to the

212

contexts, social and political, in which the main legal rules are set. This can only be provided by the universities and polytechnics. The need for such courses is apparent but as yet unrealised by these institutions. Secondly, if the approach taken to the teaching of welfare and labour law on professional law courses were to be followed in teaching immigration and nationality law, the professional lawyer would probably be no better off than he or she is today. At present, welfare law is not on the professional syllabus at all and labour law merits a mere four weeks' teaching time. It is no solution to one of the basic weaknesses in our legal education system, to attempt to 'teach' this subject as an exclusively vocational one. The approach to immigration and nationality law has to be a sensitive one, and the professional stage of a lawyer's training is not the ideal time at which to attempt such a study.

In conclusion, the proper study of immigration and nationality law at universities and polytechnics is necessary both in terms of fulfilling the traditional objectives of legal education and, more importantly, as part of the proper training of future generations of legal advisers.

IV. Problems of change

The following chapter is based on the assumption that UK immigration law should be reconsidered and reformed. The aim should be not to abolish immediately all immigration control but to devise a completely new system of control, conforming to international standards, taking practical account of the character and needs of the UK as a whole, and bearing in mind the effects of one country's policy upon other countries and their peoples.

The assumption that such reform is needed is now held by a growing number of people, but to the majority such reform is an entirely unfamiliar idea. There is a widely-held assumption of quite a different kind: that there are only two alternatives open – either to maintain as it is, or even toughen the existing system of control, or to abolish control altogether.

There are two large obstacles to the reformer. One is this falsely-based assumption; it is not easy to get across to those who hold it that there is in fact a large range of possible policies lying between these two alternatives. The other is to persuade people that it is possible to debate the subject of immigration at all without racial discrimination being essential to the control system. These obstacles are particularly hard to move because they have been built up by Right, Left and Centre. It is just as hard to persuade someone on the Left that it is *possible* for what he or she sees as the racist, capitalist state to introduce nonracist controls as it is to persuade someone on the Right that controls *ought* not to be racially discriminatory. In between, in the Centre (in which I mean to include what are loosely called the right and 'soft Left' of the Labour Party and the left of the Conservative Party) the difficulty lies not so much in an ideological position as in set habits of mind. There is a firm belief, always implicit and sometimes openly stated, that the white electorate is so racist that the faintest whiff of liberalisation of immigration law would cause a landslide of votes away form the party proposing it. It is assumed that reform is not politically possible, not on the agenda. Moreover, each party, as a party, is imprisoned by its own record, to the extent that no new suggestions for reform now can emerge without party spokesmen admitting, implicitly or explicitly, that they have been fundamentally in the wrong for the last 20 years on the issue. The Liberal and Social Democratic parties are not hampered by records in office nor so hard set in old habits of thinking, but if the Alliance were ever in a position to formulate a new policy and put it into effect, the problem of explaining and commending reform to Parliament and the public would still present a formidable task. Most people would simply not understand what the reformers were talking about, so firmly entrenched are three distinct prejudices: racial prejudice itself, the pre-judged assumption that the traditional type of immigration debate is the only possible form of debate, and the pre-judged assumption that a genuine con-straint exists, preventing the exercise of one's volition in getting untied.

How to deal with these very real mental difficulties, and with some of the practical details of change besides, is the subject of the following chapter.

Agenda for Changing the Law

ANN DUMMETT

Background

In 1983, the Action Group on Immigration and Nationality[1] organised a conference in Oxford on the subject of reform of British immigration law and its administration. The purpose was to initiate a new kind of debate on the subject, and there was no question of attempting to reach agreed conclusions. Most of the earlier chapters in this book are adapted from papers written for this conference. Further information, and other suggestions and ideas, were put forward by participants during the discussions and later to me in letters and conversations. I have drawn on the taped record of proceedings, and these later informal contributions, some of them from people who were not able to attend the conference but had expressed an interest in the subject, in writing the following chapter. Some views are directly quoted and others summarised: all are attributed to their authors, and where an opinion is expressed without attribution it can be taken as my own.

But this chapter is not an account of conference proceedings: for anyone who wants such an account, a summary report is available from AGIN.[1] Instead, it asks: 'what can be done, and how, to realise hopes of reforming the law?' And this leads us into new areas, not covered above: the shape of new legislation, the structure of its administration, public opinion, the political parties, the media, and some guesswork about the likely course of political and economic events, both in the UK and in the world outside, in the next decade.

The Shape of New Legislation

It would be far too ambitious to attempt a detailed draft of a new Immigration Bill here, and yet it is not difficult, in the light of earlier chapters, to indicate what its general structure could be

216

like. To begin with, if the legislation is to conform to international standards, certain basic assumptions are already given.

One must distinguish here between (1) agreements such as the European Convention for the Protection of Human Rights and Fundamental Freedoms, and the Community Treaties, whose scope is limited to the nationals of a particular group of countries, (2) the requirements laid down in international instruments to which the UK is a party, and in particular the parts of them ratified by the UK government, and (3) the wider context of public international law as a whole, and the principles currently informing it. In the UK, most treaties have no binding effect on the courts unless given internal application by Act of Parliament. Moreover, the practice and style of UK governments has often been narrow and literal when legislating on matters affected by international agreements. For example, the UK is a party to the Convention on the Reduction of Statelessness 1961. The standard set by the Convention is clearly the principle that the domestic legislation of states should be framed so as to prevent statelessness occurring at all, and to provide access to a nationality for people who are already stateless and who come within the jurisdiction of a state which is a party to the Convention. At first, UK law was already sufficiently liberal to ensure that anyone born on UK or colonial territory had a nationality, and most children born abroad to British-born nationals were British, but a special Act was passed in 1964 to provide that illegitimate children born abroad to British mothers were not stateless. In the British Nationality Act 1981, however, British government policy was more restrictive and it is now possible to be born stateless in the UK. The UK government claimed that it was still conforming to the Convention, since procedures conforming to the minimum requirements laid down in the Convention were incorporated in a Schedule to the Act, permitting a stateless child over 10 years of age and under 22 to become British under certain conditions. At the same time, the Immigration Rules were framed in such a way that it will be very rare for a UK-born stateless child to qualify for British nationality. This is a clear example of conformity to the letter, but not the standard, of an international agreement. From the international point of view, such literalism may be found inadequate.

Over the last 15 years, international tribunals have found British immigration law wanting on many occasions. Richard Plender remarks:

> The case for considering any reform of one country's immigra-
> tion laws in the context of the regional and international system
> in which it operates is so strong, and so self-evident, that it

scarcely requires a defence. Yet it is now widely if not universally accepted that the drafting of the United Kingdom's immigration legislation has often suffered in recent years from an excessively insular approach. A series of judgments of the European Court in Luxembourg and the Commission of Human Rights in Strasbourg bear testimony to that fact.[2]

Richard Plender maintains that while governments, including the British, have continued to insist that the control of immigration is essentially within the domestic jurisdiction of states, this view is not compatible with the proposition, now generally accepted in international law, that individuals, and particularly aliens, can derive from public international law rights enforceable against states. There are now numerous multilateral agreements based on this assumption, some dealing with migrant workers, refugees and such specified groups, and others in more general terms, like the Covenant of 1966 on the Elimination of All Forms of Racial Discrimination. All of these are concerned with protecting the rights of individuals at international law. Some of the European instruments deal with actual rights of entry, as well as rights after entry to the territory of another state. The right to have one's family life respected, for example, in the European Convention is directly affected by the provisions a state may make in its immigration law on the admission of family members to join an alien already lawfully admitted. And the right of a worker from a member state to seek and take employment in another member state is established in the EEC Treaty and Regulations.

Broadly speaking, there are two different senses in which British immigration law might claim to conform to international law: first, that the letter of international instruments to which the state is a party is being observed, and secondly that the domestic law achieves the aims and standards which public international law has set. (This is admittedly an over-simplification of a complex matter, but a helpful one in looking at the broad question of reform of our domestic law.) It is plain that the UK does not always satisfy the first sense of the requirement, and it is not alone. Under the pressure of the world recession in recent years, many industrialised states have been tightening their restrictions on the rights of alien entrants and alien residents. But if we look at British immigration law in the light of the standards set by international law, the need for certain specific reforms is immediately obvious.

Most obviously, UK law fails to conform to the assumption, taken for granted internationally, that a state's own nationals have right of admission to the national territory. The first step in reforming immigration law must therefore be to reform British nationality law beforehand, or in a single Act of Parliament that deals with immigration also. Such reform of nationality could take several possible forms, so long as there are still British dependent territories in existence. A single citizenship of the UK and Colonies could be re-established, but this time with right of movement for all holders between all the territories concerned, as in French law, which allows all French citizens to move freely between metropolitan France and the Overseas Departments (and, while they were still in existence, also allowed movement between the Overseas Territories and these). It was Liberal party policy in the 1983 General Election to establish such a status, but excluding Hong Kong from the territories concerned. Or, as was argued in a Conservative Party working paper (not adopted as party policy) in 1975, separate citizenships could be established for all the remaining dependencies, with the people in each territory having right of entry to that territory but not necessarily to any other, alongside a UK citizenship. The Conservative paper did not propose that all existing British nationals should, under this arrangement, have a right of entry to *some* British territory, but the scheme could be modified to allow for this, and so provide that all British nationals had right of entry either to the UK itself or to a particular dependency. There are other variations that could be tried: the essential basis, however, has to be that all British nationals have a right of abode somewhere. The way is then clear for a new regime of immigration control over all who are not British.

Next, the UK's multilateral agreements with other groups of states could, with advantage, be acknowledged in immigration legislation. This is not the case at present. There have been attempts by Lord Wade, in Bills introduced in the House of Lords, to incorporate the European Convention into UK domestic law, but they have failed. Again, there are different ways in which its provisions could be incorporated, and one possibility might be to include relevant Articles of the Convention, concerned with aliens in the national territory, into an Immigration Act. The Treaty of Rome and European Community Regulations already have direct effect in the UK without need of domestic legislation. The UN Convention and Protocol on the Status of Refugees should be incorporated, so that applicants who had been refused would have a remedy before the courts or an immigration appeal tribunal. At whatever time a reforming Immigration Bill was introduced, other international agreements in force at the time could be looked at either with a view to incorporating some of their provisions into the Bill, or in order to ensure that specific provisions in the Bill fulfilled them in spirit as well as in letter. The European Social

Charter and the European Convention on the Legal Status of Migrant Workers are examples of such agreements.

One important effect of this approach would be to increase the scope of the courts to review and apply immigration legislation. Another would be the declaratory effect: the UK would visibly have moved from an insular and narrowly-drawn scheme to an explicit acknowledgment of international standards. Thirdly, of course, the new provisions themselves would clarify and liberalise the law and establish clear rights for migrants and yet do so without *necessarily* expanding the gross numbers of persons allowed to enter and remain. The principle of international law which says that the admission of aliens is at the discretion of each state would be unimpaired. The only modifications to that discretion that such a Bill would acknowledge would be the modifications already made by agreements to which the UK was party. For instance, so long as the UK remains a member of the EEC it is bound to admit EEC nationals under the provisions of EEC law. And if it was accepted that, in Richard Plender's words, 'There is some evidence to show that racial discrimination in the selection of immigrants may be considered as contravening a generally accepted norm or standard, if not a rule of customary international law'[3] then the framers of the Bill, in acknowledging this norm or standard, would not be surrendering the claim of the state to control immigration into its territory. They would simply have to acknowledge that whatever scheme, tight or loose, they designed, must not be racially discriminatory. At present, UK immigration law is specifically excluded from the scope of the Race Relations Acts and Equal Opportunities Act, an exclusion which has its own declaratory, and practical, effects. Explicit recognition of the principles of race and sex equality in immigration law would import into immigration control a much-needed consistency with the body of domestic law as well as with international standards.

Having got this far, however, the authors of a reforming Bill would still have a very long way to go. They would not have a complete immigration policy, only a foundation. What considerations should they next take into account?

Dr Freda Hawkin has shown[4] that Canada has been strongly influenced in its immigration legislation by foreign policy considerations as well as labour market needs, Australia by population needs, and both by an emphasis on family reunion in a broad sense: the admission of immigrants with relatives or even close friends already settled in the country. The US has moved from a concern with the national origins of immigrants towards a greater concern with protecting American labour. Éric-Jean Thomas has described Sweden's emphasis on refugee policy,[5] and the reliance of most west European countries on a guest-worker system which was expected to be a manipulation of the labour market but has turned into a pattern of permanent settlement by foreign workers and their families. In short, different countries have very different ideas about what an immigration policy is meant to achieve, and these ideals change over time. Canada and Australia, for the first half of the present century, had frankly racially discriminatory policies, which both have now reversed. The Federal Republic of Germany has had a very liberal refugee policy, recently coming under strong pressure for restriction. Sometimes immigration policies are developed without much analysis of their underlying purposes and effects; sometimes, as during the 1970s in Norway, Australia and Canada, official government enquiries are mounted to examine the whole matter and produce recommendations. All the richer countries have, in recent years and especially since 1979, experienced a rapid rise in unemployment and other economic problems resulting from the world recession, and in some of them there have been outbreaks of hostility against foreign workers. The result has been a tendency to consider tightening entry laws, increase restrictions on foreign residents and, in some countries, to exert pressure on migrants to go away. Important changes can be made to policy by administrative means instead of by new legislation.

The United Kingdom, as Usha Prashar remarks,[6] has never formulated a clear immigration policy; it has only responded at particular moments to particular pressures. There has been no consistent labour-market policy. The UK has never accepted the 'guest-worker' principle in the same way as other European countries, but nor has it recently had any organised programmes for the admission and settlement of groups of workers, apart from the European Worker programme just after the Second World War. It relied heavily up to the mid-1970s on the highly flexible supply of migrant labour from the Republic of Ireland for many of the purposes that other countries used guest-workers for: the Irish were close at hand, free from control, and would come for a few months or for longer periods, to any region where jobs were available. The low status and exploitation of Irish workers has perhaps been one of the most neglected factors in the British debate on immigration. Since 1973, however, fewer Irish migrants have come, partly because of improved opportunities in the Republic, and partly because they can and do go to other EEC countries to work. In the 1950s and early 1960s, Britain was continually short of labour and could supplement Irish labour with Commonwealth labour without mounting any special programmes, though some industries did run recruiting offices in the West Indies. Once restrictions on the free flow of Commonwealth

221

labour had been introduced, labour shortages were met by increasing the issue of work permits to aliens. But effective demand for labour was already decreasing by 1970 in the UK, long before it slackened in the rest of western Europe. It is a curious fact, pointed out by Paul Foot, that when controls on Commonwealth immigrants were first introduced in 1962, although there was no agitation about shortage of jobs, and the demands for exclusion were either explicitly racialist or complained of pressure on housing and social services, the system of control introduced was in the form of work vouchers – a system for which, at the time, there was little economic justification. In other words, despite regulations on the entry and settlement of workers, labour-market considerations have never been central to the purposes of British immigration laws in the past, even when restrictions on employment have been used as a means of controlling entry. Should they be so now? It is a question very difficult to answer in the middle of a recession whose end is not foreseeable.

Foreign policy considerations do not seem to have affected British governments' attitudes to immigration much, but there is a field within which external policies have a highly important relationship to immigration law, namely, our membership of the Commonwealth. This has a very different character from our membership of the EEC, and the Council of Europe. First, it is a relationship governed by conventions with a small 'c'. It is the creation of history and tradition, not of strict law. But, secondly, it has special claims on British consideration. The Queen of the UK is also Head of the Commonwealth, though not Head of State in all the member countries. There are still strong links between member countries, sometimes of legal tradition, sometimes of language; there are numerous Commonwealth institutions, and some shared activities like the Commonwealth Games. Moreover, Commonwealth citizens are still acknowledged to have a special position in domestic law, in that they can vote in UK elections and have certain other rights, formerly the rights of the British subject. It might seem to follow logically from our Commonwealth membership that there should be a system of Commonwealth preference in our immigration law. Instead, immigration law after 1962 established, at first by administrative means only and later by the patriality definition in the Immigration Act 1971, a system which effectively differentiated between white Commonwealth citizens and others. The permission for young working holiday makers from the Commonwealth to enter and take employment without a permit, which looks on the face of it like a general Commonwealth preference, has in practice been almost entirely confined to young white Commonwealth citizens, mostly from

Australia and New Zealand. The patriality definition has allowed many white Commonwealth citizens, holding other countries' passports, to settle in the UK without being counted in the immigration figures or regarded in any quarter as 'immigrants'. It is clear that a reforming law should recognise that there has been this racial discrimination if it is to take account of the spirit of the multi-racial Commonwealth. It might include some special concessions to Commonwealth citizens, regardless of colour (possibly work-exchange schemes, specially low student rates, or a preferential form of access to British nationality in a new Nationality Act). But some consideration of the Commonwealth link there must be, not least because there are family ties going back over generations between many British citizens and people in other Commonwealth countries. It would be refreshing if it were possible to see, in this same light, the family histories of a white Hampshire lady whose grandfather was in the Indian Civil Service and a brown London lady whose grandfather also worked under the government of India in the 1920s.

What the demands of foreign policy might be in the widest context has yet to be assessed, but it can at least be said that a move by the UK towards the international standards mentioned earlier, and to a closer Commonwealth link, would be a very significant gesture, indicating an attitude towards the outside world very different from what foreigners all too often see as characteristically British arrogance and narrow nationalism.

A policy to promote family unity would follow from observance of the international standards, likewise. The admission of spouses of either sex, to join a person lawfully settled in the UK, the admission of dependant children up to 21, of elderly dependant relatives and of distressed relatives, would meet these standards and, provided the administrative procedures for monitoring admission were drastically reformed, would transform the atmosphere of immigration control, while bringing enormous relief to the families now affected by the restrictions.

Concern for the size and structure of the population, which has for decades been an important feature in Australia's policy aims, need not be a primary concern for the UK. As David Coleman and Heather Booth have shown, migration's effect has been very small indeed on population as a whole:

> Natural increase has always been much more important than net migration in the development of Britain's population. Given that, the second point is that net migration has always been negative: more people are leaving Britain than are entering Britain and this has almost always been the case except for odd

periods. In other words, to the extent that migration has an effect on population development in Britain, it actually reduces the population size. Immigration is pretty insignificant for the development of our population.[7]

There is, therefore, no case for cutting down crude numbers of immigrants from the point of view of keeping our population down, and little argument for increasing crude numbers of immigrants suddenly, in order, say, to increase the proportion of young people in the population, since the increase would have to be very large indeed to make a significant difference. Australia's total population is only a quarter of the size of the UK's, and the migratory flow both in and out of Australia was significantly large for decades, up to the 1970s. The situation is therefore quite different though not for the reasons popularly supposed.

The argument so far has brought us to a point where we can envisage new legislation which deals with the rights of refugees, rights of resident aliens after admission, admission of family members and possibly some special, non-racial provisions for Commonwealth citizens, all based on a reformed British nationality structure. Such legislation would slightly increase the numbers of people eligible to enter the UK, but not in any demographically significant way, and the effects on the economy would similarly be slight and probably balance out. This slight increase must, after all, be seen against the background of free movement into the UK which already exists from other EC countries, including Ireland, and of British citizens returning from abroad; it must also be borne in mind that some dependant relatives and some refugees are admitted under existing law. But we have not yet tackled the question of what should inform policy on 'primary' immigration, that is, entry in order to settle and work by a person who has no claim as a family member, a refugee or a national of a community country. There is also the important issue of temporary admission of all kinds, not only of tourists, but of students, trainees, temporary workers, investors, the self-employed and the long-term visitor – say, a woman who wants to come to care for a relative here during a long illness.

Existing law already makes provision for some primary immigration, but in very small categories, strongly favouring the rich and the very highly skilled. There is a category for 'persons of independent means' and another for 'business-men and business-women', either of whom needs to have disposable capital of at least £150,000 or disposable income of £15,000 a year to qualify before meeting other conditions. Work permits are still issued, but to high-grade business executives and specialist professionals, under very close limitations. The aim appears to be mainly to control absolute numbers of entrants. Do we really want to limit primary immigration to the very rich and successful? If we had done so throughout our history, British life would be immeasurably the poorer. There are also numerous categories for temporary admission, including one for writers and artists, who are forbidden to take any employment except 'that related to his self-employment as a writer or artist' and who must be able to support themselves and their dependants from their own resources – a stiff order for many people in these professions. The rules on admission of students, taken together with the level of fees set for them by the Department of Education and Science, are such as to prevent most overseas students from coming here at all: one must either have a generous grant from one's home government or have considerable private means to have any hope of qualifying. The Immigration Rules constantly reiterate the requirement that temporary entrants must not have recourse to public funds. What policy can be deduced from the existing provisions is, in general, a determination to limit all sorts of entry as closely as possible by imposing difficult and detailed requirements, and also to see that temporary entrants cost the country nothing while, in many cases, having to contribute quite a lot for the golden privilege of admission.

The question, 'What sort of immigration policy do we want?' can only be answered in terms of, 'What sort of society do we aim to be?' The answer to the second question, as revealed in current immigration policy, appears to be something like 'A mainly white society with no free handouts and as few foreigners as possible.' Finding a new policy with a different character will be possible only for a government with new aims for national policy as a whole, whatever party, or parties, may form it. It will not be possible to formulate a reforming immigration law in a policy vacuum. This is not to say that some future government will have to work out, consciously, first its manifesto for national aims as a whole and then immigration law as a form of expression of them, but it will need to have in mind certain assumptions and ideas about the country's future of a very different kind from the uninspired and backward-looking insularity which has characterised some members of all political parties in the last decade. Because a change in many political attitudes, not just attitudes to immigration, will be essential before a reforming law can appear, and because it is impossible at present to forecast how the world economy, and the British economy within it, will be faring in a few years' time, it would be pointless to attempt detailed suggestions for a new set of immigration categories here. However, it would help to stimulate new thinking meanwhile if other countries' policies were studied for comparison. Canada's 'points' system of admissions, for everyone outside the refugee and family reunion categories, offers a flexible means of adapting broad policy aims to a general situation which changes year by year, for example. A completely different approach is demonstrated in US law, with its elaborate system of numerical quotas, types of certification, and categories within categories, reducing flexibility but also reducing the range of discretion. Many such systems could be studied, in search of the advantages and disadvantages that each has had in practice, in order to devise a system of control that succeeds in achieving the policy aims behind it. It is on these policy aims that work now needs to be done: the range of policy options is enormously wide, once one begins to think about immigration anew.

A New Administrative Structure

Freda Hawkins has emphasised[8] that the administration of the law is itself an important part of policy: 'management is deeply involved in policy-making in larger and smaller ways'. The framing of new legislation and the Rules to accompany it will not achieve reform unless the administration of the law is reformed also. The greater the flexibility and Act and Rules allow for – and some flexibility is necessary both for efficiency and for doing justice in borderline cases – the greater the scope for discretion given to the executive, which means for most of the time the discretion of paid officials.

Hitherto, both policy and day-to-day management have usually been the responsibility of the Home Office. This responsibility has not been undivided: other Departments are involved, including the Foreign and Commonwealth Office, which is responsible for entry clearance overseas; the Department of Employment, which administers work-permits; the DES on student admissions and the DHSS in various ways. But general lines of policy, and most of the administration, have lain with the Home Office's Immigration and Nationality Department. Meanwhile, 'immigration' has in the last 30 years been seen by politicians as if it consisted only of black immigration, and successive governments have attempted to promote 'integration', 'harmonious community relations' and 'racial equality', with programmes and structures that have also been absorbed into the Home Office's vast, conglomerate empire since the 1950s. The Home Office's own structure and work have therefore perpetuated the confusion between immigration issues, properly speaking, and racial issues.

As the Department of State responsible for national security, the Home Office has necessarily an irreducible role in the administration of controls. But this irreducible role is only a very small part of immigration policy and management as a whole, and there is no particular reason why the Home Office should be the policy-making Department. Indeed, one can think of many good reasons why it should not. Although its responsibilities are very varied (broadcasting, the Children's Department, fire services, etc.,) the Home Office's character is to a great extent formed by its major areas of activity: prisons, police, counter-espionage. Alongside these, immigration policy is all too often seen as a matter of restriction, of suspecting the fakes, of keeping the country safe from intruders. Whereas a Department concerned with tourism might develop a friendly attitude, one concerned with the labour market a flexible approach, and one concerned with foreign trade or foreign policy an open and informed mind towards people from other countries, the Department concerned with internal law and order is impelled by its own traditions and standards to be insular and restrictive.

The structure of government in the UK is such that a small Department has little say in major government policy decisions, and an inter-departmental committee even less. The big Departments – Foreign Office, Home Office, Treasury – are headed by senior political figures and staffed by officials accustomed to being the big fish in the pond. To establish a new department for immigration policy could have disadvantages:

> *Ad hoc* Departments or sub-Departments . . . tend to be weak and isolated and their low standing in the Whitehall pecking-order makes them particularly ill-suited to the kind of co-ordination operation required in this instance.[9]

So said Nicholas Deakin of a proposal for a new department concerned with 'integration', in 1968. He has since pointed out that the same considerations apply to immigration policy and the establishment of a new structure to deal with it:

> In a suppressed report, about seven years ago, the Think Tank pointed to the Home Office's failure as a key factor in the way policy on migration and on race relations had broken down. The Home Office has in fact no divine right to run immigration *policy*, and has not always done so. Responsibility lay at one time with the Colonial Office, and for a brief period was at the Department of Economic Affairs. The mere turnkey responsibility is only part of the whole, and there should be discussion of how departmental responsibilities could be re-allocated.[10]

Other countries vary in how they allot responsibility for immigration policy to different Departments. Canada has altered this responsibility many times over: at one time with Agriculture and Mines, more recently with Manpower, and so on. Because migration touches on so many policy issues, any government department in any country dealing with it must be involved in discussion and co-ordination with a number of other departments: the decision, whom to make responsible, must depend on what ends immigration policy in general is intended to serve. If it is racial restriction, the Home Office is a logical enough choice, though the effect of conjoining responsibility for racial restrictions on entry with policy on 'racial equality' within one Department has been disastrous. But if it is to be anything else – encouraging family unity, settling refugees, or whatever – it could make much better sense to place the main *policy* responsibility on some other large Department, such as the DHSS. It might, however, be better to have a completely fresh start, when making fundamental changes in policy and organisation. A Ministry of Migration and Tourism, which included a visibly positive role in encouraging tourism to the UK, and which also had responsibility for looking at the overall effects of immigration and emigration, would be able to make such a fresh start. Moreover, the issues would not risk getting shuffled on to a junior Minister and being ignored by his or her seniors. (Nicholas Deakin is inclined now to favour this suggestion on balance).

Who, then, would have responsibility for the immigration service, the officers at the ports and overseas ports, the interviewers and more senior officials to whom difficult cases are referred? Such a new Ministry could do so, liaising with the Home Office only on the very limited number of cases where national security might be involved. Whatever the Department responsible, there is plainly a need to reform the recruitment and training of the immigration service. It is true that a new lead from the top, a new set of goals for policy, would make a great difference. Even in the present structure, it was, apparently, noticeable when Roy Jenkins was Home Secretary, with a very different attitude to policy from most of his predecessors and successors, that the attitudes of officials, from high to low, altered a little. (No structure, reformed or unreformed, is unresponsive to the personality of the person at its head – this can, of course, mean a shift in more directions than one). A number of incidents have shown, in the last 15 years, that at least some of the members of the service allow personal views of a strongly racist kind to influence their behaviour: for example, the officer at a seaport who tried to refuse entry to a returning resident (who was in fact a senior police officer from the north of

England and happened to be black) with the words, 'We've got enough of you buggers here already.' In a case reported to JCWI in 1983, an Englishwoman arriving at a port with her Greek fiancé was asked, 'Why don't you marry one of your own kind?' It would be possible to give hundreds of similar examples. The training of officers places great emphasis on the detection of bogus applicants, and on the likelihood that many such will be from the Indian subcontinent. No new policy is going to succeed in its aims unless it is made very clear to people at every level of the service that the policy requires new attitudes and procedures on their part.

It has been argued by Christopher Husbands that such reform is not a practical idea, and that the immigration service, like the police force, attracts an authoritarian type of personality. It might, however, be argued that other types of occupation give similar opportunities to exercise power over other people's lives without unduly encouraging applicants liable to misuse it. For all such work, recruitment, training and, in addition, monitoring, and some sanction against misuse of powers, are important, but above all the general climate of opinion must be such that an individual exercising powers is aware of social sanctions against misuse. So long as racially restrictive immigration controls continue, the tone of public attitudes is set to some extent by them, and it is not surprising if officials administering immigration controls respond to what they see as the guiding social convention: no blacks wanted. If, on the other hand, a new policy were promulgated and embodied in legislation, with new Departmental responsibilities established at the same time, a large step towards reform of the immigration service would have been taken even before detailed new methods of recruitment, initial training and in-service training were put into effect. The new climate would produce new conventions of behaviour.

The Media

Is it possible, though, to create a new policy, and a new administrative structure to operate it, without *first* altering the whole political climate of opinion within which immigration law has developed since 1960? The problem is: where to break into the circle? You cannot change public opinion on immigration policy without changing the law: you cannot change the law without changing public opinion first. Suppose some future government tried to launch a new policy in a climate of opinion much like the present, how would the media react?

Several experienced journalists have contributed anonymously to the following discussion of the problem:

(1) My view is that the chances of changing the media's perceptions of immigration are minimal. There's a combination of (a) lack of imaginative awareness (possibly better described as downright ignorance) and (b) a view that the media should play up to popular fears and views, and this pernicious combination makes it almost impossible to get the Press to take ideas like immigration seriously at all. That said, the media are also enormously deferential. If a government that was reasonably okay with the media (Conservative, Alliance, or Right-wing Labour with Alliance support) took a very positive line, there would be some chance of the media backing it, but if there were backlash, I don't think you could rely on the media continuing to uphold the government line.

(2) The present government says, and the people want to believe, that the great post-war immigration has ended. Only those to whom special obligation is due are entitled to come, and there are limited numbers of them. The economic reason for immigration is no longer there, with unemployment high. The media, reflecting public opinion and the consensus, do not write any more about immigration as a political issue. It would be sad if immigration did become an inflammatory issue. I know how easily campaigns which start in one direction produce an irrational reaction against them – drama which the media must report. That is not to say that justice must not be sought . . . but you would have to consider whether the gains from a campaign in pursuit of government action would be outweighed by the loss of some racial harmony.

(3) The reaction of the media depends on the overall political situation. In a time of slump and reaction, such as the present, the attitude of the media towards immigration is hysterical. In the 1930s, hysteria was whipped up when a few onion sellers from Belgium were allowed into this country. I am sure that if there were any relaxation at all at the present of immigration restrictions, the overwhelming reaction of the media would be exceedingly hostile. When there is very little hope, and wretchedness in the air, the racists have a field day. When there is full employment, hysteria is played down: there was very little campaigning against the first waves of Commonwealth immigration into this country, and even after the 1962 Act there was a sort of truce between the media and the large scale immigration that followed. There are slight variations within the media: most newspapers are overwhelmingly reactionary and racist, but the *Guardian* and

Mirror are not. And television and radio have been rather fairer on immigration than the newspapers. But in the event of any relaxation in immigration controls – that is another matter.

Although these three journalists obviously have very different views from each other on politics and the media in general, all are equally pessimistic about the way the media would be likely to react to even a faint whiff of reform of immigration law, at any rate in the present general situation. But, of course, the present general situation[11] is precisely one in which the existing government is dead set against any reform of immigration law, and in which no political party is shouting loudly about an alternative, in which the future looks bleak all round and other issues besides immigration are to the fore. Before any government initiative, by whatever party is in power, can happen on immigration, there will certainly have had to be considerable changes in the tone of public affairs.

Who sets the tone, government – and other prominent political figures – or the Press? There is, obviously, no simple answer to such a question, but undoubtedly the Press exerts considerable influence over the impression given to the public of what politicians say and do. The manner in which Enoch Powell's 'race' speeches have been reported contrasts very sharply with Press coverage of his speeches on nuclear weapons. Edward Heath and Tony Benn, whatever they say and do, are presented as bad or absurd; Margaret Thatcher, by contrast, is treated with respect when reported even by opponents of her policies. Many politicians with important things to say are simply not reported at all. The media are quick to cast stereotypes, of both personalities and issues, and to go on using them in all circumstances. This unthinking use of stereotypes is defended as 'news sense', and seems to be an unshakeable orthodoxy, rigorously observed by all news editors. When, in addition, there is bad faith, as there clearly is with some newspapers, whose gross inaccuracies are continually reported to the Press Council, and when there are editors and feature writers with strongly racist opinions, as with several national dailies, the chance of getting immigration law reform rationally considered, or even accurately reported, looks very slim indeed.

None the less, when a government introduces a major piece of legislation, or signals a major policy change, the Press reports what the main government and opposition spokesmen actually say. To some extent, the onus is on leading politicians to set the terms in which an an issue is reported and then discussed in the Press. What, then, can be hoped from leading politicians?

Politicians and their Parties

Investigation of the history of immigration as an issue in British politics produces a depressing picture. There has been migration to the UK from many sources for centuries, much of it peaceful and fruitful, but only rarely, as when Queen Anne tried for economic reasons to encourage the entry of French Huguenots, has the response of governments been positively welcoming. Usually it has simply been indifferent. Foreign business-men, craftsmen, scientists, artists and musicians, have brought benefits over long periods without remark, but every now and again a xenophobic political response has burst out. Paul Foot[12] has drawn some striking parallels between the political campaigns of the 1890s and of the 1950s and 1960s against the immigration of specific groups: East European Jews and 'coloured' Commonwealth entrants. At both times the anti-immigrant propaganda has emanated at first from a fairly small group on the political Right, only to be accepted and taken over by leading politicians in the main political parties, and backed by some of their supporters on both sides. Even the opponents of restriction have often been equivocal. John Burns, a socialist turned Liberal, opposed Conservative demands for restrictions on poor Jews, and demanded better working conditions for all, and the abolition of child labour, to remedy the ills that anti-immigrant campaigners had detailed, but at the same time he attacked rich Jews and accused the Conservatives of making 'the Stock Exchange a new Jerusalem and Park Lane a new Mount Pisgah'[13] In the late 1950s, while some Labour MPs were advocating 'integration' measures and opposing any attempt to control Commonwealth immigration, others called openly for controls. On 2 September 1958 the *Daily Sketch* reported a Labour MP, George Rogers, as saying that the government ought quickly to introduce legislative controls over 'coloured people from the Commonwealth':

> Overcrowding has fostered vice, drugs, prostitution and the use of knives. For years the white people have been tolerant. Now their tempers are up.[14]

His was not a lone Labour voice.

In other words, anti-immigrant, racial feeling has not consistently divided the main political parties from each other. In 1961, the Labour leadership, under Hugh Gaitskell, strongly opposed Conservative immigration controls on 'coloured' Commonwealth immigrants, but only a few years later the Labour Party in office, after Gaitskell's death, tightened controls sharply in 1965 and 1968. Conservatives have throughout claimed that their opponents are soft on immigration control and would open the floodgates given half a chance, while the response of the Labour Party in Parliament since 1965 has been, while in power to prove itself tough, and while in opposition to shift ground and complain of Conservative controls as inhumane. However, although very few Conservative MPs or party supporters have opposed current controls at any time, many Labour MPs and local party members have done so, and in 1982 the Labour Party annual conference voted in favour of reforming nationality and immigration law, broadly along the lines that AGIN had been recommending. This new policy was not given great prominence in the campaign, and was ignored by the media. At the same time, the Conservative Party conference headed off a resolution from its extreme Right, but remained virtually united on current controls, and took the line that Conservatives had 'solved' the immigration question by bringing new entry, except for some close relatives of existing residents, to an end.

It has been assumed throughout by both parties that the ordinary white voter 'in the pubs and clubs' is opposed to the presence of black people; hence Conservative leaders have announced themselves as champions of ordinary people, sturdily ignoring the absurd claims of intellectuals and busybody do-good-ers, while Labour has sought to satisfy both racism and anti-racism among its voters, and has not wholly succeeded in doing either. Christopher Husbands[15] quotes a remark made by Ben Tillett in 1900 which neatly describes a continuing common attitude: 'Yes, you are our brothers and we will do our duty by you . . . but we wish you had not come to this country'. Such confusions appear regularly in opinion surveys. Christopher Husbands also records[16] that in 1961, 76 per cent of the electorate, according to Gallup, favoured the controls the Conservative Government then intended to take, yet only 31 per cent of the same sample disagreed with the attacks the Liberal and Labour parties were making on the same legislation. Several surveys suggest that the race/immigration control issue won Conservative candidates a significant number of votes in 1970. However, the Husbands analysis of surveys in the last 20 years suggests that Labour has much less to fear from desertion by voters than its leaders and managers have usually assumed would happen if the party produced a reforming policy.

The Liberal Party has not been in office since the Common-wealth immigration debate began. Cynics might say, therefore, that it is not surprising if the Liberal policy on this matter has consistently been far more clear and unambiguous in opposing racially discriminatory immigration controls than Labour, but it could just as well be argued that a small party in need of all the votes it can get might have been tempted to 'play the race card'. Though most Liberals including the leadership have remained firmly anti-racist throughout, some individual Liberal candidates in the 1970s interpreted the new fashion for 'community politics', responding to immediate local needs and wishes, as if it were an unthinking populism, and, if they found strong racist feeling among those they canvassed, responded by acquiescing in it. None the less, the Liberal position has been the clearest on the subject. The SDP, caught in the toils of an enormously complex policy-making system, has produced suggestions on immigration within its human rights programme, and these are not dissimilar to Liberal policy, though with more emphasis on legal rights and remedies and less on fundamental policy change. The SDP, early in its existence, sought and obtained some active support from members of ethnic minorities in Britain.

The political parties have, since the late 1970s, become aware of the importance of the ethnic minority vote. Though very small, adding up to less than 4 per cent of the electorate as a whole, these minorities are disproportionately represented in marginal consti-tuencies. Party managers have, therefore, considered how to appeal to them. The Conservatives have not chosen to abate any of their immigration-control policy: instead they emphasise proposals they think likely to appeal to Asian voters, such as lower taxes and a free-enterprise economy. They take very little interest in policies to attract the West Indian vote. Labour, on the other hand, has put more stress on immigration policy recently in areas with significant black populations.

The superficial picture, at present, shows a sharp line between Conservatives, on the one hand, with a policy of strict racial immigration control, and of Labour, Liberals and SDP on the other, with policies demanding reform of the Immigration Act and Rules and the British Nationality Act 1981. But below the surface the situation is much more cloudy. A few Conservatives are privately worried about the present system; a lot of Labour workers and supporters are hardly aware of their party's new policy statements. Many ethnic minority voters have become disillusioned with politicians in general. Meanwhile, the idea of looking at immigration policy in any other light than as a matter of race has had very little impact. Though the idea of thoroughgoing reform as an anti-racist measure, or a matter of human rights, has begun to take hold, it is hardly appreciated by any politicians yet that such thoroughgoing reform will require a positive policy. And this in turn requires asking many new and difficult questions about migration as a whole and its total effects.

New thinking requires new habits of mind: using the term

'immigrants' to denote every kind of entrant, for example – white Zimbabwean farmers, American and Japanese executives, settlers from EEC countries, Poles and white South Africans who have been given asylum. 'Immigration policy' has to be understood to comprehend a part of EEC law, and the regulations on issue of work permits to applicants from no matter what country. There is no sign yet of politicians changing old habits. But the old terms and assumptions of debate on immigration can produce nothing: this was vividly illustrated in a debate in the Commons on 5 March 1984. Gerald Kaufman made an excellent speech[17] condemning the effect of current Immigration Rules on family life. But when interrupted by a Conservative, Mr Nick Budgen, with a request to set out 'the principles by which a future Labour Government will or will not control immigration', he replied 'the sort of principles on which it used to operate' without adding anything to make clear what time he was referring to. The question was a gift to anyone ready with a policy to expound, however basic and rudimentary, but the opportunity to propose that there was any alternative to the existing system, other than complete freedom of entry for all, was missed. This failure allowed the Minister of State, Mr David Waddington, yet again to obscure the distinction between reformed control and complete freedom of entry:

> Immigration control in general must mean immigration control in particular . . . The right hon. Gentleman paid lip service to control, and said that the Government were running a hard control. He cannot have it both ways. If there is to be control, hard decisions will have to be made, and we must face that.[18]

Mr Waddington was, of course, skilfully playing on words here. One can perfectly reasonably complain that, while some control is necessary, a 'hard' control, in the sense of one causing hardship, is wrong. 'Hard' decisions, in the sense of difficult, borderline decisions, always come up in the application of policy, but this fact does not justify *heartless* decisions. Moreover, at the same time as sowing this confusion, Mr Waddington planted the assumption that 'control' could mean only one thing: the present system. He then went on to attack the opposition's record when in power on family cases, and to quote figures, in exactly the same style that Ministers in both Labour and Conservative Governments have done for at last 15 years when challenged. After this unpromising opening, many speakers described cases in their constituencies, and then Mr John Stokes claimed that he could not think of any other country into which entry was as easy as it was into the UK. After the inevitable reference to 'ordinary

English people' on the one hand and 'technical college lecturers' on the other, however, Mr Stokes was able to score a point:

> We have not heard one word from the Opposition . . . of what they would do or what their policy is.[19]

Mr David Alton, for the Liberals, made a very brief reference to general reform:

> Immigration control should be exercised on the basis of objective criteria, and applied without discrimination on grounds of race, colour or religion.[20]

He added some specific suggestions on appeals procedure, but few hearers would have gathered from his speech that he wanted to recommend a complete alternative plan and system of control, far less what such an alternative would be like. Other speakers, including one Conservative, asked for liberalising changes in the Rules on admission of relatives, for non-discriminatory application of existing Rules and for publication of instructions to immigration officers, without touching on the issue of new legislation as a whole. Perhaps the nearest point to a breakthrough was the remark by Mr Denis Howell, winding up for Labour:

> If any Government of which I was a member were to blame I must accept responsibility.[21]

Could this signal the difficult, but essential, step that Labour politicians – and SDP leaders who were once members of Labour governments – need to take if they are ever to offer a convincing alternative immigration policy: the admission that they have been wrong in the past?

Political prophecy is a dangerous business, and it is impossible to forecast how opposition policies – and dissentient Conservative opinion – may develop before a general election. The idea of thoroughgoing reform of immigration policy and its administration has yet to be fully grasped by most leading politicians, but there are several possible ways in which they might come to approach it. Perhaps the most likely is the time-honoured British way of gradualness. This does not necessarily mean a slow advance; it means an advance step by step. The demands for reform of the way Rules are applied, of the Rules themselves, and of the appeal system, could, once successful, be followed by demands for reform of the voucher system for UK passport holders in India, a two-clause Act to restore *ius soli* to nationality law, and give an immediate grant to British Overseas Citizens resident in the UK of British citizenship – and so on. Once an impetus had developed, and a few changes had been introduced bit by bit, the need for more systematic reform would be better known and the practical chance of achieving it would be higher. If politicians could be persuaded of such an approach, their own understanding of what more was needed could similarly proceed step by step. But such a method, of making gradual changes, can be followed only by a government in office. Is there any way for politicians to consider, and promote, the idea of reform while in opposition or on the back benches?

In 1979 AGIN petitioned the government to set up a Royal Commission on migration as a whole, and the request was turned down flat.

A Royal Commission or Committee of Inquiry is not now a practical option. Oppositions cannot establish them. A government sufficiently committed to the idea of setting one up would have come near the end of its period in office before such a body had reported. There would be no chance of its introducing major new legislation before another General Election, and therefore a risk that nothing would be done at all. However, a government committed to reform will need much more detailed knowledge, argument and draft plans at its disposal than now exists if it is to attempt major new legislation, and work towards draft plans ought to be got under way as soon as possible.

Probably the most practical way to bring about such work is for many separate studies and discussions to be undertaken simultaneously, from different points of view and in various styles. For example, academic studies are needed to provide new information; political research 'think tanks' and working parties can tackle principles and practical notions on the basis of their own general policy approaches in other fields; professional groups of lawyers or doctors can produce reports and suggestions; campaigning groups and concerned individuals can try their hand at drafting improved Rules or suggesting new guidelines for administration. Even if such efforts overlapped in places and differed on many points, they would provide an invaluable basis for policy planning when the moment came.

The four essential conditions for action are: first, for politicians and the public to understand that reform of immigration policy does *not* mean the same as abandoning control altogether; secondly, that an alternative is desirable; thirdly, that it is practical. Fourthly, work must be done on positive proposals for a reforming policy: its aims and principles, its system of categorisation and assessment, its administrative structure and the safeguards it provides for individual rights. In practice, efforts to meet all these four conditions must be made within the next two or three years if the present irrational, expensive, racially discriminatory structure is to be replaced in the foreseeable future.

Notes

1 The Action Group on Immigration and Nationality (AGIN) is a campaigning body, consisting of an executive committee composed of representatives of a number of supporting organisations. These include the Joint Council for the Welfare of Immigrants, the United Kingdom Immigrants Advisory Service, the National Council for Civil Liberties, National Association of Community Relations Councils, British Council of Churches Community and Race Relations Unit, Catholic Commission for Racial Justice, Quaker Social Responsibility and Education, West Indian Standing Conference, Standing Conference of Pakistani Organisations, National Council of Bangladeshi Organisations, National Union of Students and Indian Workers' Association, Southall. Other organisations send representatives with observer status: these include the Runnymede Trust and others. There is a small number of individual members. The purpose is to promote, by co-operation between these bodies, reform of immigration and nationality law to observe race and sex equality, to promote family unity and to provide fair legal procedures. A report of the AGIN conference and a list of other publications can be obtained for 50p plus postage from 115 Old Street, London EC1.
2 Richard Plender at the AGIN conference, July 1983.
3 Richard Plender at the AGIN conference, July 1983.
4 See Part I.
5 See Part I.
6 See Part II.
7 Heather Booth 'Immigration in Perspective: Population Development in the United Kingdom', pp. 109–142, see Part II.
8 See Part II.
9 Nicholas Deakin, *Whitehall and Integration*, a briefing paper for the Institute of Race Relations, (1968).
10 Nicholas Deakin at the AGIN Conference.
11 I.e., at the time of writing (early 1984).
12 Paul Foot, *Immigration and Race in British Politics*, (Penguin, 1965).
13 *Ibid.*, p. 96.
14 *Ibid.*, p. 169.
15 'Race and Immigration' in *Socialism in a Cold Climate*, (ed., Allen and Unwin).
16 *Ibid.*
17 See *Hansard*, 5 March 1984, cols. 659–666.
18 *Hansard*, 5 March 1984, col. 666.
19 *Ibid.*, col. 682.
20 *Ibid.*, col. 687.
21 *Ibid.*, col. 693.

The Cobden Trust

The Cobden Trust is a registered charity, established in 1963 to undertake research and education work in the field of civil liberties. It seeks the protection and extension of civil liberties in the United Kingdom and has a two fold strategy to achieve this objective: research, into the causes of injustice, and education work, informing the public about their rights and responsibilities.

How you can help
While we are able to raise funds from charitable trusts and foundations, we depend also on generous public support. As a registered charity, the Trust can recover tax from the Inland Revenue on any convenanted donation. If you would like to help us in this way or would like further information, then please write for details to the Secretary, the Cobden Trust, 21 Tabard Street, London SE1 4LA.

Black Magistrates

MICHAEL KING *and* COLIN MAY

The ideal of a lay magistracy reflecting a cross-section of the local community has never been realised. Despite the large number of people of Asian or Afro-Caribbean origin living in towns and cities througout the United Kingdom, relatively few black men or women find their way on to the justices' bench.

Is their under-representation on the bench related to the people and the processes involved in their selection and appointment? Or is it rather a symptom of black alienation from the mainstream of British society? The research which forms the basis of this report, through a combination of interviews and statistical analysis, sets out to answer these and other questions concerning the appointment of black people to the bench.

In their report, the authors provide a revealing account of the way in which the machinery of selection works. In particular they show how the often unrecognised assumptions and predilections of the selectors and those who administer the selection process can influence decisions at each stage. These factors may indicate which candidates are 'suitable' and which interest groups need to be 'balanced'. They also disclose a disturbing undercurrent of discontent and disaffection among certain sectors of the black communities with the way in which J.P.s are chosen and with the justice dispensed by magistrates' courts.

The Cobden Trust. £4.95 plus postage & packing

Books on Race Relations, Immigration and Nationality from NCCL

Race Relations Rights

A practical guide to the law on race discrimination
PAUL GORDON, JOHN WRIGHT and PATRICIA HEWITT

Race Relations Rights is a revised edition of an earlier NCCL guide to the Race Relations Act, published in 1978. It has been completely amended to take into account changes in the law since then, and developments in case law.

When the book first appeared, the Race Relations Act 1976 had been in force for less than a year, and it was unclear how its provisions would work in practice. The experience of the last few years has shown that there is little room for complaeency about the law's effectiveness and the role of the Commission for Racial Equality.

First and foremost, this remains a practical guide to the race discrimination legislation. It explains:

- How to present a case at a county court or an industrial tribunal

- What the incitement law really says

- The powers of the Commission for Racial Equality

- The meaning of direct and indirect discrimination

- How to combat racism in the media

- The positive discrimination provisions of the Race Relations Act

It is certain to be of great assistance to advisers and campaigners on race relations.

National Council for Civil Liberties. **£1.95** plus postage & packing

British Nationality

The Agin Guide to the New Law

Second edition, September 1984

ANN DUMMETT *and* IAN MARTIN

British Nationality, written by two of the country's leading experts on nationality and immigration law, has been widely welcomed as the most practical and sympathetic guide to the complexities of the British Nationality Act 1981. This new edition, completely revised and updated, takes into account the changes that have been made since the Act's commencement and the experience of two years of the Act's operation.

It is an essential handbook and reference for advisers, legal practitioners and campaigners working in nationality, immigration and race relations.

Published for the Action Group on Immigration and Nationality by the *National Council for Civil Liberties*.

£2.95 plus postage & packing